Bernie P. Randhawa
Oct. 10, 2001
B ≠ N Delivery

The cultural ideal of motherhood in Victorian Britain seems to be undermined by Victorian novels, which almost always represent mothers as incapacitated, abandoning, or dead. Carolyn Dever argues that the phenomenon of the dead or missing mother in Victorian narrative is central to the construction of the good mother as a cultural ideal. Maternal loss is the prerequisite for Victorian representations of domestic life, a fact which has especially complex implications for women. And when Freud constructs psychoanalytic models of family, gender, and desire, he too assumes that domesticity begins with the death of the mother. Analyzing texts by Dickens, Collins, Eliot, Darwin, and Woolf, as well as Freud, Klein, and Winnicott, Dever argues that fictional and theoretical narratives alike use maternal absence to articulate concerns about gender and representation. Psychoanalysis has long been used to analyze Victorian fiction; Dever contends that Victorian fiction has much to teach us about psychoanalysis.

CAMBRIDGE STUDIES IN NINETEENTH-CENTURY
LITERATURE AND CULTURE 17

DEATH AND THE MOTHER
FROM DICKENS TO FREUD

CAMBRIDGE STUDIES IN NINETEENTH-CENTURY
LITERATURE AND CULTURE

General editors
Gillian Beer, *University of Cambridge*
Catherine Gallagher, *University of California, Berkeley*

Editorial board
Isobel Armstrong, *Birkbeck College, London*
Terry Eagleton, *University of Oxford*
Leonore Davidoff, *University of Essex*
D. A. Miller, *Columbia University*
J. Hillis Miller, *University of California, Irvine*
Mary Poovey, *New York University*
Elaine Showalter, *Princeton University*

Nineteenth-century British literature and culture have been rich fields for interdisciplinary studies. Since the turn of the twentieth century, scholars and critics have tracked the intersections and tensions between Victorian literature and the visual arts, politics, social organization, economic life, technical innovations, scientific thought – in short, culture in its broadest sense. In recent years, theoretical challenges and historiographical shifts have unsettled the assumptions of previous scholarly syntheses and called into question the terms of older debates. Whereas the tendency in much past literary critical interpretation was to use the metaphor of culture as "background," feminist, Foucauldian, and other analyses have employed more dynamic models that raise questions of power and of circulation. Such developments have re-animated the field.

This series aims to accommodate and promote the most interesting work being undertaken on the frontiers of the field of nineteenth-century literary studies: work which intersects fruitfully with other fields of study such as history, or literary theory, or the history of science. Comparative as well as interdisciplinary approaches are welcomed.

A complete list of titles published will be found at the end of the book.

DEATH AND THE MOTHER FROM DICKENS TO FREUD

Victorian Fiction and the Anxiety of Origins

CAROLYN DEVER

New York University

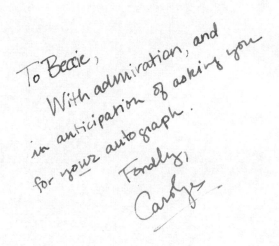

To Becsie,
With admiration, and
in anticipation of asking you
for your autograph.
Fondly,
Carolyn

CAMBRIDGE
UNIVERSITY PRESS

PUBLISHED BY THE PRESS SYNDICATE OF THE UNIVERSITY OF CAMBRIDGE
The Pitt Building, Trumpington Street, Cambridge CB2 1RP, United Kingdom

CAMBRIDGE UNIVERSITY PRESS
The Edinburgh Building, Cambridge CB2 2RU, United Kingdom
40 West 20th Street, New York, NY10011-4211, USA
10 Stamford Road, Oakleigh, Melbourne 3166, Australia

First published 1998

Printed in the United Kingdom at the Unversity Press, Cambridge

Typeset in Baskerville 11/12½ pt [VN]

A catalogue record for this book is available from the British Library

Publication of this book has been aided by a grant from the Abraham and Rebecca Stein
Faculty Publication Fund of New York University, Department of English

ISBN 0 521 62280 8 hardback

For Kathryn

Contents

Preface

The ideal mother is the ghost that haunts the Victorian novel. Paradoxically, the world of Victorian fiction, so preoccupied with women's power in the context of the domestic sphere, only rarely embodies that power in the figure of a mother. Instead, Victorian novels almost invariably feature protagonists whose mothers are dead or lost, swept away by menacing and often mysterious outside forces. The maternal ideal in fiction thus takes its shape and its power in the context of almost complete maternal absence, and I would argue, through the necessary vehicle of such a void. This is a book about representations of the loss of the mother, about the ambivalent compensatory structures that emerge in the wake of her departure, and finally, about the revealing disruption of those structures at the inevitable point at which the repressed returns.

The mid-nineteenth century is a period in which narrative fictions and rhetorics of the maternal ideal flourish side by side. It is surely noteworthy, then, that the maternal ideal *within* narrative fictions is a rule honored more often in the breach: the predominant domestic topos in the Victorian novel is a family represented in terms of maternal death or desertion. The mother's absence creates a mystery for her child to solve, motivating time and again the redefinition – in the absence of role-models – of female decorum, gender roles, and sexuality. In the absence of the mother, the child is left with a personal mystery, too, that motivates a formal search for "origins" in narratives ranging from the orphan discovering the truth of family history to the natural philosopher explicating, in somewhat larger terms, the origin of species.

The iconography of the maternal ideal achieves its cultural power through a poetics of abandonment and ambivalence, as the representational conundrum of the eroticized adult female is accommodated in the disguise of a dead – and therefore virtuous, pure, noble, and true – mother. And symbolically within fictional worlds, the crisis of maternal loss enables the synthesis of questions of originality, agency, erotic and

xi

scientific desire, returning always to a point of ending that becomes, generically, the point of beginning. The mother is the actual and symbolic site of generation, the earliest influence on development, and the domestic anchor of the most basic socioeconomic unit; she is central to the emerging theories of Darwin, Freud, and Marx – yet throughout nineteenth-century narratives she is almost always already gone. Domestic and detective fictions, scientific and political concerns converge in the maternal quest, as texts ranging from *Oliver Twist*, *Vanity Fair*, and *Middlemarch* to *The Origin of Species* and *The Interpretation of Dreams* return again and again to the space, the problem, of the mother who is not there.

The narrative structure that follows maternal loss proves profoundly influential over the course of the nineteenth century, describing the melancholic construction of an ideal through the loss of the living object, the embodied mother. The most immediate beneficiary of this narrative structure is Freud: in his theories of subjectivity, Freud presents the metaphor of maternal loss as the prerequisite for adult subjectivity and "normative" sexuality, reading all relationships of desire as repetitions of the original trauma of lost love, separation from the mother. Psychoanalytic methodologies as well as narrative forms are structurally dependent on the symbolic figure of the missing mother, and the implications of this fact are developed in post-Freudian object-relations theories that situate the mother, rather than the father, at the center of erotic and developmental pathologies. While this book offers a psychoanalytic perspective on Victorian fiction, it also considers the shaping influence of Victorian fiction on psychoanalytic theories of gender, language, and desire, exploring, in both genres, the impulse to construct the origins of subjectivity in the event of maternal loss.

In the two introductory chapters that follow, I consider the cultural, historical, and literary contexts that produce Victorian and psychoanalytic narratives so preoccupied with motherless children. Within the development of the Victorian novel, as within the institutional history of psychoanalysis, the ideological stakes of maternal loss are revealed most dramatically in the context of startling and unexpected events of maternal return. Thus from popular fiction to Victorian obstetrics, from Freud's "*fort-da* game" to Melanie Klein's theory of the "epistemophilic impulse," I read maternal absence as a dynamic signifying presence that exposes issues at stake in the containment of all that is potentially transgressive in the mother embodied.

Pursuing the implications of Freudian and object-relations paradigms in the chapters that follow, I argue that Victorian novels that represent the *return* of the missing mother after staging her death or disappearance enact subversive responses to the social, psychological, and narrative structures consolidated through her loss. The emphasis on the mother's return suggests a challenge to the psychoanalytic models of subjectivity predicated on the ideal of maternal absence, revealing the insistence of maternal embodiment, agency, and subjectivity. Predicting the fate of D. W. Winnicott's ideal "good-enough" mother, the more aggressively the mother returns, the more aggressively she challenges exclusionary structures of signification and narrative. The narrative *fort-da* of disappearance and return troubles the cultural ideal of the good mother even as it galvanizes a continued fascination with the mother as the central object of desire.

The novels I examine in detail, Dickens's *Bleak House*, Collins's *The Woman in White*, and Eliot's *Daniel Deronda*, each invoke the formal structures of fictional autobiography and detective novel; Dickens, Collins, and Eliot deploy the device of maternal absence in order to exploit its formal and psychological possibilities. In each of these texts, maternal loss prompts anxieties that undermine a protagonist's efforts to construct an identity, to consolidate a life story; it therefore motivates the act of detection. The function of maternal absence, and even more problematically, the function of maternal return, indicate a crisis of origin that is configured as a crisis of causality. But as the autobiographical narrative of Esther Summerson in Dickens's *Bleak House* suggests, the agendas informing the retrieval of a lost mother complicate the relationship between autobiography and causality. In Wilkie Collins's "detective" novel *The Woman in White*, the mother functions as an embattled signifier of stability; the progress of the detective plot maps the unraveling of a maternal ideal in exchange for a notion of the mother as the source of debilitating secrets and transgression. In contrast, George Eliot's last novel, *Daniel Deronda*, describes a narrative world in which all characters construct the terms of desire as longing for a lost mother. The figure of the mother is implicated in a deconstruction of gender roles, erotic object choice, and empowerment; her return represents the final collapse of the fictional frameworks supporting bourgeois ethics of Victorian maternity.

I further pursue the ideological formulation of "origin" through an analysis of *The Autobiography of Charles Darwin*, in which the politics of originality emerge through Darwin's construction of the origin of both species and individual as a male parthenogenetic transaction. My conclusion turns to Virginia Woolf's *To the Lighthouse*, arguing that Mrs. Ramsay's death marks Woolf's consolidation of Victorian and psychoanalytic plots. Through Woolf, the concerns of this project come full circle, returning to the introductory tensions between Victorian and psychoanalytic narratives, between mothers and melancholia, between maternal loss and the politics of representation.

This book has several central goals: to analyze a symptomatic structure ubiquitous in Victorian narrative; to address the implications of psychoanalytic appropriations of this story; and to place these fictional and theoretical narratives in a continuum that demonstrates larger cultural anxieties about the function of gender in the construction of origins. I am concerned not only with the understanding of a powerfully central figure in Victorian fiction, but also with the pursuit of this figure through the discourses that have shaped ideas of normative development, gender roles, and sexuality. These narratives tell the story of the "maternal death" at the beginning of every life. Considered together, they reveal a great deal about one another, as well as about the ideological implications of a maternal ideal paradoxically strongest in its absence.

During the production of this book, I benefited from the generous financial support of an American Council of Learned Societies Fellowship, a Goddard Fellowship from New York University, a Mellon Fellowship in the Humanities, and fellowship aid from Harvard University. I would also like to thank the Dean and Department of English at Vanderbilt University for providing institutional support during the 1996–7 academic year.

The first and most influential readers of this project were Barbara Johnson and Marjorie Garber, to whom I will always be grateful for offering such powerful models of theory and practice.

At New York University, I have been fortunate to teach a remarkable array of graduate and undergraduate students whose energy of mind has had tremendous influence over this book. A number of colleagues at NYU have supported the work, including Mary Carruthers, Una Chaudhuri, Margaret Cohen, Dustin Griffin, Phillip Brian Harper, Perry Meisel, and Mary Poovey. I am particularly grateful to Josephine Hendin, John Maynard, and Jeffrey Spear for their generosity as readers and mentors.

I am indebted to a group of extraordinary friends at Boston College who provided early and constant support; my thanks go especially to

Rosemarie Bodenheimer, Carol Hurd Green, Robin Lydenberg, Frances Restuccia, and Judith Wilt. I have profited from many years of impassioned conversation with David Hirsch and Marvin Taylor, and from the friendship and editorial eye of Sarah Blake. I would also like to thank Lisa Appignanesi, Tita Chico, Kimberly Christopher, Lydia Alix Fillingham, Barbara Claire Freeman, Teresa Goddu, Adrienne Munich, Cheryl Nixon, Susan Schwarz, and Mark Wollaeger.

It seems particularly important in a book about mothers to acknowledge actual mothers, and I am fortunate to have two; my thanks go to Kristine Dever and Diane Dever, as well as to Frank Dever, Mark Dever, and the rest of my family.

Finally, my love and thanks to Kathryn Schwarz.

A NOTE ON THE TEXT

A version of chapter 3, "Broken mirror, broken words in *Bleak House*," appeared in *Studies in the Novel* 27:1 (1995), and a version of chapter 6, "Calling Dr. Darwin," appeared in *Victorian Literature and Culture* 24 (1997). All quotations from the work of Sigmund Freud refer to *The Standard Edition of the Complete Psychological Works of Sigmund Freud*, trans. and ed. James Strachey, twenty-six volumes (London: The Hogarth Press and the Institute of Psycho-Analysis, 1986), and are cited by title, volume, and page number.

CHAPTER I

The lady vanishes

I merely desire information. Until yesterday I had no idea that
there were any families or persons whose origin was a Terminus.

Oscar Wilde[1]

Our starting-point will again be the one situation which we believe
we understand – the situation of the infant when it is presented with
a stranger instead of its mother.

Sigmund Freud[2]

To write a life, in the Victorian period, is to write the story of the loss of
the mother. In fiction and biography, autobiography and poetry, the
organizational logic of lived experience extends, not from the moment
of birth, but from the instant of that primal loss. From *Emma* through *To
the Lighthouse*, but most dramatically in the fiction of mid-Victorian
Britain, stories of family and individual development, as well as narratives of mystery, intrigue, and desire, almost invariably occur in the
immediate context of maternal death or desertion. The significance of
maternal loss in the construction of subjectivity, domesticity, and desire,
and the ideological implications of this representational practice, are the
concerns of this book.

It is paradoxical that the predominant generic template of the nineteenth-century British novel blatantly undermines those ideologies of
the family it is commonly thought to uphold. Structured principally *not*
as a celebration of family unity, or even of the sanctity of the domestic
sphere, the Victorian novel conventionally opens with a scene of family
rupture, frequently a maternal deathbed or a tale of wanton maternal
abandonment. The scenario is familiar: the narrative will pursue the
story of a child or adolescent protagonist who, motherless, is left to
decode the mysteries of the world, and most provocatively of the
mating-process, alone. I want to suggest that this paradigm opens up a

series of representational possibilities ranging from the conservative to the radical; in the space of the missing mother, novelists from Austen through Eliot are free to reinscribe the form and function of maternity according to highly idiosyncratic agendas, and thus to reformulate both conventional roles for women and conventional modes of narration.

The structural centrality of maternal loss enables mid-Victorian writers to consider complex questions of female subjectivity and sexuality. And largely because their plots occur in the context of the manifest *failure* – whether willful or not – of successful maternity, this narrative structure addresses larger ideological problems of femininity. Reflecting the structural and thematic patterns of her own fiction as well as her contemporaries', Elizabeth Gaskell, for example, constructs the death of Maria Brontë as the organizing principle, central crisis, and source of dramatic tension in the early chapters of her *Life of Charlotte Brontë*. While Gaskell's first chapter climaxes in the graphic reproduction of the Brontë family tombstone in Haworth Church, the first name of that too-long list offers the central trope through which Gaskell structures her version of the Brontë children's youth: "HERE LIE THE REMAINS OF MARIA BRONTË, WIFE OF THE REV. P. BRONTË, A. B., MINISTER OF HAWORTH."[3] Thus the young Brontë children, from the first moment of the biography, are characterized as "six little motherless children,"[4] the eldest, young Maria Brontë, acting in her mother Maria's stead. That mother herself, however, is present in Gaskell's text – and, Gaskell would have it, in her children's lives – as only the vaguest of figures: "according to my informant, the mother was not very anxious to see much of her children, probably because the sight of them, knowing how soon they were to be left motherless, would have agitated her too much."[5]

Elizabeth Gaskell does not argue that Charlotte Brontë's life begins with the death of her mother; rather, it is Gaskell's *text* that requires this event in order to begin. For the specter of the motherless, vulnerable child envisioned so vividly by the dying Maria Brontë is the paradigmatic subject of nineteenth-century British narrative, the ensuing *Bildung* mapping the child's negotiation back into a domestic space – and defining, along the way, the parameters of that domestic space and the male and female subjects that inhabit it. These texts consistently bracket the question of the mother herself as an embodied and vocal human figure; indeed, the ideology of the domestic articulated in the context of maternal loss appears to depend fundamentally on that loss as one of its constitutive principles.

This narrative structure has far-reaching implications. The consolidation of Victorian subjectivity in the domestic context reaches its most coherent form not in nineteenth-century fiction, but with Freud's appropriation of the *Bildungsroman* as the form structuring "normative" development.[6] Psychoanalysis, and in particular object-relations theory, provides a useful lens through which to consider the phenomenon of maternal loss in Victorian fiction. However, as I argue in the next chapter, the narrative mode through which Freud structures normative psychoanalytic development is itself a direct reflection of mid-Victorian tropes, with similar representational and ideological investments in maternal loss. In fact, Victorian concern with maternal loss offers psychoanalysis its most basic vocabulary for human development: in psychoanalysis, maternal loss simply shifts from a representational motif to a psychological mandate, as all permutations of mature subjectivity and sexuality emerge from the negotiation of the predicament of "abandonment." From the basic concept of infantile differentiation to the phallic mother and the structure of fetishism, from the inexplicability of female heterosexual desire to the *Unheimlich*, the narrative of "origins" in psychoanalysis begins with the crisis precipitated by the mother as a figure for loss. Whether the "loss" in question is the event of actual maternal death, the recognition of the female genitals as "castrated," or simply the mother's momentary but anxiety-producing absence, the maternal body figures an essential failure: the child, object-relations theorists argue, *must* eventually read the mother as inadequate in order to constitute a subject-position independent of hers. I will argue, then, through the chapters that follow, that the analysis of Victorian fiction has as much to teach us about psychoanalysis as psychoanalysis teaches us about the Victorian novel; indeed, in many instances, Victorian representational paradigms pose provocative and revealing challenges to the narcissistic empire of the psychoanalytic subject.

Mastering abandonment by translating it into renunciation, that subject is eternally engaged in pursuit of the original object, the lost and idealized mother visible only in the negative, in the inadequacies of substitution. In *Beyond the Pleasure Principle*, Freud writes of the child engaged in the game of *fort-da*, in which the boy constructs his mother's symbolic departure and return; Freud interprets the baby's babble as the German *fort*, or "gone," followed by *da*, or "there":

At the outset he was in a *passive* situation – he was overpowered by the experience; but, by repeating it, unpleasurable though it was, as a game, he took on an *active* part. These efforts might be put down to an instinct for mastery that was acting independently of whether the memory was in itself pleasurable or not. But still another interpretation may be attempted. Throwing away the object so that it was "gone" might satisfy an impulse of the child's, which was suppressed in his actual life, to revenge himself on his mother for going away from him. In that case it would have a defiant meaning: "All right, then, go away! I don't need you. I'm sending you away myself."[7]

The shift from passivity to activity, from victim to master, characterizes the origin of psychoanalytic subjectivity. This is in essence a narrative of revenge, bound to repeat the moment of abandonment in an ambivalent celebration of the triumph of survival. Such a compulsion to repeat, as Freud and later Lacan would have it, characterizes the conditions of subjectivity itself: all objects of desire, all symbols of triumph, exist in a structure referential to this instantiating rupture. Normative subjectivity, in the psychoanalytic model, is articulated through a poetics of loss. And the fundamental lost object is, practically or symbolically, the mother.

The melancholic structure of psychoanalytic subjectivity reflects the poetics of loss that shapes the Victorian narrative tradition. In both genres, narrative dependency on maternal loss displaces or attenuates questions of female sexuality and subjectivity, of infancy and relatedness, and of all that is representationally challenging about the spectacle of maternity itself. In Victorian novels, representations of maternal loss produce structures of displacement and operate as examinations of the objects substituted in the breach: servants and siblings, father, friends, lovers, orphanages, and texts – tombstones, letters, wills – all of which stand in a profoundly secondary relationship to the original lost, maternal object. Paradoxically, perhaps, the powerful Victorian ideal of maternal beneficence is constructed as an untested abstraction that is fundamentally dependent on a context of loss for its articulation.

Indeed, in "Mourning and Melancholia," Freud explicitly links the pathology of melancholia with the normative developmental phase of orality, and through this connection, situates the mother at the epicenter of both. Discussing melancholia, through the work of Otto Rank and Karl Abraham, as a narcissistic disorder characterized by the ego's inability to forsake a loved object, Freud writes:

This substitution of identification for object-love is an important mechanism in the narcissistic affections . . . It represents, of course, a *regression* from one type of object-choice to original narcissism. We have elsewhere shown that identification is a preliminary stage of object-choice, that it is the first way – and one that is expressed in an ambivalent fashion – in which the ego picks out an object.

The ego wants to incorporate this object into itself, and, in accordance with the oral or cannibalistic phase of libidinal development in which it is, it wants to do so by devouring it. Abraham is undoubtedly right in attributing to this connection the refusal of nourishment met with in severe forms of melancholia.[8]

The desire to introject the lost object is a symptom of the melancholic subject and the melancholic text alike. Notably, the oral mother–child relationship provides Freud with a template for melancholia: the child's struggle toward individual subjectivity entails the need to separate from the nutritive mother, even as that separation itself entails a potentially devastating loss. The melancholic narrative framework offers a solution to this double bind, a formula for independent subjectivity in which the object of desire is "devoured," metaphorically taken into the body, suspended, protected, abstracted, idealized, and potentially mastered. Freud's theory of melancholia situates loss not in the past, but right in the present, suggesting a logic by which the mother as an artifact is readable in the "present" of a text, even when that narrative's opening trope attempts to contain her in the historical past through the representation of her death. Just as melancholic subjectivity acts under the influence of the introjected idealized object, melancholic narratives, too, take their shape not after that instantiating loss, but precisely *through* it.

Judith Butler pursues Freud's identification of the internalized melancholic object with the construction of an abstract ideal, suggesting in the process a theory that locates loss as fundamental to the codifying tropes of subjectivity:

If melancholia in Freud's sense is the effect of an ungrieved loss (a sustaining of the lost object/Other as a psychic figure with the consequence of heightened identification with the Other, self-beratement, and the acting out of unresolved anger and love), it may be that performance, understood as "acting out," is significantly related to the problem of unacknowledged loss. Where there is an ungrieved loss in drag performance (and I am sure that such a generalization cannot be universalized), perhaps it is a loss that is refused and incorporated in the performed identification, one that reiterates a gendered idealization and its radical uninhabitability.[9]

Butler's mimetic theory turns on a notion of the performative that is pertinent to psychoanalytic and Victorian narratives alike. The "performed identification" that "reiterates a gendered idealization and its radical uninhabitability" presents categories of subjectivity in terms of tropes that are doomed to failure, always demonstrating their inability to achieve an abstract ideal. Identity, in other words, is not natural or grounded; it is a mimetic process constructed in the breach, in an attempt to compensate for loss by becoming – through performance motivated by nostalgia – a caricature of the lost object.

Rigidly idealized categories of identity – the Victorian ideal of maternity, for example – depend precisely on the absence and the ineffability of the original model, and thus the trope of maternal absence is one of the most powerful tools in the maintenance of the nineteenth-century maternal ideal. For Victorian narratives so relentlessly invested in the spectacle of maternal loss participate in the construction of a domestic ideology through their introjection of the dead mother, representing that mother in those structures of gender and desire shaped with reference to her disembodied ideal. Butler writes: "In the experience of losing another human being whom one has loved, Freud argues, the ego is said to incorporate that other into the very structure of the ego, taking on attributes of the other and 'sustaining' the other through magical acts of imitation."[10] The "magical acts of imitation" that work so effectively to perpetuate, to reanimate the lost object are the foundational acts upon which Victorian domestic ideologies are constructed. The representation of maternal loss is necessary to the reciprocal emergence of the maternal ideal, cause not effect of a codifying system; indeed, the nostalgia created in the wake of the mother's death simply increases the urgency with which the text seeks to idealize that lost object.

Victorian dead-mother plots facilitate a number of cultural processes, functioning most prominently, perhaps, as a means of addressing the question of origins in terms at once physical and psychological. Reflecting concerns most famously articulated in *The Origin of Species*, fictional texts in the mid-nineteenth century express the epistemological crisis of origins through the representation of maternal loss, in a translation of Darwin's phylogenetic theory to an ontogenetic scale. Interestingly, the translation works in reverse, as well: as I will argue below, when Darwin himself reverses the terms of his investigation by returning from phylogeny to ontogeny, describing his *own* origins in his posthumously published *Autobiography*, the death of his mother is the source of the curiosity in the boy that later makes the explorer and naturalist of the man.

As the examples of Elizabeth Gaskell and Charles Darwin indicate, the structuring principle of maternal loss operates across conventions of genre. Gaskell's *Life of Brontë*, like *Mary Barton*, *North and South*, and *Wives and Daughters*, is the *Bildungsroman* of a young woman who loses her mother, while Darwin's *Origin of Species*, like his *Autobiography*, is an attempt to investigate backward, to read history – whether personal or that of an entire species – in order to interrogate structures of cause and effect. Consistently, and without regard to genre, Victorian dead-mother texts engage such a reversal of causal and historical conventions. Reading the historical present as the effect of a hidden cause, narratives from *Oliver Twist* to *Daniel Deronda* relentlessly seek that cause – which invariably devolves upon some secret possessed by a strategically missing mother – as a means of decoding the psychological predicament of the protagonist. While Austen's *Emma* and *Persuasion* invoke the trauma of maternal loss as clues to the psychological constitution of their respective protagonists, not until Dickens, first in *Oliver Twist* then more dramatically in *Bleak House*, does maternal loss develop from a structural device to a psychological phenomenon. Consolidating tropes from earlier realist and Gothic conventions of maternal loss, and particularly from the example of Austen, Dickens exploits literary historical precedents that enable the unique and historically specific realization of a maternal ideal achieved in absence.

Dickens's significant contribution here, which is reflected and developed throughout the next forty years of literary history, entails a generic hybrid of mystery narrative and fictional autobiography. Raising the stakes of mystery by mapping it onto the crisis of a young, orphaned boy or girl, Dickens constructs profoundly melancholic biographical narratives, in which the understanding and management of loss is endemic to adulthood. And like the Freudian analytic narrative, in which the forward-looking trajectory of the *Bildung* is crossed with the backward-looking quest for original trauma, Dickens's formal innovation involves such a temporal duality. By psychologizing the detective plot and by making a mystery of the biographical form, Dickens hints at the melodramatic intrigue and transgressive potential lurking even in the most bourgeois lives, such as those of the domesticized Oliver Twist and Esther Summerson. Within this powerful hybrid genre, "mother" is a synecdoche for physical and psychological origin; by taking her out of the picture, Dickens constructs a crisis in which self-understanding, represented as the ability to craft a coherent life story or autobiography, is entirely dependent on the solution to a mystery. And just as for Freud, for Dickens, all roads return to the missing mother, the only question and the only answer in life stories that are also mysteries.

Such relentless recourse to a mysterious and absent figure underscores the sense in which fiction of this period, beginning most dramatically with Dickens, seeks to place, codify, and occasionally demonize the mother, a task so challenging it is most notoriously effected in the near-total absence of actual examples. Historically, the representational paradoxes of maternity were produced by rigid and anxious ethics of motherhood and female decorum. Even from the topmost reaches of Victorian culture, the maternal paradox is clearly visible and begs consideration.[11] In mid-Victorian England, the cultural construction of the bourgeois family, and by extension, of middle-class subjectivity, is predicated on a static ideal of maternal subjectivity that trickles down through the ranks from the level of Queen Victoria herself, the woman who "ruled her nation as a mother and her household as a monarch."[12] Adrienne Munich argues that the coincidence in Victoria of monarch and mother led to iconographic confusion:

Something appears to be wrong at the top of the pyramid of authority. Although an idealized mother, a madonna, is vested with great spiritual authority, unvirginal mothers, unlike fathers, are less imaginable as representing temporal monarchy; maternal monarchy seems absurd. By being so confoundingly physical and fecund, Victoria's female body does not lend itself to translation as a madonna, to assimilation into a personification, such as Britannia, or to veneration as a moral sage.[13]

The anxiety focused on Victoria, writes Munich, produces an analogy between the Queen's excessive body and the nation's excessive empire: "Queen Victoria's body, loved yet ridiculed, became a representation for the excess of a body politic with the largest circulation in the world."[14] But the equation of maternal body and body politic fails to address anxieties focused on the issue of excess; dual impulses of expansion and circumscription consistently overwrite representations of the Queen Regnant. The overdetermined identification of Victoria as domestic ideal, as a woman who figures for all women the propriety of "place," responds precisely to the anxiety of a woman who is clearly and powerfully *out* of place. As a woman on the throne of England, Victoria represents both the desire and the danger of female power taken to its illogical extreme: belonging at once to wife and mother, woman and queen, Victoria's body must reify the ideal that her position threatens to subvert. Only after the death of Prince Albert is there a successful iconographic resolution to the representational paradox of the Queen/Mother, Munich argues, as virginity is recuperated through the metaphor of widowhood in an idealization of pristine, asexual maternity that reflects an ethical investment similar to that of the melancholic novel. Munich writes: "Despite maternal monarchy's seeming paradox, the image of the widowed mother solves some of the representational difficulties in conceptualizing a Victorian queen. Victoria no longer had to face her problem of anomalous authority in regard to a husband. The Mother Victoria image as a holy mother eventually subsumes, even mutes, that of the wife."[5]

The metaphor of Victoria's rule within the "home" becomes central to explanations of her role as ruler of the nation, while also lending a vocabulary of maternal sovereignty to more conventional domestic spheres; Victoria, Munich argues, manipulates and capitalizes upon the iconography of maternity as the Angel in the Palace. In his 1864 address "Of Queens' Gardens," John Ruskin extends the metaphor of the home toward that of the palace; women are the queens of a domain only literally smaller than the domain of Victoria Regina:

So far as she rules, all must be right, or nothing is. She must be enduringly, incorruptibly good; instinctively, infallibly wise – wise, not for self-development, but for self-renunciation: wise, not that she may set herself above her husband, but that she may never fall from his side: wise, not with the narrowness of insolent and loveless pride, but with the passionate gentleness of an infinitely variable, because infinitely applicable, modesty of service – the true changefulness of woman.[16]

According to the metaphor Ruskin sets forth here, a system of moral order is dependent on a woman's entrance into the social contract of subjection, her acceptance of self-renunciation, unerring supportiveness, and modesty. Although all that is "good" and "right" proceeds logically from the structure of maternal virtue, women's power is necessarily invisible, tangible more in terms of its effects than the immediacy of proximate causality. The virtuous Victorian mother haunts the citizens of mid-century England, male and female alike, a profoundly disembodied voice and a powerfully absent presence. The popular advice writer Mrs. Ellis comments:

It has often been said that no man, however depraved or vicious, need be utterly despaired of, with whom his mother's influence still lingers on the side of virtue. On the couch of sickness, the battle-field, and even the gloomy scaffold, it is the image of his mother which still haunts the memory of the dying man; and in the hour of strong temptation, when guilty comrades urge the treacherous or the bloody deed, it is to forget the warning of his mother's voice, that the half-persuaded victim drinks a deeper draught.[17]

A culture's superego, the mother's influence is ideally strong even – or especially – in her absence. A culture's ghost, the mother lurks unseen but powerfully heard in the recesses of the Victorian conscience.

Arguing that Britain's economic, legal, and medical institutions depend on such an ideology of "True Womanhood," Mary Poovey contends that the domestic ideal relies on the censuring of female desire and ambition in favor of "natural" maternal love:

The place women occupied in liberal, bourgeois ideology also helps account for the persistence in the domestic ideal of the earlier image of women as sexualized, susceptible, and fallen. The representation of women not only as dependent but as needing the control that was the other face of protection was integral to the separation of spheres and everything that followed from it, because this image provided a defensible explanation for inequality. If women were governed not by reason (like men), but by something else, then they could hardly be expected (or allowed) to participate in the economic and political fray. Increasingly, from the late eighteenth century, the medical model of reproductive difference was invoked to define this something: when it was given one emphasis, women's reproductive capacity equaled her maternal instinct; when given another, it equaled her sexuality.[18]

Poovey suggests that the Victorian medical community's construction of the female body reflects the logic of female disenfranchisement: ruled by their bodies, the medical model suggests, women can be separated from the spheres of politics and intellect – perhaps ironically, considering the status of Victoria Regina. The danger, however, of circumscription predicated on the body is the implication of maternal embodiment as an eroticized spectacle. Poovey describes an important distinction between the cultural construction of maternal instinct as "natural" and that of female sexuality as perverse, dangerous, and uncontrollable. This distinction illustrates the fault-line of a central ideological paradox. Mid-Victorian representations of the domestic ideal exist in proportion to anxieties about the opposite, the image of the sexualized, susceptible, fallen woman; the doubleness that inheres within representations of that domestic ideal, therefore, signals a complexity of representational concerns challenged by stereotypes of Victorian maternity. The index entry for "Woman" in Walter E. Houghton's historical study, *The Victorian Frame of Mind*, reads, "*See also* Family, Home, Marriage, Purity."[19] This belies the period's concern – represented consistently and aggressively in its narrative fictions – with women's implication in orphanage, anomie, illegitimacy, and sexual transgression.

Narratives of mortality are central to medical discourses of maternity, and especially of childbirth, and these narratives negotiate the fine line between the canonization of the mother and their engagement with the material and often horrifying implications of her embodiment. But stories of maternal mortality in medical literature retain agendas very different from – and revealing of – those belonging to fictional texts, for the death rate of mothers in the Victorian novel is elevated far beyond the mortality rates among the same population of living women during this period; it is far more dangerous to give birth in a fictional world than in any region, under any conditions, within any social class in Victorian Britain. Actuarial discourses of maternal mortality, however, particularly in the literature of obstetrics, labor under a mandate similar to the fictional investment in the preservation of an abstract maternal ideal, even if the means by which women's bodies, voices, and agency are constructed is radically different. Irvine Loudon writes of maternal mortality in Victorian obstetrics:

Deaths in childbirth were always different from other deaths. Childbirth was the only major cause of mortality that was not a disease, and in that way it stood apart. It was always a tragedy. When a maternal death occurred it was swift, unexpected, and a sudden and brutal disruption of a family. Time and again, medical practitioners, hardened by the hundreds of illnesses they were unable to cure and which ended in death, testified to the special quality of a maternal death. They were the deaths which, in a lifetime of medical practice, they never forgot.[20]

Contemporary medical discourses on this emotionally loaded topic are concerned largely with the medicalization of childbirth, particularly following James Y. Simpson's pioneering use of ether in an obstetrical context on 19 January 1847, followed by his endorsement of chloroform as the anesthetic of choice.[21] Debates about the dangers and ethics of anesthetics accompanied concerns about disease at lying-in hospitals, most of which provided care for poor, urban women. Writing about the dangers inherent in the modern understanding of childbirth, Florence Nightingale comments:

It is dangerously deadening our senses to this fact – viz., that there ought to be *no* deaths in a lying-in institution – if we connect it in the least degree with the name of hospital, as long as a hospital means a place for the reception of diseases and accidents . . . In French statistics, this confusion of ideas, were it not ghastly, would be ludicrous. "Admissions," under the head "Malades," include not only the lying-in women, but the new-born infants, which appear to be "admitted" to life and to hospital together, as if life were synonymous with disease, so that, e.g., 4,000 "Admissions," in such a year, to the Paris Maternité would mean 2,000 deliveries, 2,000 births – [and – how many deaths?].[22]

Nightingale's task in *Introductory Notes on Lying-In Institutions* (1871) is to trouble the conceptual link between childbirth and disease, and simulta-

neously, to interrogate the sense in which major urban lying-in wards
have actually succeeded in confirming this impression by making birth
into a disease that is too often mortal: "for every two women who would
die if delivered at home, fifteen must die if delivered in lying-in hospitals
. . . The evidence is entirely in favour of home delivery, and of making
better provision in future for this arrangement among the destitute
poor."[23]

The major problem in lying-in institutions, and the greatest challenge
in mid-century debates around maternal mortality, is the epidemic
status of puerperal fever, also known as childbed fever, blood-poisoning,
or metria. Despite widespread disagreement over the means of transmission of this disease, and even over whether it constituted a single
disease at all, one thing was certain: puerperal fever, when it struck –
and it struck all too often – was almost always fatal. In an 1835 midwives'
manual, Robert Collins, M.D., writes:

The ordinary symptoms of puerperal fever are, a cold shivering fit; acute pain in
some part of the abdominal cavity, with great tenderness on pressure; rapid pulse,
varying from 120 to 140. In many instances the abdominal distress sets in without
any previous shivering fit; thus of the 88 cases, only 33 commenced in that
manner. In the very early stage, the tenderness is often the most acute over the
uterine region, but it generally diffuses itself rapidly over the entire of this cavity.

In hospital, the female, (perhaps from fear,) will at times insist that she is
quite easy and free from pain, though the presence of the disease is most clearly
pronounced, even by external symptoms. The appearance of the countenance,
of itself, particularly where there is much watchfulness, leaves to the experienced eye but little doubt. As the disease advances, the abdomen becomes
distended, in some to a great amount, in others it is inconsiderable.

The disease seems to run its course with great rapidity in most instances. In
fifty-six deaths in the Hospital, it proved fatal at the following periods after the
date of the seizure, viz.: – *Two* in 24 hours; *one* in 27; *one* in 36; *nine* on the 2d day;
fifteen on the 3d; *thirteen* on the 4th; *four* on the 5th; *five* on the 6th; *three* on the 7th;
two on the 8th; and *one* on the 11th day.[24]

Puerperal fever was devastating to parturient women, usually even more
so than the mortality rate here, fifty-six deaths among eighty-eight
women, would indicate; the Dublin Lying-In Hospital, better known as
the Rotunda, was a very good hospital indeed. Robert Collins believed
that puerperal fever was spread through unsanitary physical contact,
and like some of his colleagues, believed it was preventable; in 1829, he
took the unprecedented step of closing the Rotunda and scouring it
thoroughly, repainting woodwork and washing walls and ceilings with
lime. When the hospital reopened, he segregated sick patients from

healthy, and thus between 1829 and 1833 lost not a single woman to childbed fever.[25]

Happily, Collins's practices proved influential over a number of colleagues, who took similar steps in maternity wards elsewhere in Britain. However, there was far from a consensus of opinion about the contagious nature of puerperal fever; as D. C. O'Connor writes as late as 1864:

Of all epidemic diseases – the contagious character of which is doubtful – none has excited so much interest as puerperal fever, from the belief entertained by many, that the physician, whose duty it is to cure, often carries to his patient a most malignant disease. And still the evidence afforded of this fact is such as would not stand for one moment in the ordinary affairs of the world. If a man were sent to trial for manslaughter, on similar testimony, the question of his guilt would not be entertained for one moment; and why should old women's stories, told by timid physicians, be accepted as arguments by the medical profession?[26]

Unusually defensive about the anecdotal authority of "old women's stories," O'Connor makes manifest the fact that tensions persisted – along lines of class as well as gender – concerning the relative roles of physician and midwife. However, his conviction that puerperal fever is simply an "accidental" phenomenon, caused by bruising of the uterus during childbirth, is countered strongly by such influential interlocutors as Nightingale, who writes:

Puerperal women, as everyone knows, are the most susceptible of all subjects to "blood-poisoning." The smallest transference of putrescing miasm from a locality where such miasm exists to the bedside of a lying-in patient is most dangerous. Puerperal women are, moreover, exposed to the risks of "blood-poisoning" by the simple fact of being brought together in lying-in wards, and especially by being retained a longer time than is absolutely necessary in wards after being delivered, while to a great extent they escape this entire class of risks by being attended at home.[27]

Nightingale argues that childbirth itself is not only not a miasmic disease, it is not a disease at all, and that "midwifery statistics point to one truth; namely, that there is a large amount of preventable mortality in midwifery practice."[28] As O'Connor's metaphors of litigation and culpability indicate, the very preventable nature of childbed death, particularly in a historical period so shaped by ideologies of womanhood, inflects medical documents with palpable anxiety about the relative guilt of obstetricians and midwives. Therefore in genres ranging from the midwife's manual to the annual statistical report of the Registrar-General, descriptive language is overdetermined by defensiveness on the part of the physician–narrator. Nightingale, with characteristic forthrightness, writes: "Lying-in is not a fatal disease, nor a disease at all. It is not a fatal accident, nor an accident at all . . . Unless from causes unconnected with the puerperal state, no woman ought to die in her lying-in; and there ought, in a lying-in institution, to be no death-rate at all."[29] If the physician, "whose duty it is to cure," not only fails to save a new mother, but is the active agent behind her death, then his burden of guilt is enormous; "Whose character," writes J. Matthews Duncan, M.D., "can endure or survive the divulging of the truth about it?"[30]

The anxiety of medical culpability in mother-slaying inflects even the driest statistical tabulations of mortality rates, and this constitutes the primary site in medical texts – otherwise remarkably scientific, disinterested, and humane – in which the pressure of the maternal ideal is visible. The question of maternal mortality was therefore of critical interest to William Farr, whose letters on causes of death in England in the Registrar-General's annual reports from 1847 until 1880 contain careful analyses of childbed death statistics. Farr's concern with childbed death is at once compassionate and professional: he was involved in a revealing debate over whether medical practitioners reported maternal mortality rates accurately and honestly. This debate originated with an article by Robert Barnes, M.D., in an 1859 issue of *The Dublin Quarterly Journal of Medical Science*, which argued for a radical skepticism over the reliability of childbed death statistics; more rigorous record-keeping, argued Barnes, would dictate improved modes of treatment for puerperal women. He writes:

The Registrar-General publishes weekly a summary of the London mortality returns, which is scanned with interest by many persons. These circumstances concur to invest the London mortality returns with an authority which I fear is not merited generally. The fallacy of large generalizations, unchecked by individual experience, may be seen from the following example. It is stated in the Registrar-General's Report for 1856, that the mortality in child-birth in England and Wales, in 1847, was 1 in 167, and that it had fallen to 1 in 227 in 1856. Now, having applied to Dr. Elkington for the puerperal statistics of Birmingham, I learn that the Registrar of that town says that "no one ever specifies the deaths in child-birth or from puerperal fever." May it not be that in 1847 there was less repugnance in giving correct certificates than in 1856? Certain it is, that here, as in every other medical inquiry, we must fall back upon individual observation.[31]

The Birmingham Registrar's soon to be notorious response – "'no one

ever specifies the deaths in child-birth or from puerperal fever'" –
reveals the burden of this culture's powerful maternal ideal. Obstetricians and midwives alike have a great deal at stake in evading the blame
and guilt associated with the death of an *accouchée*, particularly in the
context of debates concerning the transmission of infections such as
puerperal fever, while definitions of "childbed death" were cast vaguely
enough to offer ample alternatives for the death certificate. Even Farr,
despite his outraged, prolonged, and uncharacteristically illogical rejection of charges of underreporting, defensively acknowledges the psychological stakes of obstetrical practice: "There may be an indisposition in
some cases to record the child-birth as the cause, but there is no reason
to believe that practitioners have generally shrunk from the performance of their duty."[32] Charles Meigs, addressing that "indisposition,"
writes in 1848, "There is something so touching in the death of a woman
who has recently given birth to her child . . . It is a sort of desecration for
an accouchée to die."[33]

Sentimentalized rhetoric only occasionally appears in midwives' narratives of childbirth and maternal death, and physicians writing these
manuals only rarely acknowledge maternity as a "special" category.
They are more often struck by the psychological force of the *accouchées*
themselves, as they periodically exercise the power to will themselves to
death, largely due to extenuating life circumstances in the apparent
absence of any empirical cause; the female mind, quite astonishingly,
retains hegemony over the empirical – and thus theoretically control-
lable – domain of the female body. Granted, these are usually women
seduced, and the implication is that their shame is too great for them to
go on living; it is noteworthy, however, that the rhetoric of mysterious
recovery does not appear in these texts. Otherwise credible, physicians are
all too willing to accept credit for a job well done, and to credit female
psychology with the occasional failure. "No. 131" in Robert Collins's
book is typical: "No. 131. – Was a poor woman who had been seduced;
when about to leave the hospital, she had become very depressed in
mind; she had no local distress or apparent disease, yet her situation so
much affected her, that she became gradually more feeble, and sunk on
the 28th day, evidently from the effect of grief."[34] "No. 24" in Sinclair
and Johnston's influential *Practical Midwifery* (1847) is similarly troubled,
though married:

No. 24. – The second stage of labour in this case was excessively short, only a
few minutes, and the placenta was naturally expelled in due course. Soon after
her delivery it was discovered that something was preying on her mind. On

inquiry it was found that previous to her marriage she had occupied a respectable position in life: that she had formed an alliance much beneath her, and was consequently deserted by her friends, and of her husband, who was a sailor, she had received no tidings for a period of eight months. On the second day after her delivery she had a severe rigor, but there was no tenderness; her bowels had been freed; there was a full secretion of milk, and the lochial discharge was normal; but the pulse was quick and full. The next day the pulse was 120, and full; the abdomen somewhat tympanitic. Considerable pain was experienced on pressure over every point of the abdominal surface, and the secretion and discharge were absent.

Third day. She passed a good night, and her pulse had fallen twelve beats; but the symptoms were otherwise unimproved, and she complained of acute lancinating pain coming on in paroxysms along each side of the abdomen. The tympany increased during this day, and towards evening the stomach became irritable; green vomiting then set in; the pulse increased to 130, and became small; respiration became hurried, and she died early in the morning on the fourth day from the rigor. Her intellect was perfect up to the moment of death.

Treatment. – Free venesection; mercury combined with opium; the latter also in full doses, uncombined; mercurial inunctions, turpentine enemata, turpentine stupes, bran poultices, mild nutrition, and stimulants.
No autopsy was permitted.[35]

The tragic stories of No. 131 and No. 24 invoke the basic narrative frameworks of fictional maternal death – unjust life circumstances beyond the maternal victim's control, the triumph of the psychological over the physical. In fact, No. 131's story is a plausible alternative scenario for Gaskell's Ruth Hilton, while surely Anne Elliot's friends envisioned for her a fate such as that of No. 24 had she married Wentworth the first time around. But these narratives also reveal the signal difference between medical and literary discourses: novels, poems, and biographical texts invoke maternal loss in order to explore its effect on the bereaved offspring, while for these medical texts, the mother herself, and largely the mother herself as a physical entity, is the center of attention. Did the infants of No. 24 and No. 131 live or die? Were they male or female? And who refused to allow the autopsy of No. 24? Did her friends relent, in time to mourn – and perhaps to raise her child – if not to forgive? Or did her husband's ship dock at Plymouth, having survived hurricanes in the Antilles, allowing him to race to her bedside – arriving, perhaps, just a moment too late? Without question, nineteenth-century obstetrical writing objectifies the mother – as in the Victorian novel, she rarely speaks, and she seldom has a name – but it objectifies her as and through her body in order to diagnose, and ideally to save.[36] Literary writing of this period, however, objectifies her as a "mother," reducing her entire subjectivity to this single function; killing her off, then, enables the laboratory of bereavement and melancholic displacement that constitutes the paradigmatic Victorian narrative.

William Farr's outraged response to Barnes's suggestion that childbed deaths were underreported participates, in some sense, in the desire to market motherhood positively to young women: "Such a[n inflated mortality] rate, if general, would represent marriage and childbearing as a most perilous ordeal for a young woman to encounter."[37] Ironically, perhaps, the young woman in question was more likely to read the domestic and sentimental fiction of the day than the Registrar-General's report, and maternal mortality rates in fiction, for childbirth and in later life, are far more grossly inflated than Barnes would ever dream; indeed, given the extent to which Victorian maternity is widely represented as a culture of death, it is remarkable that marriage and childbearing continued apace throughout the period. Maternal death in Victorian England was certainly a matter of grave concern, for women contemplating childbirth and for medical practitioners. But in Victorian fiction, the mother is at much greater risk, and the fictional investment in maternal morbidity accommodates agendas ranging from the misogynist to the proto-feminist.

A sampling from the catalogue of missing mothers in nineteenth-century fiction reveals a broad range of texts, from a variety of sub-genres, that participate in the melancholic paradigm. From Mrs. Woodhouse to Mrs. Brooke, the list includes Mrs. Frankenstein, Mrs. Snow, Mrs. Eyre, Mrs. Crimsworth, Mrs. Helstone (temporarily), Mrs. Earnshaw, Mrs. Marjoribanks, Mrs. Fairlie, Mrs. Cohen, Mrs. Hale, Mrs. Gibson, Mrs. Greystock, the Lady Mount Severn, and both Mrs. Pirrip *and* Mrs. Joe Gargery. Other examples within the Dickens canon alone include Agnes, mother of Oliver, and Mrs. Dombey, mother of Paul, who depart this earth in the opening scene, while Clara Copperfield Murdstone takes her infant son with her, dying on her elder son David's birthday. And in *Bleak House*, Esther Summerson believes her mother is dead from the beginning, but only discovers her dead at the end.

Generally speaking, dead or missing mothers in Victorian fiction – as opposed to nonfictional discourses – are not ugly, poor, angry, guilty, or the victims of violence, domestic or otherwise; they *are*, in general, beautiful, middle-class, repentant, misguided martyr-figures separated from their children by some circumstantial tragedy or dread wasting disease. The major exception to this rule, an exception that marks the end of an era and alters the parameters of Victorian fiction, is the figure of Alcharisi in George Eliot's *Daniel Deronda* (1876). Franco Moretti writes of developments in the *Bildungsroman* during this period, "George Eliot . . . and everything changes,"[38] and indeed, Alcharisi, Daniel's mother, was a reluctant mother all along, and willingly and explicitly exchanges her child for her career. Through the figure of Alcharisi, Eliot confronts the trope of maternal loss directly, and exposes a radically alternative set of motives inspiring the maternal decampments that are more norm than exception throughout this period.

"This is a deep, dark, and continuous stream of mortality," writes Farr, not about the novels of his day, but about the potential of standardized midwife training to reduce maternal death. "How can it be accounted for?"[39] Chalking this "stream of mortality" up to such causes as poor medical training, dirty hospitals, unwashed doctors and midwives, poverty, and chance, Farr is in the peculiar position of having to defend suspiciously low death rates while also arguing that these rates are inflated and many of the deaths preventable. Whether actual maternal death rates are higher or lower than reported – and Loudon writes that "Published figures of maternal deaths were never exaggerated – they underestimated the true level"[40] – they are in fact, as already noted, dramatically lower than the fiction of this period would suggest. According to Farr's statistics, in the thirty-year period from 1847 to 1876, 106,565 women died in childbirth, one to every two hundred children born alive.[41] Even adjusting for Farr's almost certainly low rate of reporting, childbed death rates in Victorian Britain consistently remained well below 1 percent, and between 1837, when such statistics were first gathered, and 1937, when rates began to drop rapidly, the official figure remained almost constant at .45 percent. In a 1986 essay titled "Did the Mothers Really Die?," Roger Schofield writes, "Undoubtedly the risk of dying in childbed was much higher than it is today, and many women died needlessly because of the inadequate obstetrical skill of those who attended them. But childbearing . . . turns out to have been a rather less mortal occasion than we may have been inclined to believe."[42]

The drastically inflated popular image of childbed death is a credit to the culture of death that pervades Victorian fictions of maternity. The issue at stake in fiction is not motherhood for the sake of the mother, but motherhood for the sake of its emotional impact on those around her, particularly the bereaved children and husband, forced to struggle on after her death without her as their reliable moral compass. While medical discourses on the subject of childbed death, as well as women's mortality more generally, have a particular agenda with regard to the female body, its functions and vulnerabilities, the imperatives of fiction are dramatically different, and here that female body is a means to an end; this distinction begins to justify the discrepancy in death rates between the historical record and literary representation.

Novels of this period are infected with a puerperal fever of their own, involving the impossible reconciliation of a maternal ideal with the representation of embodied – and potentially eroticized – female subjects. As John Hawkins Miller argues in an article about Victorian attitudes toward childbirth:

The medical profession was only too aware of the truth of St. Augustine's observation that we are born *inter faeces et urinam*. This anatomical fact, combined with the religious view of women in childbirth as ritualistically unclean, partially explains why Victorians viewed childbirth as unseemly . . . On the other hand, the state of motherhood – presided over by the image of the Madonna and Child – is pure and undefiled . . . These two comments . . . one on the disagreeableness of childbirth and the other on the glory of motherhood, reflect Tertullian's observation about the duality of women – *templum aedificatum super cloacam*, a temple built upon a sewer.[43]

The mother, Miller argues, represents built-in conflict between an iconographic ideal – the Madonna – and the insistence of physicality – the visceral spectacle of childbirth. Like the paradoxical figure of Queen Victoria – at once fat, fecund, and unavoidably physical and regal, all-powerful, and untouchable – the combination in the bourgeois mother of bodily excess and cultural ideal remains a representational paradox throughout this period. Victoria, then, or any mother, represents the central figure of cultural desire overwritten by inaccessibility. Representations of the maternal ideal must necessarily get past the body; thus what emerges is a maternal ideal constituted in the breach, in the amazing superabundance of good mothers represented as dead or missing. Indeed, in the mid-Victorian period, it could be argued, the *only* good mother is a dead mother.

Persistent idolizations of maternal virtue figure an entrenched anxiety focused acutely on the body and on female eroticism. Reflecting the conclusions of Mrs. Ellis, Walter Houghton writes of the Victorian struggle toward chastity and the repression of the erotic, a struggle whose standard was the virtue of the chaste mother:

But of all women in the world, the most pure – and the most useful as a sanction for adolescent chastity – was Mother. Every young Victorian heard his father's voice sounding in his conscience, "Remember your dear, good mother, and never do anything, think anything, imagine anything she would be ashamed of." In that way, filial love, already increased in the Victorian family by the repression of sexual emotions, was exaggerated in the cause of moral censorship and control.[44]

The incest taboo is thus turned outward and applied to all objects, erotic and otherwise. The extension of filial logic to the broad spectrum of non-familial relationships facilitates the policing of borderlines and the maintenance of cultural order. Thus within the conventional structures of Victorian fiction, a crisis emerges around the issue of maternal representation: as the original "split subject," as well as the original split object, Victorian mothers signify as public and private, erotic and chaste, the first object of desire and the first site of anxiety. The crisis of culturally instantiated "doubleness," the tension between an ideal and its anxious opposite, produces the tropes of maternal death, absence, and loss, for at this cultural moment, the good mother is simply *too* good to be true.

As Nina Auerbach has argued, the splitting of characteristics between pairs of women, demon and angel, virgin and whore, Becky Sharp and Amelia Sedley, Anne Catherick and Laura Fairlie, is a common approach to the paradox of femininity.[45] I want to add to this argument, however, that the need to articulate an ethic of maternal virtue through the extermination of the maternal body is symptomatic of the form of power that derives from such a notion of "virtue." Novelists such as Dickens, dependent on a naturalized idea of female virtue for their generalizations about maternal goodness, follow a long narrative tradition of female disembodiment. Richardson's *Clarissa* (1748–9) is perhaps the clearest source for the monitory ethic of disembodied femininity found in Victorian melancholic texts. Richardson's novel discovers an important pattern of narrative introjection, which makes internal – and thus invisible, insidious, and "natural" – an ideology of self-discipline that is associated concretely with the feminine, becomes coded through this process of naturalization as "virtue," and is translated in the Victorian period as a generalized and felicitously invisible notion of maternal goodness.

The novel's primary vehicle for the establishment of this ideological pattern is its gradual erasure of Clarissa Harlowe's body after her rape, an erasure superimposed against an increasingly powerful Clarissa-voice or Clarissa-function that serves the goal of moral discipline. Belford chides Lovelace:

How many opportunities must thou have had of admiring [Clarissa's] inestimable worth, yet couldst have thy senses so much absorbed in the WOMAN in her charming person as to be blind to the ANGEL that shines out in such full glory in her mind? Indeed, I have ever thought myself when blessed with her conversation, in the company of a real angel: and I am sure it would be impossible for me, were she to be as beautiful and as crimsoned over with health as I have seen her, to have the least thought of sex when I heard her talk.[46]

When Belford distinguishes between "WOMAN" and "ANGEL," he does so to support the division of Clarissa's grossly embodied state from her apparently transcendent "voice." In doing so, he identifies and participates in the novel's larger project, the manufacturing of an *abstract* ideal of virtue, and that quality of abstraction inheres precisely in its immaterial, disembodied nature.

For when Clarissa dies, the community of mourners consolidated around her memory – including the community of readers of the mammoth tombstone that is the novel *Clarissa* – is able to retain, and indeed to internalize, the "voice" of its dead "ANGEL." For Clarissa's agency, formally embodied in the figure of Belford, the executor of her "will," achieves the peak of its powers after her death. Clarissa is posthumously constructed for Anna Howe, Belford, Lovelace, her parents, and all those who came in contact with her actually or through reputation, as "conscience." The model of Clarissa's virtue, powerful in its singular martyrdom, is formalized by Anna's testimony to Clarissa's homely aphorisms and her skills as an "excellent ECONOMIST and HOUSEWIFE" (1468). Although circumstances dictate that Clarissa never act as "ECONOMIST and HOUSEWIFE" during the novel's action, she is represented posthumously as a domestic figure *par excellence*.

The memory of Clarissa serves a monitory function to those she has left behind, particularly to those who did her wrong. Through their internalization of Clarissa as an icon of virtue, her friends and family assume masochistic positions of self-discipline in their attempt to mimic the abstract ideals for which she stands. Like the father-slaying sons in Freud's *Totem and Taboo*, the community that has "consumed" Clarissa in some very real sense *becomes* Clarissa, constructing itself out of guilt in a rigidly overdetermined duplication of her model. The novel's introjection of the dead Clarissa facilitates the establishment of a disciplinary mode, regulating behavior and internalizing self-control through the construction of Clarissa-as-conscience. Recalling Foucault's discussion of Bentham's Panopticon, discipline in *Clarissa* becomes an internal mechanism, physically divorced from Clarissa herself as the agent of its administration:

Hence the major effect of the Panopticon: to induce in the inmate a state of conscious and permanent visibility that assures the automatic functioning of power. So to arrange things that the surveillance is permanent in its effects, even if it is discontinuous in its action; that the perfection of power should tend to render its actual exercise unnecessary; that this architectural apparatus should be a machine for creating and sustaining a power relation independent of the person who exercises it; in short, that the inmates should be caught up in a power situation of which they themselves are the bearers.[47]

More powerful as an agent of discipline after her martyrdom than in life, "Clarissa" at the end of the novel emerges as a symptom of secularized power. To appropriate Foucault's terms, "a power relation" sustained "independent of the person who exercises it" consolidates the monitory function of disembodied female virtue in a clear prediction of the dead mother's status in Victorian fiction.

Maternal absence is a plot device familiar in periods before and after the Victorian. From the birth of Athena full-blown from the head of Zeus to Shakespeare's *King Lear* and *Pericles*, from Burney's *Evelina* and Austen's *Persuasion* to Disney's *Bambi*, *Cinderella*, and *Snow White*, to television situation comedies that revel in the exploits of bumbling single fathers, maternal absence, often so normative as to go unnoted, is a sign that something is different – and perhaps amiss – within the individual, the home, and the world. Working from the paradigm of virtue disembodied established in *Clarissa*, however, and in service of a range of ideological and representational agendas, this story achieves new cultural prestige in nineteenth-century Britain. Victorian melancholic fictions trace their genealogy to earlier novels, including texts by Behn, Fielding, Radcliffe, Edgeworth, Burney, Austen, and Shelley, which feature centrally missing mothers. The *structural* advantages of maternal loss develop from the consolidation of several subgenres of eighteenth-century fiction – namely, novels of sensibility, the *Bildungsroman*, and the Gothic – that invoke maternal absence. However, the complex *ideological* core of Victorian melancholic narrative emerges directly from the regulatory ethic of disembodied virtue articulated in *Clarissa*, and not until the late 1830s, when this ideological formation coincides with narratives structured around maternal absence, consolidating the mother as the powerfully disembodied figure behind the fiction, do the full implications of the Victorian dead-mother plot appear.

The formative power of emotion over reason is particularly over-determined in the *à la carte* approach to feelings found in fictions of sensibility, a genre that first begins to capitalize on emotion as a power structure, in a direct anticipation of Dickens. Emblematized in Sterne's *A Sentimental Journey* (1768), and drawing a political and philosophical vocabulary from Locke and Shaftesbury, Hume and Rousseau, novels of sensibility codify an extremity of emotional response both within and to the novel. Patterning themselves after the conspicuous display of emotion that follows Clarissa Harlowe's death, such texts construct moral virtue as a by-product of deep feeling, an ethic that will be translated in the mid-nineteenth century into the rhetorical conflation of death, virtue, and emotion. Among other, often more arbitrary occa-sions for grief, novels of sensibility frequently stage familial death-scenes for the expression of acute but productive emotional crises; Elizabeth Inchbald's *A Simple Story* (1799), for example, begins with the death of a father, while her *Emmeline, Orphan of the Castle* (1788) and Mary Woll-stonecraft's *Mary* (1788) open with the deaths of a mother-figure and a mother, respectively. Linked with a political ethic that privileges emo-tion over reason, fictions of sensibility ground liberal subjectivity in an ethic of empathic identification. Similar to their nineteenth-century descendants in their concern with the psychological constitution of self through emotion, they locate determining cathexes everywhere, rather than in a single, constitutive event such as the death of the mother.

Similar in its focus on a promiscuous, mobile protagonist who wan-ders from one scene to the next, the eighteenth-century *Bildungsroman* provides the Victorian novel with its vocabulary of adolescent alien-ation. Franco Moretti argues that the *Bildungsroman* emerges in the eighteenth century as "the 'symbolic form' of modernity" embodied in images of restless, ambitious youth, "epitomized . . . in mobility and interiority."[48] As the tropes of romance develop into narratives of worldly ambition, the demands both of exogamy and ambition require the fracture of the family unit; the loss of the mother through death or desertion thus facilitates – by necessity – the protagonist's construction in terms of radical individualism. For characters such as Fielding's Tom Jones, Burney's Evelina, or even Edgeworth's Belinda, the status of "motherless" child enables a range of comic possibilities that include a picaresque mode engendered by the immediate fact of homelessness; incest plots engineered by comic family mysteries; and battles over inheritance and paternity. From the very earliest moments of this narrative model, the English novel writes its way from an essentially anomic notion of the subject into stability; it makes a virtue of necessity (and arguably, a necessity of virtue) by appropriating abject orphanage into worldly independence.

The distinction, however, between such novels and their mid-Victorian descendants inheres in their relatively low level of investment in the question of the mother herself. Cut loose from the family structure almost immediately, the picaresque protagonist of the *Bildungsroman* neither mourns nor sentimentalizes that family, and nor does he or she construct the mother as the idealized symbol of psychological unity; rather, the mother is simply the means to a highly pragmatic end for an offspring far more concerned with the ideology of individualism than domestic virtue. The exception to this trend, and another structural source for mid-Victorian fiction, is the Gothic novel; in the novels of Anne Radcliffe, in Mary Shelley's *Frankenstein* (1818), and most dramatically in Matthew Lewis's *The Monk* (1796), maternal death – usually a mystery or a grotesque – prompts melodramatic, psychosexually inflected plots in which the mother, as presence and as absence, is an immediate problem for her child, especially if that child is a daughter. Claire Kahane writes, "What I see repeatedly locked into the forbidden center of the Gothic which draws me inward is the spectral presence of a dead–undead mother, archaic and all-encompassing, a ghost signifying the problematics of femininity which the heroine must confront."[49] Maternal death is codified in the Gothic novel as a token of erotic danger, and in response to that endangerment, young heroines, akin to Clarissa Harlowe, must begin to articulate their own versions of womanliness.

From the implications of maternal death in the Gothic novel, the mother is constructed as an emblem of the safety, unity, and order that existed before the very dangerous chaos of the child's Gothic plot. While Gothic novels rely on fractured domestic structures in order to construct the erotic crises that eventually produce stability, the *Bildungsroman* of narrative realism relies on maternal loss to set the young protagonist free to construct selfhood independently of parental constraint. And fictions of sensibility institute the equation of emotion and virtue as a worldly trope, constructing a formula that Victorian novelists will translate into the constitutive trope of the domestic sphere – even though that domestic sphere is always already represented as fractured, in the history of the novel as in the Victorian narrative tradition.[50]

Within the first two decades of the nineteenth century, Jane Austen contributes the penultimate development to the plot of maternal mortality that will become so overdetermined in the Victorian novel. In almost every novel – most dramatically, perhaps, in *Persuasion* and *Emma*, but also in texts that feature living mothers – Austen begins the efficient fusion of realist and Gothic structural devices even as she engages the tropes of sensibility by satirizing their extremity.[51] As in the Gothic novel, maternal death or decampment – literal or just figurative – betokens extreme vulnerability for Austen's heroines, a vulnerability that is more often than not enacted through a crisis of sexuality. For Anne Elliot, for instance, as for Emma Woodhouse, and even for Lydia Bennet, Austen's novels display the extent to which daughters do not understand how to conduct their own courtship plots, a dangerous fact in a context in which mothers are consistently too unavailable or too unwise to intervene.

Austen neither sentimentalizes nor especially psychologizes mothers, however, and in this regard she draws on the structural advantages afforded by the more picaresque, episodic plots of eighteenth-century literary realism without regard to the ideology of female power in death consolidated in *Clarissa*. For Austen, unlike the Victorian novelists who depend so heavily on her example, the mother is not immediately implicated in the construction of her child's identity, and therefore her death or failure does not precipitate an identity crisis per se. As I will argue in more detail below, Austen deploys motherlessness, whether by death (*Persuasion*, *Emma*), abdication (*Mansfield Park*), vacuousness (*Pride and Prejudice*), or ineffectuality (*Sense and Sensibility*), as a generic rather than a psychological convention. The delightful exception to omnibus maternal absence is *Northanger Abbey* (1818), in which the mother's sensible *presence* is among the first cues to the novel's satirical mode. Catherine Morland's mother is of a sort rarely to be found in fictions of Gothic pretensions – namely, as Austen acerbically notes, alive: "Her mother was a woman of useful plain sense, with a good temper, and, what is more remarkable, with a good constitution. She had three sons before Catherine was born; and instead of dying in bringing the latter into the world, as any body might expect, she still lived on – lived to have six children more – to see them growing up around her, and to enjoy excellent health herself."[52] Catherine, on the other hand, "in training for a heroine," is schooled not in the ways of the world but in the ways of fiction, and for an adolescent girl of her vocation, a mother who is both living and sensible is a liability of the first degree. Indeed, her mother's

robust presence is perhaps the most conspicuous index to the preposter-
ousness of Catherine's fiction-induced delusions, but for Austen even in
this case, the mother remains a generic formation disassociated from the
sphere of psychological influence. Instead, the rare metonym of maternal presence indicates the romantic – and by this point, fully consolidated – nature of the tropes that follow the structural convention of
maternal decampment.

Dickens's *Oliver Twist* was published in 1837, the same year Queen
Victoria acceded to the throne, and this, I would argue, is the first fully
"Victorian" novel, marking the complete articulation of the
psychologized, sentimentalized plot of the dead mother. Dickens com-
pletes the response to eighteenth-century narrative models first engineered by Austen, in a far more earnest and less satirical fusion of these
three formal precedents, even as he participates in the symptomatic
canonization of a dead woman modeled in *Clarissa*. Like the protagonists of Austen and her eighteenth-century precedents, young Oliver is in
many kinds of danger because of his orphanage; similar to the plots of
his eighteenth-century counterparts, Oliver's plot unfolds into the revelation of Oliver's "true" – meaning family or genetic – identity. But
Dickens brings a new literalism to the phenomena of both female
disembodiment and female virtue, and the distinction that makes *Oliver
Twist* so unique is the radical and explicit idealization of the mother, not
only in her death, but quite remarkably, *through* her death.

Beginning with *Oliver Twist*, three specific agendas emerge within the
larger form of the Victorian melancholic novel. The first of these is a
sentimental form emblematized in this novel, which uses maternal
absence to invent a deeply emotional and abstract vocabulary of
motherhood and family. The second, which exists in its purest – if least
sentimental – form in Austen's *Emma*, is the erotic, a form that uses the
structural space of maternal absence as a staging-ground for the drama
of adolescent sexual selection. In the final form, the emancipatory novel,
which evolves directly into the New Woman novel, novelists exploit
maternal absence to construct radical new visions for female potential.
Each of these subgenres exploits the convergence, enabled most dramatically by Dickens, of mystery and life story or autobiography; even
Austen's Mr. Knightley delves into Emma Woodhouse's past to justify
Emma's will to power, thwarted only by her long-dead mother and
flourishing untamed in the succession of substitutes who fail to fully
replace that mother. Through their demystification of personal origin,
each narrative form constructs a strategically and politically distinct

notion of subjectivity. Appropriated for the endorsement of "family values" as radically distinct as the endings of *Oliver Twist* and *Jane Eyre*, the narrative vehicle of maternal loss proves a flexible tool in the construction of a range of ideological positions.

In the first formal appropriation of the dead-mother narrative, texts such as *Oliver Twist, Bleak House*, and Elizabeth Gaskell's *Wives and Daughters* construct a blank slate on which the cultural ideal of sentimental maternity can be firmly reinscribed. *Oliver Twist* (1837) opens with a scene of both birth and death, in which the protagonist, Oliver, comes into the world a foundling in a poorhouse. After hearing her infant scream, Oliver's anonymous mother speaks for the first and last time: "'Let me see the child, and die.'"[53] The narrator then reports, "She imprinted her cold white lips passionately on its forehead, passed her hands over her face, gazed wildly round, shuddered, fell back – and died" (46). The mother's kiss operates as a form of baptism for Oliver; even this brief moment of connection with his mother establishes her definitively as the standard of goodness and virtue for the boy. Orphaned almost immediately, Oliver faces a life of enforced anonymity: a foundling in a poorhouse, he is named by the state and left to fend for himself, first in the orphanage, and later in London's East End. What Dickens's text is concerned with, I want to argue, is precisely the invention of a rhetoric of sentimental domesticity: the low condition of Oliver's birth is contrasted with his poor mother's urgent – and virtuous – desire to kiss her child. The aim of the narrative is thus foregrounded by contrast, directed toward the goal of Oliver's transcendence over the morally and economically impoverished conditions of his existence. This goal is characteristically represented through the symmetrical recuperation of the dead mother at the end of the novel, in which a tombstone is erected in her name – although her actual body is never recovered. That tombstone, marking the fact of maternal virtue, but marking it over an empty space, is emblematic of the profoundly disembodied nature of the maternal ideal.

In the author's preface to the novel, Dickens declares his desire "to show, in little Oliver, the principle of Good surviving through every adverse circumstance, and triumphing at last" (33). The condition of motherlessness is invoked throughout *Oliver Twist* as the ultimate "adverse circumstance." Acts of fortune or kindness directed toward the boy are inevitably followed by the recurrence of the orphan-trope. For example, in his first employment, with Sowerberry the undertaker, Oliver comes to blows with his rival, Noah Claypole, who has taunted him about the mysterious circumstances surrounding his mother's death. The narrator describes the scene:

A minute ago, the boy had looked the quiet, mild, dejected creature that harsh treatment had made him. But his spirit was roused at last; the cruel insult to his dead mother had set his blood on fire. His breast heaved; his attitude was erect; his eye bright and vivid; his whole person changed, as he stood glaring over the cowardly tormentor who now lay crouching at his feet; and defied him with an energy he had never known before. (88)

Oliver's radical tumescence occurs in defense of an ideal, persistently represented throughout the text as "maternal." A moment formative of his own personal ideals, Oliver's attack on Noah costs him a job and thrusts him forth, alone, into London's underworld. But as a moment that articulates the moral value-structure of the novel as well as its protagonist, Oliver's defense of his mother's (as yet unknown) "good name" predicts the formal recuperation of that name at the novel's conclusion.

Through the narrative of *Oliver Twist*, Dickens constructs a model of sentimentalized filial behavior by means of contrast: the very abjection of Oliver's condition is distinguished from the high moral tenor of his impulses; all he lacks is an object for his affections. The mystery of the dead mother's identity, of her name, functions as the novel's informal detective plot; as Mr. Bumble explains soon after Oliver's birth," 'we have never been able to discover who is his father, or what was his mother's settlement, name, or condition' " (51). Oliver's advocates and enemies alike seek the answer to this mystery, and so return no less than four times to re-narrations of the scene of maternal death; the story is told differently each time, until it is revealed that the dead woman left a wedding-ring inscribed with the name "Agnes." This clue is enough to confirm Oliver's identity; to ensure him a portion of his father's wealth; to affirm his instinctive connection to a mother-substitute, who he learns is his mother's sister Rose; and to install him inextricably in a secure, rural environment with a newly formed, happy – and motherless – substitute family:

Mr. Brownlow adopted Oliver as his son. Removing with him and the old housekeeper to within a mile of the parsonage-house where his dear friends [the newlyweds Rose and Harry] resided, he gratified the only remaining wish of Oliver's warm and earnest heart, and thus linked together a little society, whose condition approached as nearly to one of perfect happiness as can ever be known in this changing world. (476)

The novel's conclusion of pastoral paradise rewards Oliver's virtuous impulses under adverse conditions, and the ultimate icon of the pastoral is the mother, recuperated. In the final revision of the death-scene with which it opens, *Oliver Twist* concludes with the formal recognition of Agnes's goodness:

Within the altar of the old village church there stands a white marble tablet, which bears as yet but one word: "AGNES". There is no coffin in that tomb; and may it be many, many years before another name is placed above it. But, if the spirits of the Dead ever come back to earth, to visit spots hallowed by the love – the love beyond the grave – of those whom they knew in life, I believe that the shade of Agnes sometimes hovers round that solemn nook. I believe it none the less because that nook is in a Church, and she was weak and erring. (479–80)

From the death of the mother to her "burial," *Oliver Twist* traces a path from impoverished abjection to bourgeois sentimentality; the fallibility of Agnes only underscores the importance of her transcendence, and her ghostly presence at the novel's close confirms her spectral presence throughout the text. Within the context of nineteenth-century fiction, *Oliver Twist* stands out as an example of carefully constructed domestic sentimentality, in which the novel's accession to the domestic occurs in direct proportion to its ability to recuperate the dead mother, not as a living woman, but as a good woman. That recuperation facilitates the establishment of the period's central, most powerful moral abstraction, an ideal of maternity explicitly divorced from the problematic of female physicality.

The second form of structural advantage presented by maternal loss occurs in narratives of courtship and sexual desire. Such texts as Jane Austen's *Emma* and *Mansfield Park*, Trollope's *The Eustace Diamonds*, and Mrs. Henry Wood's wildly popular sensation novel *East Lynne* exploit the protagonist's motherlessness as a token of erotic vulnerability (which is in turn parodied by Thackeray's descriptions of Becky Sharp's machinations in *Vanity Fair*). For the female protagonist in each of these novels, the absent mother and the future husband stand in a complementary relationship to one another. The equation of mother and suitor offers each heroine a contained moral framework for the expression of desire. Further, the period between mother and marriage functions within each text as an opportunity to experiment with alternative forms of power; in each case, the heroine uses this opportunity to test the limits of her social, political, and discursive agency.

Thus *Emma* (1816), for example, establishes a paradigm that will be enormously influential in the Victorian period, opening with a doubly inscribed scene of loss: not only is Emma Woodhouse's mother dead, but Emma has also lost her long-time governess, Miss Taylor, who has married Mr. Weston that very day. Emma sits alone, dejected, with only her father for company: "It was on the wedding-day of this beloved friend that Emma first sat in mournful thought of any continuance. The wedding over and the bride-people gone, her father and herself were left to dine together, with no prospect of a third to cheer a long evening."54 That "third" is, of course, Mr. Knightley, who intervenes in the father–daughter dyad both on this particular evening and permanently, at the end of the novel, when he marries Emma and moves into her father's home.

Establishing from the beginning the desirability of the triangular structure, Mr. Knightley, as the third term, exists in a multiply over-determined relationship to Emma's dead mother. Not only does he occupy the position that was originally hers; he is identified explicitly as like her, and as like Emma herself. As the only person in the novel capable of coping with Emma, Knightley identifies the late Mrs. Wood-house as the only other person ever to have had that capacity:

"Emma is spoiled by being the cleverest of her family. At ten years old, she had the misfortune of being able to answer questions that puzzled her sister at seventeen. She was always quick and assured: Isabella is slow and diffident. And ever since she was twelve, Emma has been mistress of the house and of you all. In her mother she lost the only person able to cope with her. She inherits her mother's talents, and must have been under subjection to her." (32–3)

Knightley's marriage to Emma represents a reassertion of the structure of "subjection" that was removed with the removal of her mother. The symmetrical equation of maternal object and love-object, reflective of the Freudian ethic of erotic substitution, is suggestive of the complex relationship between structures of desire and structures of power. There is an implication in Knightley's comment of a distinction between subjection and subjectivity; indeed, while Emma is motherless and single, she produces an excess of plot, drama, and activity. In her analysis of maternal loss in *Emma*, Marianne Hirsch argues that "plot itself demands maternal absence," but that the "female family ro-mance" of *Emma* produces marriage, Emma's subjection to another rule, and the cessation of her drama.55 That the space of maternal loss is the space of sexual desire suggests that each of these relationships exists within conflicting dynamics of subjection and subjectivity. For Emma, marriage equals the reinscription of the domain of "maternal" hegemony; the condition of motherlessness represents a fecundity of possibilities for her future.[56]

The third form of melancholic text, the narrative of opportunity, exists in close relationship to those novels pursuing an examination of marriage and courtship. Such texts as Margaret Oliphant's *Miss Marjoribanks*, as well as Charlotte Brontë's *Jane Eyre* and *Shirley*, and Elizabeth Gaskell's *North and South*, utilize the protagonist's motherlessness to produce revisionary, often proto-feminist, representations of marriage, the family, and women's roles. Here it is precisely the *absence* of a maternal role-model that allows these texts to challenge conventions of female behavior. In a discussion of Jane Eyre as a motherless heroine, Adrienne Rich argues for the revisionary feminist potential of narratives that lack the embodiment of a pre-existing ideology of women's place and desire: "Jane Eyre, motherless and economically powerless, undergoes certain traditional female temptations, and finds that each temptation presents itself along with an alternative – the image of a nurturing or principled or spirited woman on whom she can model herself, or to whom she can look for support." Jane's separation from any stable, permanent mother-figure enables her, Rich argues, "to move forward into a wider realm of experience," and therefore to enter into her marriage on her own terms, without sacrificing her subjectivity:

In *Jane Eyre* . . . we find an alternative to the stereotypical rivalry of women; we see women in real and supportive relationship to each other, not simply as points on a triangle or as temporary substitutes for men. Marriage is the completion of the life of Jane Eyre, as it is for Miss Temple and Diana and Mary Rivers; but for Jane at least it is marriage radically understood for its period, in no sense merely a solution or a goal. It is not patriarchal marriage in the sense of a marriage that stunts and diminishes the woman; but a continuation of this woman's creation of herself.[57]

Rich's conclusion about the concessions Jane makes in her relationship to Rochester is certainly debatable. Her identification, however, of a relationship between motherlessness and women's mutual supportiveness locates a valuable asset of the structure of substitution entailed in a dead-mother plot: because characters exist in less conventional relationships to one another, they are free to critique and revise conventions more generally.

Lucilla Marjoribanks, the protagonist of Margaret Oliphant's novel *Miss Marjoribanks* (1866), demonstrates a subtle but definitive cultural critique. The text opens with the line, "Miss Marjoribanks lost her mother when she was only fifteen, and when, to add to the misfortune, she was absent at school, and could not have it in her power to soothe her dear mamma's last moments, as she herself said."[58] Lucilla goes on to analyze this crisis in terms informed exclusively by literature:

[Lucilla], however, was only fifteen, and had floods of tears at her command, as was natural at that age. All the way home she revolved the situation in her mind, which was considerably enlightened by novels and popular philosophy – for the lady at the head of Miss Marjoribanks [*sic*] school was a devoted admirer of *Friends in Council*, and was fond of bestowing that work as a prize, with pencil-marks on the margin – so that Lucilla's mind had been cultivated, and was brimful of the best of sentiments. She made up her mind on her journey to a great many virtuous resolutions; for, in such a case as hers, it was evidently the duty of an only child to devote herself to her father's comfort, and become the sunshine of his life, as so many young persons of her age have been known to become in literature. Miss Marjoribanks had a lively mind, and was capable of grasping all the circumstances of the situation at a glance. Thus, between the outbreaks of her tears for her mother, it became apparent to her that she must sacrifice her own feelings, and make a cheerful home for papa, and that a great many changes would be necessary in the household – changes which went so far as even to extend to the furniture. (25–6)

Lucilla's rank opportunism, as well as her impulse to redecorate, are the lessons of novels. Well schooled, like Catherine Morland, in the romances of fiction, Oliphant's narrator is conspicuously less gentle than Austen's about the implications of such impracticality: "novels and popular philosophy" have only educated Lucilla for a disingenuous display of emotion and generosity toward her "dear papa." As she satirizes Lucilla's responses, however, Oliphant, like Austen, also exploits the narrative conventions of maternal death, which provide opportunities for orphans and narrators alike.[59]

Q. D. Leavis makes explicit Lucilla's participation in the historical continuum of strong fictional heroines of the nineteenth century; perhaps not coincidentally, this tradition is populated by young women whose mothers have died. Leavis writes: "Lucilla is a triumphant intermediary between Jane Austen's Emma and George Eliot's Dorothea and, incidentally, more entertaining, more impressive and more likable than either."[60] Oliphant's Lucilla indeed shares many affinities with Emma and Dorothea, but most notably, *Emma*, *Miss Marjoribanks*, and *Middlemarch* are all texts that announce the death of the mother in their opening pages; in *Middlemarch* (1872), the first chapter describes Dorothea and Celia plundering their mother's "casket," her jewel-box, dividing her treasures and anticipating, as Emma does, the imminent arrival of a lover.

Lucilla's opportunistic excitement at her mother's death is based on the assumption that motherlessness is the equivalent to womanhood: "Miss Marjoribanks managed to influence the excellent woman who believed in *Friends in Council*, and to direct the future tenor of her own education; while, at least, in that one moment of opportunity, she had achieved long dresses, which was a visible mark of womanhood, and a step which could not be retraced" (33). What this notion of womanhood entails is a new level of autonomy (for Lucilla now stands in the structural position of homemaker), agency about the ways in which she fills her time, and independence in her selection of a mate. Consistently, though, what Lucilla wants is not marriage but a political voice and a position of power within her community; she wants to occupy a role that doesn't yet exist by definition, and she struggles acutely with the fact of such category crisis. Indeed, the novel's most pointed critique of gender roles occurs when Lucilla seems destined to remain a spinster, a "redundant female," forever:

When a woman has an active mind, and still does not care for parish work, it is a little hard for her to find a "sphere." And Lucilla, though she said nothing about a sphere, was still more or less in that condition of mind which has been so often and so fully described to the British public – when the ripe female intelligence, not having the natural resource of a nursery and a husband to manage, turns inwards, and begins to "make a protest" against the existing order of society, and to call the world to account for giving it no due occupation – and to consume itself. (395)

When Lucilla is faced with the specter of "spherelessness," however, she manages to convert her circumstances into both occupation and opportunity for the betterment of the community. She manages the successful campaign of a candidate for Parliament from the town of Carlingford, and in fact, only under the rubric of this campaign, of finding "the best man for Carlingford," does she finally, secondarily, find the "best man" for herself, and marry. But her husband is her cousin, Tom Marjoribanks; thus she and her name both remain unchanged. Although at the end of the novel she stands quite literally in the place of her mother, as *Mrs.* Marjoribanks, Lucilla, like Eliot's Dorothea, holds a vision of her married life that is far from the convention of the domestic. Oliphant's narrator writes, "at the moment of taking leave of her, there is something consoling to our own mind in the thought that Lucilla can now suffer no change of name. As she was in the first freshness of her youthful

daring, when she rose like the sun upon the chaos of society in Carlingford, so it is now as she goes forth into the County to carry light and
progress there" (498–9). Lucilla is another lady with a lamp, her vision
oriented outward, her proper sphere of influence quite clearly the
sociopolitical as well as the domestic, in excess even of Dorothea, who
by the end of *Middlemarch* is simply wife to a Member of Parliament, her
horizon of ambition dramatically curtailed. The distance between this
Mrs. Marjoribanks and her predecessor is measured in the fact that
Lucilla's mother lay on the sofa for years prior to her expiration; the
daughter's first act is to reupholster that sofa in a flattering shade of
green.

The representational issues surrounding maternity in the nineteenth
century are at once complicated and paradoxical; the extremes of public
and private, chaste and erotic, ideal and embodied meet in a single
figure, while there remains an enormous investment in keeping them
separate. Ironically, therefore, representations of maternal *loss* –
through abandonment, accident, or death – become a culture's way of
negotiating these paradoxes, and the narrative invention of a domestic
ideal is almost invariably predicated on the prior condition of maternal
abandonment. As a means of constructing an ideal or dismantling it, or
as a vehicle for the narration of adolescent sexuality and courtship, the
death of the mother in nineteenth-century fiction creates a structural
environment of instability that allows the narrative to progress into an
internally sanctioned ideal of stability. As I will argue in the next
chapter, within Freudian and post-Freudian psychoanalysis, the vocabulary of maternal loss similarly figures the terms of subjective stability by staging that loss as the child's first and most significant rite of
passage. While the practical implications of Victorian fiction and
psychoanalysis are different, these two distinct modes of narration
deploy the same figure to similar ends: the passage from anxiety to
stability, from loss to mastery, occurs by appropriating maternal loss.
For each genre, this appropriation facilitates a representational anxiety
in which the division of prohibition and desire, of abstraction and
embodiment, is negotiated.

Between each of the chapters that follow, I have inserted epigraphs
from mid-nineteenth-century British midwives' manuals. I want these
quotations to demonstrate a sense of generic contrast, to suggest alternative contemporary modes of understanding motherhood and the phenomenon of maternal loss. However, they should also underscore an
important point I made earlier, that novels of Victorian Britain featur-

ing maternal absence, whether through death or abandonment, are in almost no sense concerned with the woman behind the mother they mourn. Insofar as they are concerned exclusively and graphically with that woman, these epigraphs offer the opportunity to view her through another lens, through a medical instead of a melancholic narrative. For better or for worse, this alternative perspective provides a glimpse into a world almost never broached in Victorian fiction, the embodied representation of the female subject as a mother.

Puerperal Mania. – No. 7. October 27, 1857. – A pluripara, delivered normally. Mania appeared on the third day; she got out of bed and went into the street, thinking "her husband wanted to do away with her"; she was still suckling her child; she was removed to an asylum.

Robert Barnes, M.D., "Clinical History of the Eastern Division of the Royal Maternity Charity, During the Year Ending September 30, 1858," *Dublin Quarterly Journal of Medical Science* 28 (1859), 118.

CHAPTER 2

Psychoanalytic cannibalism

There is no getting round the fact that each man and woman *came out of a woman*. Attempts are made to get out of this awkward predicament. There is the whole subject of couvade, and in the original harlequin myth there is a man who gives birth to babies. And the idea of being born out of the head is often found, and it is certainly easy to jump from the word "conception" to the concept of "conceiving of."

D. W. Winnicott[1]

As the site of each individual's physical and psychological origin, the mother is necessarily central to the analysis of infancy, development, and trauma. Paradoxically, however, the mother is most often represented within the conventions of Freudian psychoanalysis in terms of disappearance. In order for human development to occur in an orderly fashion, the infant's primal cathexis onto the mother must be ruptured, and the mother replaced by alternative physical, psychological, and erotic objects. When the mother appears in psychoanalysis, then, she is destined to disappear; she is the original object of desire and of prohibition, the site of both origins and loss.

This chapter aims to elucidate the theoretical underpinnings of my larger analysis of dead and missing mothers in the Victorian novel. At the same time, however, I remain concerned with the extent to which psychoanalytic theories *duplicate* the narrative paradigms of Victorian fiction, a fact that is both clarified and problematized in post-Freudian revisions of psychoanalytic developmental models, particularly in the predominant field of British psychoanalysis, object-relations theory. The discussion of psychoanalysis that follows will consider Freud's treatment of maternal absence in the context of the work of Melanie Klein and D. W. Winnicott, both of whom intervene powerfully in the field of infant and child analysis, and both of whom work in language

amenable to – and occasionally identical to – literary critical methodologies.

Melanie Klein is a figure interposed historically between Freud and
Winnicott, and her work, which focuses on dynamics of ambivalence
between mother and child, clarifies the terms in which psychoanalysis as
a narrative form recapitulates tropes of Victorian fiction. While the
historical trajectory of twentieth-century psychoanalysis tends toward
an increased focus on the mother, it also describes the ideological
construction of the mother in familiar terms, as a passive, disembodied
ideal divorced from the material responses of living women. For Freud,
the mother is the figure at the center of every form of desire, and for
Klein, the mother is a figure whose symbolic presence is legible at every
point of adult life; for Freud and Klein alike, she is the referent toward
whom all rhetorics and all desires tend. For Winnicott, however, the
mother is potentially dangerous to her child, a powerful figure who
requires discipline and containment for the good of the vulnerable
infant – and for the world order that follows that good. By considering
Freud, Klein, and Winnicott in the historical context of psychoanalytic
theory, then, the terms of each analyst's investment in maternal "loss"
reveal striking agendas that at once call forth and revise ideological
formulations generated in and lingering from the Victorian period.

FREUD AND THE LOSS OF THE MOTHER

In his 1926 essay *Inhibitions, Symptoms, and Anxiety*, Freud argues that the
etiology of all anxiety is traceable to the loss of the original object, the
mother:

Only a few manifestations of anxiety in children are comprehensible to us, and
we must confine our attention to them. They occur, for instance, when a child is
alone, or in the dark, or when it finds itself with an unknown person instead of
one to whom it is used – such as its mother. These three instances can be
reduced to a single condition – namely, that of missing someone who is loved
and longed for . . . Here anxiety appears as a reaction to the felt loss of the
object; and we are at once reminded of the fact that castration anxiety, too, is a
fear of being separated from a highly valued object, and that the earliest anxiety
of all – the "primal anxiety" of birth – is brought about on the occasion of a
separation from the mother.[2]

The extent to which the child is able to manage its "primal anxiety" is
precisely the extent to which it is capable of functioning as a subject.
What this management entails, then, is the expulsion of the mother

before the fact of her loss: if the child voluntarily forsakes the object of its desire, voluntarily assumes a cathexis of substitution, he or she emerges victorious over the threat of paralyzing anxiety.

The two options presented to the child in the individuation process are describable as masochistic and sadistic; namely, the choice between inflicting pain (rejection) *on* the mother, or being inflicted with pain (rejection) *by* the mother. In "Mourning and Melancholia" (1917), Freud describes the management of loss. While normal mourning is characterized by the eventual ability to recognize the loss of a loved object, and therefore to forsake the object, pathological melancholia is characterized by the desire to introject the object of loss, and therefore to punish the self for the transgressions of the loved one, thereby occupying a masochistic relationship to the event of loss itself. As in the communities consolidated in memory of the dead heroines of Richardson's *Clarissa* or Rousseau's *La Nouvelle Héloïse*, a poetics of life becomes a poetics of loss in which every event refers back to an overdetermined, abstract, idealized version of the dead object. Freud writes of melancholia: "The ego wants to incorporate this object into itself, and, in accordance with the oral or cannibalistic phase of libidinal development in which it is, it wants to do so by devouring it."[3] The analogy to the oral phase of development, in which the child's desires are fixed exclusively on the mother, makes explicit Freud's argument that later-life attitudes toward traumatic loss are shaped by the primal loss of infancy. As I will discuss shortly, Melanie Klein argues that the child's "cannibalistic" relationship to the mother represents the ambivalence of the child's desires for an all-powerful, nutritive mother, and its aggressive impulses against the mother who deprives it of food, allowing it to grow hungry or uncomfortable.

Throughout *Inhibitions, Symptoms, and Anxiety*, however, Freud attempts to refute the claims made by Otto Rank in his 1926 book, *The Trauma of Birth*. Rank, working from Freud's claim in *The Interpretation of Dreams* that *"the act of birth is the first experience of anxiety, and thus the source and prototype of the affect of anxiety,"*[4] argues that the birth-trauma is the original and prototype for all later forms of neurotic and psychotic fixation. He writes:

Our concept attempts to replace the theory of different places of fixation, which are supposed to determine the choice of neurosis, by *one* traumatic injury (producing various forms of reactions) in a single place of fixation, namely, the mother (parturition). There is, then, according to our view, only one fixation place, namely, the maternal body, and all symptoms ultimately relate to this primal fixation, which is given to us in the psychobiological fact of our Unconscious. In this sense we believe we have discovered in the trauma of birth the primal trauma.[5]

In his counter-argument, Freud focuses mainly on the infant's inability to have formed an object-relationship to the mother at the moment of birth; desire provoked by loss cannot come into being without a primary object-relationship.[6] The battle between Rank and Freud devolves into a classic "chicken or egg" debate concerning the nature of "primal" in the primal trauma. At the end of *The Ego and the Id*, Freud writes: "Here, moreover, is once again the same situation as that which underlay the first great anxiety-state of birth and the infantile anxiety of longing – the anxiety due to separation from the protecting mother."[7] However, Freud's privileging of maternal loss here is the exception to the rule; he is consistently careful to present "loss" as a strictly phallic phenomenon. Yet throughout his work, descriptions of "phallic loss" tend to slip back into the metaphor of maternal loss: whether the lost mother is a phallic mother or whether the Oedipal child's castration anxiety produces an aggressive turning away from the erotic mother, some form of maternal loss, if not maternal lack, is implicated in this formative psychodrama. This begs the question of the relationship of mother and phallus, and also potentially recasts the politics of gender and power within the developmental paradigm, which is precisely the site of Klein's intervention in Freudian discourse. The *fort-da* game Freud plays with the mother – now you see her, now you don't – is inflected with the same markers of anxiety and mastery in crisis modeled by the child in *Beyond the Pleasure Principle*. In both cases, the elaborately reinforced scaffolding of metaphor – *fort-da*, the phallus – replaces the object so tragically missing.

For even castration anxiety, the most central determining structure of Freudian psychoanalysis, is traceable to the loss of the mother. Freud argues in *Inhibitions, Symptoms, and Anxiety*:

The significance of the loss of object as a determinant of anxiety extends considerably further. For the next transformation of anxiety, viz. the castration anxiety belonging to the phallic phase, is also a fear of separation and is thus attached to the same determinant . . . The high degree of narcissistic value which the penis possesses can appeal to the fact that that organ is a guarantee to its owner that he can be once more united to his mother – i.e. to a substitute for her – in the act of copulation. Being deprived of it amounts to a renewed separation from her, and this in its turn means being helplessly exposed to an unpleasurable tension due to instinctual need, as was the case at birth. But the need whose increase is feared is now a specific one belonging to the genital libido and is no longer an indeterminate one, as it was in the period of infancy. It may be added that for a man who is impotent (that is, who is inhibited by the threat of castration) the substitute for copulation is a phantasy of returning to his mother's womb.[8]

The valuable "lost object," the mother of the oral phase, turns into the phallus of the genital organization of the libido; in each case, the child's anxiety-level exists in direct proportion to his – or her – perception of the object's permanency or efficacy. Ironically, however, for Freud's impotent man in particular, cathexis onto the mother creates a double-bind. Although "the substitute for copulation is a phantasy of returning to his mother's womb," this phantasy can only ever perpetuate his castration anxiety through the equally strong fear of the father's revenge for the theft of *his* object. The example of the impotent man, Freud's would-be "normative" (that is, male, heterosexual) subject, makes clear the sense in which desire is aggressively oriented away from the mother, but at the same time toward her, since it is directed toward her substitute or analogue. This formulation is the origin of the chiasmus of pleasure and pain, possession and loss, that constitutes desire: the subject, oriented teleologically toward *thanatos* or death, ironically seeks an ideal object of *eros* located firmly in the past. The mother, site of ambivalence for the child in the convergence of plenitude and the power to devastate, is not the only "split subject" of the developmental psychodrama; the child itself, split between future and past, mother and father, introjects the division initially projected outward onto the mother figure.

Freud's argument here makes clear a significant, and significantly double, structure of substitution: the "phallus," an object-replacement for the mother, signifies for the male child access to another mother-substitute, the erotic object with whom he copulates. This double structure of substitution, of phallus for mother and erotic object for mother, illustrates the most literal sense in which the psychoanalytic mother is in essence a rhetorical impossibility, a theoretical figure alone. As Freud argues elsewhere, the "phallic mother" represents the phantastic figure of "completeness" in the mind of the child; the phallic mother is the all-powerful, all-giving source of life that embodies both mother and father, breast and phallus. Freud's description of the phallic mother offers him a single term to describe a double scene of loss: the coincidence of separation from the mother and anxiety about the status of the phallus produces the "phallic mother" retrospectively as the spectral phantasy of anterior fulfillment.9 The anxiety operative during the Oedipal or phallic phase, the loss of the phallic mother, is character-ized by entry into a more precarious dependency-structure. At the same time, however, the Oedipal configuration makes clear that for boys and girls alike, their erotic cathexis onto the mother must be ruptured in favor of substitutes that circumvent both the incest taboo and the fear of the rival, punishing father.[10] The child is thus doubly prohibited from "desiring" the mother: the structure of phallic identification is predicated on what the mother lacks; the structure of erotic develop-ment is predicated on a re-cathexis of desire onto a substitute figure.

While Freud sees all categories of subjectivity and all forms of sexual desire as forms of desire for a lost mother, the only possible exception he makes to this rule is the category of female heterosexuality. Indeed, Freud's theory of the "transition" that must occur from one "sexual zone" – the clitoris – to the other – the vagina, represents a convoluted attempt to justify the woman's turn from the mother as the symbolic object of desire, as well as to explain the ideal of feminine erotic passivity that is in direct opposition to a normative theory that equates subjectiv-ity with erotic mastery: "A female's first object, too, must be her mother: the primary conditions for a choice of object are, of course, the same for all children. But at the end of her development, her father – a man – should have become her new love-object. In other words, to the change of her own sex there must correspond a change in the sex of her object."[11] For Freud's mother-centered psychoanalytic paradigm of erotic development, female heterosexual object-choice seems a most unlikely choice: "Only if her development follows the third, very circu-itous, path does she reach the final normal female attitude, in which she takes her father as her object and so finds her way to the feminine form of the Oedipus complex."[12] To desire the father-object, for Freud, is to repudiate the mother both literally and symbolically, a "maternal loss" that is far more extreme than he can countenance as "normal." This only underscores the extent to which, in psychoanalytic paradigms as in Victorian fiction, normative maternal loss is in fact a site of maternal presence, maternal power: to "lose" the mother is simply to embrace her symbolically, metaphorically, through a structure of endlessly sub-stitutable erotic objects. In Freud's conception of female heterosexual-ity, however, adult women must reject not only the actual mother, but also, problematically, the mother-*symbol*. The loss of this symbolic struc-ture is tantamount to the loss of language itself, and with it the loss of subjectivity aggressively constituted through the masterful manipulation of the metaphors *fort* and *da*. For Freud, the symbolic missing mother is the linchpin of successful psychic functioning: in a dazzling literalization of the central trope of Victorian fictional narratives, the embodied mother is completely irrelevant within the psychoanalytic *Bildungsroman*, while the metaphor of maternal benevolence, constructed through and as her willful passivity, is essential.

The overdetermined conventions of the Oedipal paradigm suggest, therefore, two different senses in which the psychoanalytic mother is necessarily "lost" to the child: because she is the phallic mother, castration anxiety makes clear the untenability of the original phantasy; because she is the erotic mother, the socially conditioned structures of erotic development indicate a necessary move away from her, a displacement in favor of substitutes that exist in a relationship of repetition and difference. "Phallic mother" represents a physical impossibility captured on the level of rhetorical description alone, a useful gesture toward a utopic phantasy of completeness for child and analyst alike; as the "maternal ideal" of psychoanalysis, the phallic mother exists within the framework of ideal-in-absence represented in the Victorian cult of domesticity. Further, within the bounds of symbolic, post-Oedipal discourse, the "erotic mother" is a similarly paradoxical, untenable figure; anxiously represented in the Victorian period through the iconography of maternal chastity, maternal eroticism remains a similar source of anxiety and prohibition within psychoanalysis.

The psychoanalytic child protects itself from the fact of maternal loss with the weapon of language, a concept suggestive for the rhetorical analysis of maternal loss in narrative fictions. In *Beyond the Pleasure Principle* (1920), Freud's presentation of the *fort-da* game makes explicit the equation of maternal loss and subjective articulation. He observes a young male child's manipulation of a wooden reel pulled by a piece of string. The game is inevitably accompanied by the child's apparently pleasurable cry of "'o-o-o-o,'" which Freud and the baby's mother agree represents the German word *fort*, or "gone": "What he did was to hold the reel by the string and very skillfully throw it over the edge of his curtained cot, so that it disappeared into it, at the same time uttering his expressive 'o-o-o-o'. He then pulled the reel out of the cot again by the string and hailed its reappearance with a joyful '*da*' ['there']. This, then, was the complete game – disappearance and return."[13] In Freud's description, the boy's game occurs on two levels – his manipulation of the reel over the precipice of his "curtained cot," and his equally pleasurable description of the event in marginally intelligible infantile language. Freud, like the child, connects the act itself and its description; it is the child's use of descriptive language, in fact, which provides Freud with the means of reading the symbolic significance of the activity.

The dynamic of the *fort-da*, Freud argues, "was related to the child's great cultural achievement – the instinctual renunciation (that is, the renunciation of instinctual satisfaction) which he had made in allowing his mother to go away without protesting. He compensated himself for this, as it were, by himself staging the disappearance and return of the objects within his reach" (15). The monumental significance of this event for Freud – as well as for the child – exists as a shift in the terms of power: it is the child, through the act of symbolic representation, who renounces the mother, thus inoculating himself against vulnerability to her rejection. The child's "instinctual renunciation" or "renunciation of instinctual satisfaction" represents his ability to master his bodily impulses and desires, which have been, up to this point, oriented consistently toward his mother.

The child's puzzling (to Freud) yield of pleasure from the apparently innocuous game with the reel represents the establishment of an economy of pleasure based on the acknowledgment of loss and necessary substitution; as compensation for his efforts, the child rewards himself with the pleasurable experience of representation. Freud describes this shift as the child's appropriation of the active position:

At the outset he was in a *passive* situation – he was overpowered by the experience; but, by repeating it, unpleasurable though it was, as a game, he took on an *active* part. These efforts might be put down to an instinct for mastery that was acting independently of whether the memory was in itself pleasurable or not. But still another interpretation may be attempted. Throwing away the object so that it was "gone" might satisfy an impulse of the child's, which was suppressed in his actual life, to revenge himself on his mother for going away from him. In that case it would have a defiant meaning: "All right, then, go away! I don't need you. I'm sending you away myself." (16)

Whether it is cast as the representation of mastery or the representation of revenge, the *fort-da* game functions for both Freud and this child as the replacement of the mother's power with the power of symbolic representation, and therefore of the mother's power with the child's power. The child's assumption of language – his pleasurable verbal description of the event he enacts – is equivalent to his appropriation of the discourse of rejection. For Freud, then, the gesture of rejection and the appropriation of loss signify the expulsion of the mother in exchange for the birth of independent, masterful subjectivity.

In his own symbolic representation of the *fort-da* game, Freud gives this child language on two separate occasions. It is his interpretation of the child's utterance "'o-o-o-o'" that connects this phoneme with the signifier *fort*. And it is Freud himself, not the child, who overlays the *fort-da* game with the discourse of revenge; the words "'All right, then, go away! I don't need you. I'm sending you away myself'" are the analyst's, not the child's. While Freud's personal implication in the drama he describes has been amply documented (the child is his grandson; the missing mother is Freud's now-dead favorite daughter Sophie), his investment in both interpretation and symbolic representation places him in a position of identification with the little boy; they are identical in the invocation of language as a structure of substitution for a critical loss.[14] Within the context of the Oedipal drama, the child's "rejection" of the mother, the object of his "instinctual satisfaction," would ordinarily result in his identification with the father; similarly, for little girls, rejection of the mother entails the appropriation of the mother's heterosexual desire for the father. For the child of the *fort-da* game, however, it is the father who is literally absent, taken from the family to fight in World War I; Freud reports:

A year later, the same boy whom I had observed at his first game used to take a toy, if he was angry with it, and throw it on the floor, exclaiming: "Go to the fwont!" He had heard at that time that his absent father was "at the front," and was far from regretting his absence; on the contrary he made it quite clear that he had no desire to be disturbed in his sole possession of his mother. (16)

The child's antagonism toward his absent father nonetheless belies an investment in the structure of identification; a year after the original *fort-da*, the child exists in "sole possession of his mother." The rhetoric of possession and mastery effectively triangulates the mother–infant dyad; the implicit equation of father and language occurs at the expense of maternal loss. If language is the tool of the father, it exists as a structure of identification that comes into being through the literal renunciation, and the symbolic expulsion, of the mother. The primary structure described in the oscillation of *fort* and *da* is the compensatory or complementary equation of maternal absence and linguistic presence.

Lacan argues that a structure of loss consistently underpins language from the beginning; as the *fort-da* game illustrates, the act of primary symbolization is in its essence a gesture away from the mother, rather than the articulation of a relationship to her:

There can be no *fort* without *da* and, one might say, without *Dasein* . . . If the young subject can practice this game of *fort-da*, it is precisely because he does not practice it at all, for no subject can grasp this radical articulation. He practices it with the help of a small bobbin, that is to say, with the *object a*. The function of the exercise with this object refers to an alienation, and not to some supposed mastery, which is difficult to imagine being increased in an endless repetition, whereas the endless repetition that is in question reveals the radical vacillation of the subject.[15]

In his description of the *fort-da* game, Lacan exchanges Freud's con-clusion – that the subject achieves mastery – for a reading that insists on alienation; the child's bobbin, in Lacan's interpretation, is the *object a* or the sign of "otherness" that enables the child to consolidate an identity. In Lacan's argument, the most critical signifier is the hyphen separating *fort* from *da*; for the hyphen is the graphic representation of loss, absence, and alienation. The *Dasein* of Lacan's description represents the aggres-sive assertion of subjectivity, a metaphysical claim to being or existence produced only through the experience of inalienable loss. This, accord-ing to Lacan, is the story of the game.

In another analysis of the *fort-da* scenario, however, Lacan appropri-ates the voice of the mother in order to articulate the relationship among the mother, the symbolic, and the child-subject. In "Tuché and Automaton," he writes:

I, too, having seen with my own eyes, opened by maternal divination, the child, traumatized by the fact that I was going away despite the appeal, precociously adumbrated in his voice, and henceforth more renewed for months at a time – long after, having picked up this child – I have seen it let his head fall on my shoulder and drop off to sleep, sleep alone being capable of giving him access to the living signifier that I had become since the date of the trauma.[16]

The Lacanian/maternal voice that narrates this passage describes the post-traumatic physical reconnection of "mother" and infant. The persistence of the voice over the head of the sleeping child makes a subtle equation between the maternal signifier and the language of the unconscious: the "mother" speaks while the child sleeps, and the "mother" speaks the child's anxieties, vulnerabilities, and phantasies, the maternal voice introjected and analogous to the dream. For the post-*fort-da*, post-Oedipal child, access to the "living signifier" – the lost object, the maternal absent presence – occurs only in sleep. For this child, sleep represents an abdication of agency, an abandonment of physical rigidity, and the emergence of the language of dreams; within the realm of the symbolic, the maternal voice subtends conscious discourse, lurking behind, beneath, below, above the signifier.

The structure that Lacan sketches out here, in which the mother-signifier exists in/as the unconscious, unseen but heard, is consistent with Julia Kristeva's theory of the semiotic. Kristeva argues that symbolic, post-Oedipal discourse exists in a synchronic relationship to the language of the semiotic, the unintelligible language that passes between mother and infant in the pre-Oedipal or choric phase of development. Kristeva's reorientation of linguistic models in favor of maternal inclusion is indebted to the work of Melanie Klein, and in particular to Klein's emphasis on the long-term significance of the pre-Oedipal phase: "Psychoanalysts acknowledge that the pre-Oedipal stages Melanie Klein discusses are 'analytically unthinkable' but not inoperative; and, furthermore, that the relation of the subject to the signifiers is established and language learning is completed only in the pregenital stages that are set in place by the retroaction of the Oedipus complex (which itself brings about the initial genital maturation)."[17] In Kristeva's terminology, the symbolic and the semiotic (reductively, the paternal and the maternal) are two modalities that work together to produce signification, figuring the present and absent components of the sign. She writes:

As a precondition to the symbolic, semiotic functioning is a fairly rudimentary combinatorial system, which will become more complex only after the break in the symbolic. It is, however, already put in place by a biological setup and is always already social and therefore historical. This semiotic functioning is discernible before the mirror stage, before the first suggestion of the thetic. But the semiotic we find in signifying practices always comes to us after the symbolic thesis, after the symbolic break, and can be analyzed in psychoanalytic discourse as well as in so-called "artistic" practice . . . In taking the thetic into account, we shall have to represent the semiotic (which is produced recursively on the basis of that break) as a "second" return of instinctual functioning within the symbolic, as a negativity introduced into the symbolic order, and as the transgression of that order.[18]

The synchronic nature of the Kristevan semiotic offers a means of taking into account the contribution of anterior, prelinguistic experience within the paternal order; recalling the theory of melancholic narrative I discussed earlier, Kristeva seeks a methodology in which to read structures of subjectivity as shaped, in some very direct sense, by an active if ineffable maternal principle. Extrapolating from the model of the *fort-da* game, she proposes a way of factoring the maternal into a paternalistic model of discourse; before either *fort* or *da*, there was the choric, instantiating, mother–child dyad. Traces of the chora are readable in the realm of the symbolic; indeed, since the act of "reading" itself presupposes a subjectivity grounded in the symbolic, the semiotic is only ever accessible through its symbolic traces.

But far from serving as a means of recuperating the mother for psychoanalysis, Kristeva's theory of the semiotic potentially only succeeds in underscoring the *fort-da* dialectic within the symbolic. Only ever existing in the realm of "theoretical supposition,"[19] the semiotic is to a certain extent the exclusive creation of the symbolic, providing the index of otherness, of negativity or transgression, and institutionalizing conclusively the subjective empire of the symbolic, in a position of mastery analogous to that of Freud's *fort-da* baby. By now formally, institutionally marginalized, her impact "'analytically unthinkable,'" the mother's sphere of influence is limited to the always already, the anterior.

Despite the importance it grants the semiotic and the influence it grants the maternal, Kristeva's argument subtly reinscribes the equation of subjectivity and maternal absence. This is a formulation challenged in those Victorian novels, such as *Bleak House* and *Daniel Deronda*, in which missing mothers return, forcing their children into the uncomfortable accommodation of their psychic demands; this is one means by which Victorian fiction proves instructive to the understanding of psychoanalytic paradigms, facing more frequently the challenge of representing maternal subjectivity as an active and visible force, despite ambivalence about the implications of such agency. Jane Gallop argues in an article about psychoanalytic feminist literary criticism that "the institution of motherhood is a cornerstone of patriarchy."[20] As a cornerstone of *psychoanalytic* patriarchy, the institution of motherhood is a temporarily useful, quickly obsolete means of describing the origins of the individual, and later of the speaking subject. Just as Freud is implicated in the game played by the *fort-da* subject, the institution of psychoanalysis is implicated in a larger *fort-da* game, in which the "mother" is perpetually relegated to the patriarchal sideline. If, as Freud argues, the anxiety of maternal loss is the source of all anxiety for the psychoanalytic subject, then a related form of anxiety informs the analyst's desire to marginalize, contain, and expel the mother.

Theoretical and narrative structures predicated on the fact of maternal loss displace or attenuate questions about female subjectivity, female sexuality, and the exclusionary practices of language and culture.

If the absent mother lurks in the unconscious, then the institutional anxiety is not that of her departure, but rather that of her return; not for her *fort*, but perhaps ironically, for her *da*. Formally coded as transgressive, the phantasmagoric return of the missing mother represents the opportunistic deconstruction of the discursive practices that imposed those codes in the first place and a direct challenge to the achievement of phallic mastery constituted in her absence – hence the profound significance of the challenge that object-relations theorists, and in particular Melanie Klein, pose to the Freudian establishment. As the cornerstone of patriarchal discourse, the circumscription of the mother is a structural necessity; if that circumscription should fail, if that absence should become a presence, the entire structure comes tumbling down.

OBJECT-RELATIONS THEORY AND THE CHALLENGE TO FREUD

In the paradigm of psychoanalytic object-relations theory, the loss of the mother is at once inevitable, catastrophic, desirable, and traumatic. Subjectivity, as well as etiology, springs full-blown from the child's ability to reconcile the polarity of desire and catastrophe. It is the task of the psychoanalyst to describe the relative success or failure of that reconciliation.

In several significant ways, the construction of a theory of object-relations represents a major departure from orthodox Freudian paradigms of development; Laplanche and Pontalis go so far as to defend Freud's familiarity with the theory, although they claim that the idea of the object-relationship "plays no part in Freud's conceptual scheme."[21] Object-relations theory was developed initially by psychoanalysts in Britain and Europe around the time of World War II. These analysts, most prominently Klein, worked primarily through the study of infants and children, extrapolating their conclusions to apply to the study of adult neuroses and psychoses. Perhaps their most dramatic departure from Freudian paradigms of development is the de-emphasizing of the importance of instinctual drives in exchange for an emphasis on the influence of social context and interaction, a shift that anticipates the most popular and populist forms of behavioral theory in the later decades of the twentieth century, including behavior modification, ego psychology, and contemporary pop psychology.

Melanie Klein's early work in infantile object-relationships presented unique challenges to the Freudian establishment, not least the claim to the centrality and power of the mother. Klein claimed that a version of the Oedipus complex occurred much earlier than Freud believed; for her, the dialectical relationship of pleasure and distress in the oral phase is paradigmatic of later relationships, while the relative resolution of this dialectic during the oral phase predicts the fate of all future psychodynamic processes. The early erotic relationship between mother and child, Klein contends, anticipates the dramas that constitute the later, Oedipal-genital phase. Thus orality, not genitality, provides the primary template for adult neuroses; and further, the child's cathexis onto the mother, rather than the father, provides the initial encounter with the superego and predetermines the course of adult behaviors and transferential relationships.[22]

When Klein moves the line of Oedipal identification back to an earlier point in time, she both participates in the major contemporary trends in psychoanalytic theory and anticipates later feminist reinterpretations of Freudian paradigms. The question of infant and child analysis was hotly debated in European psychoanalysis between the world wars; after the publication of Freud's *Three Essays on the Theory of Sexuality* (1905), the arena of early childhood development was opened up and the complexity of early childhood participation in the narrative of erotic development began to be extrapolated. Analysts' interest in infancy and childhood, particularly in Britain, prompted questions about the viability of early treatment and even calls for the standardized, prophylactic psychoanalysis of children. Klein and Anna Freud were leaders in the actual treatment of children, diverging most notably in terms of their opinions about child transference; Klein claimed that children could and did develop salutary positive and negative transferential relationships, while Anna Freud argued that children remained under the authority of parents, and that the analyst served a pedagogical rather than a transferential function.[23]

But perhaps the most dramatic effect of the interest in child analysis was the focus on the central determining importance and power of the maternal relationship. The replacement of the father with the mother as the determining figure of identity and relationship also entailed the displacement of the castration complex as the index against which all ego-formations occur. Institutionally in the world of psychoanalysis, such undermining of the castration complex began to address widespread concerns about phallocentrism. As early as the 1920s, in fact, the psychoanalytic establishment was contending with allegations of phallocentrism, and that, combined with interest in childhood sexuality, prompted an increase of favor for theories about female anatomical determinism. In a paper delivered to the Innsbruck Congress in 1927, Ernest Jones declared that "There is a healthy suspicion growing that men analysts have been led to adopt an unduly phallo-centric view of the problems in question, the importance of the female organs being correspondingly underestimated."[24] In the book *Mothering Psychoanalysis*, Janet Sayers argues that a generation of female analysts working in this period, including Klein, Anna Freud, Helene Deutsch, and Karen Horney, engineered a massive reconsideration of the omnipotence of the father and the phallus in psychoanalysis.[25]

In the model of anatomical determinism, however, the breast and the phallus are comparable: as objects that function simultaneously as signifiers constituted in an ambivalent relationship to physical referentiality, breast and phallus alike offer a logic of signification based on equivocation. Joan Riviere writes of the breast:

Without some degree of dissatisfaction with our mother's milk and her nipples or with our bottles, we none of us ever grow up mentally at all. By turning away, and also by subdividing our aims and distributing them elsewhere, the needs both of hunger and of sexual pleasure become detached from the mother. Food for the body and for pleasure of eating and drinking is gradually found elsewhere, while on turning away from the breast erotic pleasure is also rediscovered elsewhere.[26]

Like the castration complex, the efficacy of the breast, and by extension of the maternal object, exists in and as the potential of loss. But significantly, while object-relations analysts consistently claim that the mother is figured in terms of both "good breast" and "bad breast," they never draw attention to the fact that most women actually *have* two breasts. The implications of this fact help to distinguish the referential structures of the breast from those of the phallus: good breast and bad breast alike usually exist on the female body, which is therefore symbolically sufficient unto itself. In contrast, the phallus, as a signifier of absence and presence, requires for its illustration the phantastic convergence of two bodies, one male, signifying presence, and one female, signifying lack. The phallus can never be bodied forth in a single figure, and the fact that it is necessarily a theoretical abstraction should underscore the frightening physical and psychic potency of the mother.

Because it is a theoretical construct that reads forward from the infantile, object-relations consistently recurs to the physical connection between mother and child, and the postnatal drama of weaning, in order to describe the processes of differentiation; in other words, all referential structures in object-relations theory point to a mother who is necessarily absent, but whose psychic presence threatens to overwhelm. D. W. Winnicott, a theorist of object-relations indebted to the work of Klein but much more directly ideological and didactic, suggests the long-term gender politics of such physical, and later psychic, dependency:

We find that the trouble is not so much that everyone was inside and then born, but at the very beginning everyone was *dependent* on a woman. It is necessary to say that at first everyone was *absolutely* dependent on a woman, and then relatively dependent. It seems that the pattern of your mental health and mine was laid down by a woman at the start who did what she had to do well enough, at that stage when love can only be expressed physically if it is to be meaningful to the baby . . . Now it is very difficult indeed for a man or woman to reach a true acceptance of this fact of absolute and then relative dependence in so far as it applies to the actual man or woman. For this reason there is a separated-out phenomenon that we can call WOMAN which dominates the whole scene, and affects all our arguments. WOMAN is the unacknowledged mother of the first stages of the life of every man and woman.[27]

Winnicott's description of "absolute dependency" makes clear how very powerful a figure this mother is: unacknowledged or not, she has determining power over all allegedly adult functionings. But for Winnicott, it remains critical that "WOMAN" is a "separated out" phenomenon and that the "unacknowledged mother" remain in the background or in the hazy reaches of the past. Winnicott suggests what the child might have at stake in maintaining the objectified status of the mother-object; in a discussion of the praiseworthy but unsung activities of the "good mother" in society, he argues:

Is not this contribution of the devoted mother unrecognized precisely because it is immense? If this contribution is accepted, it follows that every man or woman who is sane, every man or woman who has the feeling of being a person in the world, and for whom the world means something, every happy person, is in infinite debt to a woman. At the time when as an infant (male or female) this person knew nothing about dependence, there was absolute dependence . . . If there is no true recognition of the mother's part, then there must remain a vague fear of dependence. This fear will sometimes take the form of a fear of WOMAN, or fear of a woman, and at other times will take less easily recognized forms, always including the fear of domination.[28]

Winnicott suggests that the subject's fear of dependence might lead to misogyny more generally. Similarly, Klein, through her discussion of the "epistemophilic impulse," argues that sadism and aggression toward women work as a preemptive response to the fear of domination and dependence. To "recognize the mother's part," it would seem, is not to exorcise the tensions determining the fate of the object in subjective functioning.

The terminology of loss in the object-relations paradigm is thus different from that of the castration complex. First of all, the source of potential violence is the child-subject, who phantasizes violent retaliatory strategies against the internalized "bad object," the breast that does not satisfy on demand. The *location* of revenge, however, is permanently displaced onto the body of the mother through the mechanism of aggressive projection. Riviere describes the unsatisfied infant:

In a certain degree the baby becomes aware of his dependence; he discovers that he cannot supply all his own wants – and he cries and screams. He becomes aggressive. He automatically explodes, as it were, with hate and aggressive craving. If he feels emptiness and loneliness, an automatic reaction sets in, which may soon become uncontrollable and overwhelming, an aggressive rage which brings pain and explosive, burning, suffocating, choking bodily sensations; and these in turn cause further feelings of lack, pain and apprehension.[29]

When desire confronts dependency, the resulting conflict produces aggression. But in a notable contrast to the castration complex, the object of violence and aggression is the object externalized in a phantasy in which the maternal object is destroyed. In Freud's theory of castration, the *child's* body is the site of potential or actual loss, albeit "loss" modeled on the child's perception of its parents' bodies. But in the object-relations paradigm, it is precisely the child's resistance to loss and the critical projection of aggressive feelings onto the maternal body that implicate and empower the child as an economic agent.

Because the mother–infant interaction exists as the "first and basic" alignment of imagination and reality, the epistemological framework Klein produces is paradigmatic for future episodes of dialectical reasoning. The young sadist is empowered as a creative agent within the drama of his – or her – ego-formation; the terms by which the mother is constructed and annihilated belong to the child and to the child alone. Klein describes the "epistemophilic impulse" as a sadistic impulse consisting of the phantastic construction and prompt destruction of an "object." Again, the figure that is necessarily missing is necessarily central: Klein suggests the dependence of epistemological structures on the violent destruction of a mother-symbol, and thus the importance of and the anxiety provoked by that mother within epistemologies. For the oral infant, she argues, the first "object" is the mother that bears the stuff of life, and the child's preoccupation with the mysterious contents of the maternal body prompts the drive to explore, to possess, to destroy. Klein writes, "The child expects to find within the mother *(a)* the father's penis, *(b)* excrement and *(c)* children, and these things it equates with edible substances."[30] Not only are these things (to the child's perception) "edible" substances, they are potential rivals to the child for the mother's attention; to consume these objects is to consume the dangerous, fickle mother and to secure stability. The infant is a little cannibal, oriented to and dependent on the mother's breast for survival, whose desire to incorporate the maternal body represents a drive to "epistemology" predicated on the assimilation of a multiply symbolic object and the assumption of a position as controller and interpreter of these symbols. The child's relative success at the "epistemophilic impulse" determines "the subject's relation to the outside world and to reality in general." Klein explains that the sadistic phantasies directed against "the inside of [that mother's] body constitute the first and basic relation to the outside world and to reality. Upon the degree of success with which the subject passes through this phase will depend the extent to which he can subsequently acquire an external world corresponding to reality."[31] At the heart of ego-formation, then, is the production and destruction of a symbolic object personated by the child as "mother." It is, in fact, the construction of a *rhetoric* of maternal loss, specifically in terms of metaphor and symbol, that constitutes the grammatology of the psychoanalytic subject.

The phenomenon that Klein describes is in essence a philosophy of knowledge built on a relationship of empowerment over a maternal object constructed as a symbol; subjectivity is a sadistic formulation, and the ability to configure, to destroy, and to recall the object signifies the terms of the episteme. But in the context of post-Freudian psychoanalysis, the "epistemophilic impulse," the claim to a description of the means by which knowledge is produced, implicates the theory itself. The generation of psychoanalytic theorists who founded the study of infant and early-childhood analysis was forced by the circumstances of their practice to provide their subjects with language; to work with not-yet-verbal subjects required the therapist to reconfigure the analytical scene to accommodate these analysands, recalling Freud's interpretation of baby babble as the articulation of *fort* and *da*. Klein's influential solution to this problem was the development of "play therapy," in which she kept a locked box of toys for each analysand and extracted the analytical narrative from her observations of the child's play. On the most literal level, the analyst provides the child with "objects," then constructs "object-relations theory" as an interpretation of the child's representational construction of narrative through play. It is the analyst, though, not the child, who designates the significance of objectification as "maternal," and who is the primary constructor, reader, and interpreter of symbols. For although the analyst "reads" the child's play as a symbolic representation of psychological conflict, it is the analyst herself who actually supplies the object, both object-as-toy and object-as-mother. Melanie Klein's construction of the "epistemophilic impulse" is precisely the construction of her epistemological framework, implicated, like Kristeva and Freud, in a *fort-da* game with the mother-symbol. And with its emphasis on the symbolic and the metaphorical, narrative interpretation and the implication of the "reader"-analyst, Klein's theory of infant analysis is quite immediately a paradigm of literary interpretation.

MELANIE KLEIN, AESTHETICS, AND INTERPRETATION

When Klein speaks of interpretation, she does so in terms of a strategic intervention into a therapeutic scene: "Constant interpretation, the gradual solving of resistances and the constant tracing of the transference to earlier situations – these constitute in children as in adults the correct analytic solution."[32] The analyst's interpretive "reading" of the psychic conflict represented in the child-patient's play should ideally inoculate the analysand by making conscious previously unconscious processes. As Freud writes in *The Interpretation of Dreams*:

I have been engaged for many years (with a therapeutic aim in view) in unravelling certain psychopathological structures – hysterical phobias, obsessional ideas, and so on. I have been doing so, in fact, ever since I learnt from an important communication by Josef Breuer that as regards these structures (which are looked upon as pathological symptoms) unraveling coincides with removing them. If a pathological idea of this sort can be traced back to its elements in the patient's mental life from which it originated, it simultaneously crumbles away and the patient is freed from it.[33]

The importance of interpretation, for both Klein and Freud, occurs not only in the activity, but also in its communication. The accuracy of the analyst's reading is only significant in the context of the "therapeutic view." The key to interpretation is to gain access to the "original," to the instantiating moment of a trauma or an idea. Psychoanalysis is always in the process of reading backward into infancy. Under the rubric of object-relations theory, this reading process entails the analysis of the moment and the terms of maternal loss and maternal "fiction."

While it is clear that Klein's strategy of play-interpretation is informed by Freud's theory of dream-interpretation, it is also clear that the different representational issues at stake in child analysis produce an alternative set of hermeneutical challenges. The nature of the reading that occurs in child analysis is complicated by the discursive challenges posed by the analytic scene; the child's interaction with toy objects must come to represent a readable text. In "The Psycho-Analytic Play Technique," Klein describes this challenge:

> My attention from the beginning focused on the child's anxieties and . . . it was by means of interpreting their contents that I found myself able to diminish anxiety. In order to do this, full use had to be made of the symbolic language of play which I recognized to be an essential part of the child's mode of expression . . . The importance I attributed to symbolism led me . . . to theoretical conclusions about the process of symbol formation. Play analysis had shown symbolism enabled the child to focus not only interests, but phantasies, anxieties and guilt to objects other than people.[34]

Unlike dream-work, play-work is a conscious activity, but like dream-work, play-work presents the analyst with a form of "narrative" to interpret. Klein's "theoretical conclusions" about the process of symbol-formation indicate a relationship between rhetoric and anxiety: symbolic formations accumulate as a means of displacing anxiety from the primary referent. The reading process that Klein both describes and models is an attempt to read back to that originary structure, using the rhetorical as a vehicle toward the maternal referent.

In 1937, Melanie Klein and Joan Riviere published a book entitled *Love, Hate and Reparation*, in which, explains John Rickman in the preface, "An attempt is made to convey in everyday language some of the deeper mental processes which underlie the everyday actions and feelings of normal men and women."[35] The conclusions in this book represent the logical extremes of object-relations theory. The two authors' concern with the structural issues at stake in the construction of symbols and objects reveals the primary logic of Klein's theoretical paradigms. As an analysis of the origins of imagination and creativity, the two essays that comprise the book present themselves as an effort at aesthetic theory, suggesting the repetition, in thematic concerns as well as methodology, of melancholic subjectivity foregrounded in Victorian fictional representations of maternal loss. And as an analysis of literary texts and discourse, Klein and Riviere present both a description and a theory of literary interpretation.

If object-relations theory is predicated on a logic of inextricable binary opposition, with the bad object counterbalanced against the good, then that logic is acted out in a larger sense throughout this text. The two analysts divide their subject in two, with Riviere writing about "Hate, Greed and Aggression," and Klein taking "Love, Guilt and Reparation." Within this configuration, Riviere occupies the place of the bad object, describing "some of the ways in which we endeavor to deal with and obtain *security* against the dangerous disintegrating forces of hate and aggression in ourselves which, if too strong, may lead to painful privations or even to extinction" (LHR, 4). Klein, on the other hand, represents the good object, the salutary mother, attempting "to give a picture of the equally powerful forces of love and the drive to reparation" (LHR, 57). It is quite clear from the start, however, that it is not possible to discuss one half of this opposition without invoking the other: that the aim of Riviere's piece should be to describe the trajectory from aggression to security, and that Klein's analysis of love should only exist in terms of the drive to reparation, indicates the interdependency of the oppositional terms. Klein writes:

In separating our topic in this way we cannot perhaps clearly convey the constant *interaction* of love and hate; but the division of this vast subject was necessary, for only when consideration has been given to the part that destructive impulses play in the interaction of hate and love, is it possible to show the ways in which feelings of love and tendencies to reparation develop in connection with aggressive impulses and in spite of them. (LHR, 57)

In other words, within division, there is sameness; within the clarity of an articulated impulse lurks the oppositional structure. The two analysts model the child's predicament in the pattern of oscillation between two poles.

If Klein and Riviere are attempting to act out on the level of the narrative the explicit tenets of the psychological activities they describe, they are also, in many ways, attempting to argue for a universal logic. Riviere writes in her introductory comments:

Two of the ultimate sources of these familiar emotional manifestations are the two great primary instincts of man: hunger and love, or the self-preservative

and the sexual instincts . . . Now, to present a picture of the interaction of
self-preservation, pleasure, love and hate adequately would be the same thing
as to describe and explain every manifestation of human life. Our efforts to
sketch a rough outline of it in these two lectures must necessarily be oversimpli-
fied and schematic to a high degree, and full of gaps. (LHR, 3)

The root of the universal experience is infancy; to begin to describe a
universal *fort-da* game, then, is to begin with infancy, and with the
infant's experience of – and creation of – the mother's body.

In Riviere's analysis of infantile logic, the moment of distinction is the
moment of maternal loss. To return to her description of infantile
desperation and aggression:

A baby does not recognize anyone's existence but his own (his mother's breast
is to him merely a part of himself – just a sensation at first) and he expects all
his wants to be fulfilled. He (or she) wants the breast for love of it, so to speak,
for the pleasure of sucking the milk, and also to still hunger. But what
happens if these expectations and wants are not fulfilled? In a certain degree
the baby becomes aware of his own dependence; he discovers that he cannot
supply all his own wants – and he cries and screams. He becomes aggressive.
He automatically explodes, as it were, with hate and aggressive craving.
(LHR, 8)

It is significant that the scream, the voice, is constituted in the moment
of abandonment; in the terms that Riviere sets up here, the moment of
absence marks the advent of desire, for absence signals the first indication of non-satisfaction and therefore of need. The fact that the first
love-object is the maternal object is significantly related to the connection between desire and loss; the reinstantiation of original satisfaction is
the aim of the scream. If both voice and desire are implicated in the
scene of maternal loss, then narrative, narrative desire, and narratives of
desire emerge from a relationship to the maternal object.

Riviere describes in graphic detail the torturous condition of original
desire:

The baby cannot distinguish between "me" and "not-me"; his own sensations
are his world, *the* world to him; so when he is cold, hungry or lonely there is no
milk, no well-being or pleasure in the world – the valuable things in life have
vanished. And when he is tortured with desire or anger, with uncontrollable,
suffocating screaming, and painful, burning evacuations, the whole of his world
is one of suffering; it is scalded, torn and racked too. This situation which we all
were in as babies has enormous psychological consequences for our lives. It is
our first experience of something like death, a recognition of the *non*-existence
of something, of an overwhelming loss, both in ourselves and in others, it seems.

And this experience brings an *awareness of love* (in the form of desire), and a *recognition of dependence* (in the form of need), at the same moment as, and inextricably bound up with, feelings and uncontrollable sensations of *pain and threatened destruction* within and without. (LHR, 9, italics in original)

In the apocalyptic moment of maternal desertion, desire and need emerge as separate entities, fueled, respectively, by the ability to distinguish the good object from the bad, the breast of plenty from the breast of negation. But what the dual discourses of desire have in common with one another is an originary moment that is basically the horrifying awareness of dependence, the awareness of the determining agency of the maternal object and the disenfranchised status of the nascent subject. The emergence of dialectical reasoning, what Klein terms the "depressive position,"[36] occurs as the attempt to resolve a power-struggle for the position of independence.

Once again, however, the terms of that power-struggle are implicated in the anxiety produced by the question of agency; as Klein explains:

If, however, the early conflict between love and hate has not been satisfactorily dealt with, or if guilt is too strong, this may lead to a turning away from loved people or even a rejection of them. In the last analysis it is the fear that the loved person – to begin with, the mother – may die because of the injuries inflicted upon her in phantasy, which makes it unbearable to be dependent upon this person. (LHR, 83)

The drive to independence originates as a fear of love, as well as an aggressive impulse; because of this anxiety, "the child is driven toward weakening his attachment to the all-important person, his mother" (LHR, 84). The resolution of the dilemma of control for Klein, as for Riviere and the babies they describe, is through the vehicles of phantasy and symbol-creation. By producing a rhetorical mother to expel, the subject can aggress with impunity, just as the production of a rhetorically expelled mother allows the psychoanalyst to analyze the originary drama of ego-formation.

In Klein's description, the production of a symbol – a mother-object, a phantasy – enables the displacement into fiction of the question of pain. She writes:

The baby's impulses and feelings are accompanied by a kind of mental activity which I take to be the most primitive one: that is phantasy-building, or more colloquially, imaginative thinking. For instance, the baby who feels a craving for his mother's breast when it is not there may imagine it to be there, i.e. he may imagine the satisfaction which he derives from it. Such primitive phantasy-

ing is the earliest form of the capacity which later develops into the more
elaborate workings of the imagination. (LHR, 60)

As a coping mechanism, "imaginative thinking" is a safe replacement for
the aggressive response to maternal abandonment and infantile dependency. Within the broader context of object-relations theory, symbolic
discourse is the locus of the analytic text, and the psychoanalyst is the
reader and interpreter of the "imaginative thinking" conducted in play
therapy. As an additional producer of analytic text, the psychoanalyst as
interpreter is also engaged in the act of "imaginative thinking"; and as the
producer of a text that deploys the discourse of symbolism and aesthetics,
the object-relations theorist stands in an overdetermined relationship to
the metaphor of maternal abandonment. Again, the Kleinian epistemophilic impulse, which is, ultimately, the impulse to rout the maternal body of all its phantasied contents, underpins the drive to analysis
and articulation. As a narrative theory, the epistemophilic impulse
understands aggressive claims to subjectivity as "cannibalistic" acts,
compulsively recalling the double-bind of relation to the mother.

Klein extrapolates forward from this logic to generate a theory about
all aesthetic production, all scientific production, and ultimately, all
forms of epistemological understanding. "The process by which we
displace love from the first people we cherish to other people is extended
from earliest childhood onwards to things," she writes in explanation of
the unconscious signifying powers of objects.

> By a gradual process, anything that is felt to give out goodness and beauty, and
> that calls forth pleasure and satisfaction, in the physical or in the wider sense,
> can in the unconscious mind take the place of this ever-bountiful breast, and of
> the whole mother. Thus we speak of our own country as the 'motherland'
> because in the unconscious mind our country may come to stand for our
> mother, and then it can be loved with feelings which borrow their nature from
> the relation to her. (LHR, 102–3)

In this symbolic economy, signifiers inevitably return to the mother.
Psychoanalysis, shaped like the Victorian novel in its melancholic impulse toward such a return, is a discourse that relies upon loss; to narrate
the story of a life, whether the genre in question is the case-study or the
domestic novel, is to start with and, invariably, to return to the mother.
Yet that mother is also a menacing emblem of the too-fluid borderlines
of the self, and the return to her domain is conditioned by the need to
escape again into a less precarious state of self-sufficiency. The *fort-da*
dialectic continues.

Klein's most extended analogy of maternal recuperation occurs in her description of the exploration narrative, and the dual drives of desire and acquisition that motivate the explorer.

In the explorer's unconscious mind, a new territory stands for a new mother, one that will replace the loss of the real mother. He is seeking the "promised land" – the "land flowing with milk and honey" . . . In his pursuit the explorer actually gives expression to both aggression and the drive to reparation. We know that in discovering a new country aggression is made use of in the struggle with the elements, and in overcoming difficulties of all kinds. But sometimes aggression is shown more openly; especially was this so in former times when ruthless cruelty against native populations was displayed by people who not only explored, but conquered and colonized. (LHR, 104)

Klein's invocation of colonialism suggests the terms by which the power dynamic of infancy is recuperated in adulthood. The equation of the "new mother" with the "native populations" who were conquered and colonized suggests, however, that the maternal object exists distinctly outside of the terms of "subjectivity" that originate, in some sense, with her. If the goal of recovery is a goal of mastery, subjectivity is hegemony in which the original object is the original subject; in the profoundly imperialistic itinerary of subject-formation, the will to power implicates physical and psychic, as well as narrative, control.

Klein argues that the motivating impulse behind the constant recuperation of the maternal object is the drive to reparation born out of guilt, fear, anxiety, and repressed aggression:

If the baby has, in his aggressive phantasies, injured his mother by biting and tearing her up, he may soon build up phantasies that he is putting the bits together again and repairing her. This, however, does not quite do away with his fears of having destroyed the object which, as we know, is the one whom he loves and needs most, and on whom he is entirely dependent. (LHR, 61–2)

A series of scattered fragments is readable for Klein as the repaired, roughly constructed maternal object; the mother plays monster to the infant's Victor Frankenstein. But as the fragments are readable only metonymically as mother, Klein reverses her terms: "mother" becomes "symbol," while "object" functions as "source." "The sculptor who puts life into his object of art, whether or not it represents a person, is unconsciously restoring and re-creating the early loved people, whom he has in phantasy destroyed" (LHR, 106). The adult infant has the power of animation and creation over the originary figure. The effect of "imaginative thinking," in this paradigm, is autobiographical omnipotence. Sculptor and writer alike revise the question of where babies come from with their reversal of the causal logic of ontology.

Given the prominence of the symbolic and the metaphorical throughout object-relations, it is in some sense logical that Klein's ultimate example of maternal recuperation should occur in an act of literary criticism. In the place in her writing where a case-study usually appears, she provides a reading of Keats's sonnet "On First Looking into Chapman's Homer." The advantage of this particular poem to Klein's larger argument is twofold. First of all, the narrator's description of travel, and his invocation of Cortez ("with eagle eyes/He star'd at the Pacific") extend the metaphor of exploration as recuperation. Further, the self-consciously aesthetic nature of the sonnet, a poem about reading, provides Klein with the logical end-point to her gradually evolving theory of symbolic language and maternal loss. She writes:

In Keats' perfect poem the new world stands for art, and it is clear that to him scientific and artistic enjoyment and exploration are derived from the same source – from the love for the beautiful lands – the "realms of gold." The exploration of the unconscious mind (by the way, an unknown continent discovered by Freud) shows that, as I have pointed out before, the beautiful lands stand for the loved mother, and longing with which these lands are approached is derived from our longings for her. (LHR, 106)

Not only does the new world stand for art, it stands for the mother, loved and lost. And further, not only does scientific and artistic pleasure originate in the aesthetic value of the "beautiful lands – the 'realms of gold,'" but the realms of gold find their aesthetic and economic value in their metonymic relationship to the mother. Keats's sonnet, a text *en abîme*, stands *en abîme* within Klein's text, while the object receding within these frames is the mother. The act of aesthetic production for Klein's psychoanalytic subject, like the act of life-writing in the Victorian novel, returns time and again to the same question: the question of the mother. And the act of analytic interpretation for object-relations theory, like the process of detection in Victorian fiction, has only one answer; that answer, ever problematic and tautological, is also the mother.

WINNICOTT'S GOOD-ENOUGH MOTHER

D. W. Winnicott builds upon conclusions suggested by Klein's theories of the symbol. In what is perhaps his best-known work, the theory of the transitional object and transitional relating, he argues for a process of infantile transition from identification with the mother to identification oriented outward to the subjective world, a process mediated through inanimate objects such as dolls or teddy-bears, which the child uses to learn how to break away from the mother. This is another version of the familiar psychoanalytic formulation that posits an opposition between mother and outside world. But Winnicott takes this formulation to its extreme; his later writing, which reacts with antipathy to the implications of feminist movements of the 1960s, marks a polemical and ideologically explicit return to the rhetoric of a maternal ideal that features a passive and self-abnegating mother. For Winnicott much more than for Freud, the mother's function is to serve the child's psychological needs. The mother as a desiring or desired subject is evacuated, and in turn she is constructed as a cipher whose only agency is conceived as the negative ability to damage the child through her avaricious need.

When Winnicott speaks of interpretation, he does so in the context of a discussion of "borderline cases," in which the analysand fluctuates between neurotic and psychotic states; it is the analyst's task to stabilize the patient in the neurotic. But this task is complicated, Winnicott argues, by the analyst's inevitable transferential impulse:

It is only in recent years that I have become able to wait and wait for the natural evolution of the transference arising out of the patient's growing trust in the psychoanalytic technique and setting, and to avoid breaking up this natural process by making interpretations. It will be noticed that I am talking about the making of interpretations and not about interpretations as such. It appals me to think how much deep change I have prevented or delayed in patients *in a certain classification category* by my personal need to interpret. If only we can wait, the patient arrives at understanding creatively and with immense joy, and I now enjoy this joy more than I used to enjoy the sense of having been clever.[37]

From Winnicott's perspective, the path to "immense joy" would seem to entail the repression of the epistemophilic impulse in favor of a self-patrolled passivity. The goal is the patient's achievement of creative understanding; the ideal situation is for interpretation to "be made" from the position of the analysand, and ultimately, then, for the therapeutic intervention to become gradually obsolete.

The distinction that Winnicott is attempting to draw here is one between object-relating and object-usage. The displacement of interpretation from analyst to analysand requires the patient to utilize the analyst as a functional object. He describes the distinction as follows:

Object-relating is an experience of the subject that can be described in terms of the subject as an isolate. When I speak of the use of the object, however, I take object-relating for granted and add new features that involve the nature and the behaviour of the object. For instance, the object, if it is to be used, must necessarily be real in the sense of being part of shared reality, not a bundle of projections. It is this, I think, that makes for the world of difference between relating and usage.[38]

The process of object-relating occurs internally within one particular subject, and the object to which the subject relates is the projected phantasy of his or her own psyche. But object-usage, in Winnicott's terminology, refers to a "real" object, not just a symbol or a metaphor, which is presupposed to have a subject-position in and of itself. For the "borderline cases" of Winnicott's essay, the goal of object-usage is the internalization of the analyst and the appropriation of the analytic voice: the naturalization of psychoanalysis.

Winnicott postulates that object-relation and object-usage exist in a sequential relationship to one another.

The sequence can be observed: (1) Subject *relates* to object. (2) Object is in process of being found instead of placed by the subject in the world. (3) Subject *destroys* object. (4) Object survives destruction. (5) Subject can *use* object . . . The object is always being destroyed. This destruction becomes the unconscious backcloth for love of a real object; that is, an object outside the area of the subject's omnipotent control.[39]

If "usage" signifies both internalization and intersubjectivity, the thera-peutic goal articulated within this framework is the deconstruction of the borderlines with an aim to their reinstitutionalization through the establishment of an individual subject. For the "borderline" analysand, this deconstruction is the only means to participation in "shared real-ity." The translation of the terms of relation, destruction, projection and reality into the discourse of therapy signals an important shift, for in Winnicott's paradigm, the projected object, the mother, is replaced by the real object, the analyst.

In fact, the relationship between mother and analyst, between object destroyed and object maintained or internalized, remains a tension throughout Winnicott's work. "Mothers, like analysts," he writes, "can be good or not good enough; some can and some cannot carry the baby over from relating to usage."[40] For the goal of the "good-enough mother," like the good-enough analyst, is to occupy a position of built-in obsolescence. To carry the baby to usage means that the mother's gradual withdrawal of herself as the object of phantastic projections and the center of dependency facilitates the emergence of a fully independent subject – neurotic, perhaps, but not permanently entrenched within the detached world of psychosis.

In "The Mirror-Role of the Mother and Family in Child Development," an essay that addresses Lacan's "The Mirror Stage," Winnicott argues for a reading of the mother's face as the child's primary "mirror." The mother is literally transmuted into an object when she becomes the mirror.[41] "What does the baby see when he or she looks at the mother's face? I am suggesting that, ordinarily, what the baby sees is himself or herself. In other words the mother is looking at the baby and *what she looks like is related to what she sees there.*"[42] But in this particular mimetic relationship, the discretion of the mother is entirely effaced by her relationship to the child. In other words, there is never a mother, but only the child's projection of its own reflection into the face of the maternal object; there is only ever child. From the perspective of the child, there is only maternal agency insofar as that agency functions as an extension of the child's projected imago.

What is at stake here, for Winnicott and for the child, however, is the construction of a mother who is sufficiently willing to participate in the effacement of her subjectivity. "I can make my point," Winnicott writes, "by going straight over to the case of the baby whose mother reflects her own mood, or, worse still, the rigidity of her own defences." The consequences of a maternal subjectivity that fails to reflect the child's narcissistic projection are dire:

First, their own creative capacity begins to atrophy, and in some way or other they look around for other ways of getting something of themselves back from the environment . . . Some babies, tantalized by this type of relative maternal failure, study the variable maternal visage in an attempt to predict the mother's mood, just exactly as we all study the weather . . . Immediately beyond this in the direction of pathology is predictability, which is precarious, and which strains the baby to the limits of his or her capacity to allow for events. This brings a threat of chaos, and the baby will organize withdrawal, or will not look except to perceive, as a defence. A baby so treated will grow up puzzled about mirrors and what the mirror has to offer. If the mother's face is unresponsive, then a mirror is a thing to be looked at but not to be looked into.[43]

Maternal subjectivity is equivalent to "relative maternal failure." Maternal "objectivity" is the mother's passive reflection of the child's perception; in other words, the mother's *self*-construction as object. This is, in Winnicott's argument, the form of successful mothering that produces healthy, non-pathological adults. In other words, as long as the mother is anything the child – or Winnicott – wants her to be, as long as the mother is a metaphor for anything or everything else, sanity and order will prevail.

Winnicott suggests a direct relationship between mother and analyst in this essay. He writes:

This glimpse of the baby's and child's seeing the self in the mother's face, and afterwards in a mirror, gives a way of looking at analysis and at the psycho-therapeutic task. Psychotherapy is not making clever and apt interpretations; by and large it is a long-term giving the patient back what the patient brings. It is a complex derivative of the face that reflects what is there to be seen. I like to think of my work this way, and to think that if I do this well enough the patient will find his or her own self, and will be able to exist and to feel real.[44]

If the mother is equivalent to the analyst, then the good-enough mother would appear to be one who is capable of successfully managing the countertransference onto her child. But in the larger argument of Winnicott's work, the equation of successful mother and successful psychotherapist breaks down over the question of ideology. The ana-lyst's withholding from himself of the pleasure of interpretation is only a temporary discomfort. The mother's withholding, however, proves to be a far more complicated issue, particularly in the world of post-World War II Britain, in which Winnicott writes. The displacement of the mother by a good-enough analyst, and the replacement of the mother with the analyst, becomes of tantamount importance.

It is, then, appropriate that Winnicott's most significant contribution to psychoanalytic discourse is the concept of the "transitional object," which describes the various attempts of the child to construct a path of differentiation away from the tautological, oral identification with the maternal object. In his 1953 essay, "Transitional Objects and Transi-tional Phenomena," he describes the use-value of the transitional object in terms of the construction, rather than the deconstruction, of border-lines of identity. The transitional object is the infant's first "not-me" possession; Winnicott writes:

I have introduced the terms "transitional objects" and "transitional phenom-ena" for designation of the intermediate area of experience, between the thumb and the teddy bear, between the oral erotism and the true object-relationship, between primary creative activity and projection of what has already been introjected, between primary awareness of indebtedness and the acknowledg-ment of indebtedness . . . By this definition an infant's babbling and the way in which an older child goes through a repertory of songs and tunes while preparing for sleep come within the intermediate area as transitional phenomena, along with the use made of objects that are not part of the infant's body yet are not fully recognized as belonging to external reality.[45]

The borderline that Winnicott – and the infant, as well – is trying to articulate is the line between subjectivity and objectivity, between internal and external, and to some extent, between mother and child. This is an early step in the sequence that he describes as the passage from object-relation to object-usage, for the transitional object allows the child to explore the process of differentiation without departing the space of comfort and security.

There is a direct relationship between transitional object and maternal object, but just as importantly, there is a real difference. Winnicott articulates both the relationship and the difference as one of symbolism. In contrast to Klein's theory of the symbolic, the appropriation of symbolic signifiers in Winnicott signals a moving away from the domain of the mother, rather than the maintenance of a relationship of recuperation with her. He writes, "It is true that the blanket (or whatever it is) is symbolical of some part-object, such as the breast. Nevertheless, the point of it is not its symbolic value as much as its actuality. Its not being the breast (or the mother) although real, is as important as the fact that it *stands for* the breast (or mother)" (italics mine).[46] As a discursive construct, the transitional object is a signifier whose referent is, to some extent, the mother. But as a structure of referentiality, the space of transition is the space between the "mother," the physical, need-serving body emblematized by the part-object or breast, and the symbol or metaphor, which describes the mother-function with a difference. The tropic production of "mother," therefore, facilitates the obsolescence of the physical maternal body.

Throughout Winnicott's work, the creative impulse that informs the potential subject's construction of a transitional object has been dependent on a relationship of reciprocity with the mother-object. The child's originary phantasy of omnipotent creativity, in which the breast is the object created, depends for its sustenance on the mother's competence, on her willingness to provide the breast to the child on demand.

The breast is created by the infant over and over again out of the infant's capacity to love or (one can say) out of need. A subjective phenomenon develops in the baby, which we call the mother's breast. The mother places the actual breast just there where the infant is ready to create, and at the right moment . . . From birth, therefore, the human being is concerned with the problem of the relationship between what is objectively perceived and what is subjectively conceived of, and in the solution of this problem there is no health for the human being who has not been started off well enough by the mother.[47]

All health depends on the mother's complicity in the drama of omnipotent illusion, in which that mother is constructed, first phantastically, then symbolically, by the creative agency of the infant. The condition which Klein and Riviere would call hunger, and which Winnicott describes as weaning, ultimately intervenes in the choric dyad, creating the self-protective need within the child for a transitional object as a preemptive strike against dependence and vulnerability. "The mother's eventual task," writes Winnicott, "is gradually to disillusion the infant, but she has no hope of success unless at first she has been able to give sufficient opportunity for illusion."[48] Notably, Klein's infant is far more consistently ambivalent than Winnicott's. In the Kleinian paradigm, "disillusionment" is the twin of fulfillment. For Winnicott, the ambivalence of the depressive position only emerges later, when the breast is consistently, not just occasionally, denied the infant.

It seems paradoxical, perhaps, that the task of the "good-enough mother" is to fail at her position, to create the very condition of disillusionment that it is at first her mission to forestall. Winnicott writes elsewhere of the infant's ability to articulate a *cogito*:

This stage of the beginnings of I AM can only come to actuality in the baby's self-establishment in so far as the behaviour of the mother-figure is good enough – i.e. in respect of adaptation and of de-adaptation. So in this respect she is at first a delusion which the baby has to be able to disallow, and there needs to be substituted the uncomfortable I AM unit which involves loss of the original merged-in unit, which is safe.[49]

Differentiation entails a progress from adaptation to de-adaptation for the mother, from delusion to disillusion for the child. The function of the "good-enough mother," then, recalls Winnicott's concern with the psychoanalyst's timely, not self-indulgent, interpretation in the therapeutic scene. In the mother's manual that emerges from the structures Winnicott describes, to be a good-enough mother is to have a sense of appropriate timing, and to forestall the subject-position rejection until the child has already adequately managed the terms of that rejection from the other position. To be a good-enough mother is to be rejected, not to reject, to maintain the masochistic position in order to facilitate the sadistic foundation of epistemology.

The "mother" in all her various incarnations is a much more material, embodied object in Winnicott's work than she is in Klein's; the threat of autonomous maternal subjectivity arises persistently in Winnicott's essays, if only in terms of his urgent warnings against letting it affect the vulnerable infant. While in Klein's work the mother is divided into any number of separate functions, which ultimately stand in a synecdochic relationship to the concept of "mother," in Winnicott's the mother is always constructed against the comparative yardstick of the "good enough." The overwhelming emphasis in Winnicott, in fact, is on the dangerous and inevitable fact of maternal failure and the construction of compensatory structures, such as the transitional object and the therapist, as more reliable substitutes. In an address titled "The Mother's Contribution to Society," Winnicott declares, "As for me, I can already see what a big part has been played in my work by the urge to find and to appreciate the ordinary good mother."[50] His emphasis on the urgency of *finding* such an object underscores the extent to which she remains an elusive figure throughout his work, particularly in his later work, which finds itself more often than not responding to what he perceives as feminist rejections of femininity and maternity in the 1960s.

It is interesting and problematic, for both Winnicott and object-relations theory in general, that in his work, there is a person attached to the breast – a person, that is, who is not the infant, but rather the mother. For even the metaphorical destruction of that object becomes more problematic when it is insistently personated. He writes:

It is legitimate . . . to say that at whatever age a baby begins to allow the breast an external position (outside the area of projection), then this means that destruction of the breast has become a feature. I mean the actual impulse to destroy. It is an important part of what a mother does, to be the first person to take the baby through the first version of the many that will be encountered, of attack that is survived. This is the right moment in the child's development, because of the child's relative feebleness, so that destruction can fairly easily be survived. However, even so it is a tricky matter; it is only too easy for a mother to react moralistically when her baby bites and hurts.

Although it is not entirely clear what the mother's "moralistic" response would entail, it is clear that what is most desirable is, once again, the fulfillment of the child's sadistic phantasy, the ability to aggress with impunity. Winnicott includes as a footnote to this comment, "In fact, the baby's development is immensely complicated if he or she should happen to be born with a tooth, so that the gum's attack on the breast can never be tried out."[51]

The infant born with a tooth, a young Richard III, threatens to disturb the sensitive timing of the good-enough mother if she is prompted by pain to aggress against her helpless infant – and the potential of maternal aggression haunts Winnicott's work. The desperately embattled construct of the good-enough mother comes to represent, for Winnicott as for the infants he describes, the only means by which to articulate subjectivity, the only path that is right and "natural." John Ramsbotham, in an 1842 argument in favor of the "imperious" duty of maternal suckling, demonstrates a similar anxiety at the implication that supposedly "natural" maternal instinct might involve free will:

If a mother refuse to suckle, her infant must either be brought up by hand, which is an unnatural and unsuccessful mode of nurture, or a wet-nurse must be procured. In the latter case, the babe does not suffer much injury; but an act of great injustice is done to the infant, who is thus deprived of its natural rights . . . The voluntary refusal to suckle, on the part of any woman, evinces an absence of the tenderest feelings, and a want of maternal affection for her new-born babe. But it does not merely implicate the dereliction of an obvious and most natural duty; it likewise involves an evasion of the strongest impulses of the human heart: it occasions a transfer of filial affection, gratitude, and obedience, from the mother, to a hireling, who cannot appreciate their value. Who is prepared to say, what may be the future result of this transfer?[52]

Ramsbotham's idea of appropriate maternal behavior, like Winnicott's, emerges from a defensive and overdetermined rhetoric of the "natural," a maternal ideal again articulated in the breach, in the revealing possibility of women's moral dereliction. The issues at stake for Ramsbotham, so menacingly implied in the rhetorical question that concludes this passage, become for Winnicott apocalyptic social problems.

Winnicott effectively picks up where Ramsbotham leaves off; the portentous implications that are the "future result" of maternal failure are emblematized in the menacing women's movement. In two talks, "This Feminism," given to the Progressive League in 1964, and "The Pill and the Moon," also delivered to the Progressive League, in 1969, Winnicott is particularly aggressive about the implications of feminism for the future health of society. By this time, the individual developmental paradigm has become for Winnicott a recipe for cultural survival and an ideology of gender difference that predicates all survival on the decorous behavior of its female members. Women, Winnicott argues, are foolish to take personally their physical inferiority to men, for all men know that men envy women's reproductive capacities more than any woman could ever envy a penis. "Feminism, then, can be said to have in it a bigger or smaller degree of abnormality. At one extreme it is woman's protest against a male society dominated by phallic-phase male swank; and at the other extreme it is a woman's denial of her true inferiority *at one phase* of physical development."53 The signal mistake of feminism, it would seem, is the failure to recognize that all culture is in fact a matriarchy, in which men and women alike are indebted to and initially dependent on the mother. Indeed, the world of object-relations theory *is* a matriarchy, for it is a woman, a mother, who possesses determining psychological force; Winnicott does not distinguish between women's psychological power and their historical, social, and economic struggles. For men, he argues, the memory of archaic dependency causes the crisis of identification with the "WOMAN" who is always other to them. But for women, who identify within the continuous generational progression of women, identification holds a plurality of possibilities. "I would say that feminist women look as if they envy this thing about men," Winnicott explains, "that the more men mature, the more they are unique. Some men envy women the way they need not solve the problem of an individual relationship to WOMAN because they are women as well as charmers and seducers and helpless females calling successfully on man's chivalry."54

Only in "The Pill and the Moon" does Winnicott clarify what identification with the mother might imply, and also the expectations that inform his ideology of maternal adequacy. He articulates his opinions about the birth-control pill by presenting a short poem called "The Silent Kill":

> O silly Pill for folks not ill!
> Why not wait till you know God's will?
> What's empty will in time refill
> And pregnant hill be razed to nil.
> Men! have your will, put Jack in Jill;
> Girls! drink your fill of his chlorophyll.
> Fear not the spill, you know the drill,
> You know a still and silent kill . . . the Pill.
> So take my quill I surely will:
> Don't dally dill with silly Pill,
> Just wait until what happens will!
> Then pay the bill.55

Although he concedes later that the economic effects of birth control are not only practical but desirable, this essay represents an argument about the logical extremes of birth control which, Winnicott suggests, constitutes the killing of babies. His commentary about the writing process that produced "The Silent Kill" is revealing:

It reminded me of making something with a piece of wood. It's as though you thought: I'll make a sculpture in wood, and you got a gouge and a bit of elm, and you went like this and like that, and suddenly you found you'd got a witch in front of you. It wouldn't mean that you'd thought of a witch, but that the activity in the medium altered what you were doing, so that you surprised yourself. You found you'd done a witch because the elm made the thing go that way.[56]

Unlike Klein's sculptor, who animates a statue in homage to the good object, when Winnicott writes this poem, he finds himself confronted with the specter of the evil mother, of the fairy-tale witch. Indeed, throughout the essay, women who choose birth control over babies are tantamount to the mother who eats her own children – who eats them, in other words, before they can eat her.

Further, Winnicott casts the menacing power of the mother symbolically here in terms of the desire to differentiate between "dark and light," imagery that assumes racial overtones recalling the language of imperial omnipotence in Klein's reading of the Keatsean explorer-subject. Throughout this essay, Winnicott demonstrates anxiety about miscegenation, and especially about sexual contact between white women and black men. For example, one of his patients, a young woman, had at one point almost had sex with a man to whom she was attracted: "Incidentally, he was a very black African, which didn't seem to make any difference in their family. This wasn't the heart of the problem, though it was very exciting for her to have a black man." Later, the woman announces that she has had a lovely day; Winnicott reports the following response: "And I said, 'What *did* you do?' I thought she must have had a series of black men! She said, 'We went down a lovely little stream and we caught tadpoles.' Yet from her point of view, not having the Pill and not being allowed the Pill was something she couldn't deal with."[57] As a reference back to her earlier confidence regarding the "very black African," the comment that she "must have had a series of black men" is notably peculiar. The analyst's thought, a *non sequitur* interjected between his question and his patient's oddly suggestive response, reveals assumptions about both her sexuality and her choice of partner. First of all, the conflicts surrounding the incident with the "very black African" had made her miserable; Winnicott's association of her extreme happiness with that incident represents a disjunction of thought, as does his assumption that she would have been made unproblematically happier by a "series of black men," considering that she hadn't even consummated her relationship with the first one. Further, Winnicott's identification of her lover as a "very black African" occurs "incidentally," as an afterthought, within the woman's narrative of events; that he should later attribute such significance to the man's race belies a certain anxiety about that fact in itself.

Continuing with the theme of race still later in the essay, Winnicott reports a dream he has had in which he looks at the black and white shading on a beautiful white sculpture of a child's head:

And in the dream, before I woke, I said: "This has got nothing to do with the Negro problem of black and white – it goes right behind it. It has to do with the black and white that is in the individual human being" . . . And then I saw – because I get up quite a lot in the night at the moment, and I enjoy the moon so much – that of course it was the moon. And I knew it was the moon as well because it suddenly occurred to me: "Oh damn, there's an American flag on it!"[38]

Within the iconography of this essay, "woman" and the moon are both "white" objects corrupted by the symbolic implications of the American flag and the "Negro problem of black and white." American imperialism, like miscegenation, threatens the "purity" of the white/woman, and Winnicott implicitly constructs his own position – as dreamer, as analyst, as public intellectual – as a defender of womanly purity. He writes:

But when the poets begin writing about the moon again, as if it hadn't been landed on, but it meant things, like it means to you and me when we see it in the sky and the waxing and waning of it and the majesty of it and the mystery, then we can get back to the time when we worked out what it all means, when we knew what dark and light means. If we can get back to the poetry and recover from the American landing on the moon, before it starts up on Venus, we might feel that there's some hope for civilization.[59]

The American moon landing, like the birth-control pill, like the "very black African," acts toward the demystification of two related icons, moon and woman. Winnicott writes of the implications of this demystification: "It unfortunately cannot be avoided that it involves the fantasy of the woman losing her womanliness."[60]

Winnicott's desire is to retrieve the sense of an original, stable meaning rooted in the symbolic discourse of virtuous maternal purity. In a dramatic return to the structure of the Victorian ideal *in absentia*, Winnicott, too, reacts against the possibility of women's unruliness by setting up a context in which something dramatic is at stake in their decorum – in both cases, rhetorically and ideologically, the well-being not only of the child, but of society as a whole. Within object-relations theory, the loss of womanliness is the equivalent of a culture's loss of the "good-enough" mother; the circumscription of female sexuality, in terms of the containment of sex partners, as well as the restricting of birth control, is enough to retain "womanliness," purity, and mothering alike. That the anxiety of female purity is coextensive with the fear of miscegenation suggests the nature of the "borderlines" Winnicott's transitional object helps to establish. When an ideal is articulated only in the context of its failure, it is symptomatic and overdetermined; in this case, Winnicott's investment in – and in some sense fear of – a "good-enough" mother recalls the most symptomatic imperatives of woman-hood in Victorian culture.

Metaphors of nationalism and imperialism persistently emerge from psychoanalytic descriptions of the all-powerful mother, suggesting a common series of ideological agendas for Freud, Klein, and Winnicott, and a range of responses reminiscent of the variant power dynamics operative in fictional accounts of the same phenomenon during the Victorian period. Within orthodox Freudian psychoanalysis, the mother is a figure of great complexity, a figure of enormous desirability who retains competing desires of her own. Melanie Klein reorients the axis of psychoanalysis to focus on the determining power of desire for that mother, constructing the mother as so very powerful that every element and symbol of adult life signifies her complex presence, whether she is present, temporarily missing, or dead. Winnicott, damning the implication of dependency on "WOMAN," predicates "hope for civiliza-tion" on the recovery of a remystified, repurified moon; the mother, for Winnicott, is neither desiring nor desirable, but is rather a troubling figure whose dangerous excesses must be circumscribed.

In the increasingly conservative world of psychoanalysis, the fate of the "epistemophilic impulse" becomes an imperialist desire toward the subjection of women, and this is, for John Ruskin as for Winnicott, a form of enthrallment to a figure who acknowledges her power, but chooses not to exercise it:

So far as she rules, all must be right, or nothing is. She must be enduringly, incorruptibly good; instinctively, infallibly wise – wise, not for self-develop-ment, but for self-renunciation: wise, not that she may set herself above her husband, but that she may never fall from his side: wise, not with the narrow-ness of insolent and loveless pride, but with the passionate gentleness of an infinitely variable, because infinitely applicable, modesty of service.[61]

For Ruskin as for Winnicott, nation and civilization itself derive from an ideal of female self-renunciation, but while Ruskin's praisesong reads suspiciously like a prescription, Winnicott acknowledges outright the problematic fact that the natives are restless: Winnicott longs to return to a day when he, like Ruskin, could conceivably write of such a self-abnegating queen/wife/mother-figure in the present tense.

Winnicott's return to a maternal ideal constructed *in absentia* marks the return to an ideological form familiar to readers of Victorian fiction, in which an idealized notion of adult female behavior is held up as a mandate. In the Victorian novel, however, as in the work of Freud, that mandate is almost always rejected in favor of complex and problematic *failures* of the ideal articulated through narratives of maternal loss and return. Unlike Freud and Klein, whose theories of domestic life present the mother at the center of a number of tensions involving desire and desirability, Winnicott is more concerned with an imposition of conformity. But this invariably remains a subjunctive proposition, for as in Victorian fiction, as in Freud's *fort-da* game or Klein's depressive position, the story almost always establishes itself dialectically, in explicit violation of its positive pole; even Winnicott's moon will always retain the flag of the American astronauts. The narrative complexity and energy that early psychoanalysis shares with the world of Victorian fiction consist of their respective attempts to fathom maternal excess and transgression, to comprehend structures of abandonment that prompt not disability or rage but fascination and desire. The argument about Victorian fiction that follows will focus, then, on the dynamics of such desire, on the fate of such ideological truncheons as that wielded by Winnicott in the context of the more recognizable Freudian plot of intrigue.

I was summoned to a private patient near the Mansion House, who had been, a few minutes before, attacked with a sudden flooding in the eighth month of pregnancy, while sitting with her family at tea, in the drawing-room. Upon proceeding up-stairs, tracks of blood were perceptible upon every step. In the bed-room, I found a neighbouring professional gentleman, who had been also called by the servants in their alarm at the state of their mistress; and although this unfortunate occurrence had not happened a quarter of an hour before, it had already produced such a degree of depression as I have rarely witnessed, with its concomitant symptoms. Upon a vaginal examination a little after six, I detected the Placenta to be placed immediately over the Os Uteri; some discharge was still oozing away, but there was no tendency to pain. The urgency of the haemmorrhage appeared therefore to be at present somewhat abating; and the lady for a short time seemed disposed to revive; but presently the flooding returned with its original violence. Anxiously watching its progress for a short time, and observing no diminution in the discharge, I determined on delivery; but previously I requested my professional friend to satisfy himself that the Placenta was presenting. Being answered in the affirmative, I proceeded without further loss of time to empty the Uterus. The Os Uteri was but little opened, yet it was relaxed, and permitted the passage of my hand with ease into the Uterus; but that organ showed at the moment no disposition to active contraction; having brought down the breech, the child was found to be alive; I therefore proceeded gently in its extraction; and after the child was born, the placenta was thrown off, and was soon withdrawn. The uterine tumour proved now to be irregularly contracted, and full flaccid under the hand. For a short time, this lady appeared comfortable; the discharge ceased, and she expressed her warmest thanks for my prompt assistance; but by-and-by she began to complain of her breath: "Oh! my breath, my breath!" was her urgent exclamation. There was no more flooding after delivery; yet my patient continued to sink, and expired soon after seven o'clock; so that in less than two hours, from an apparent state of perfect health, her valuable life was sacrificed to a sudden attack of haemmorrhage, in spite of the most prompt assistance. The child was lively, and promised to do well.

John Ramsbotham, M.D., *Practical Observations in Midwifery, with Cases in Illustration* (2nd edition, revised, in one volume) (London: S. Highley, 32, Fleet Street; John Churchill, Princes Street, Soho, 1842), 311–12.

CHAPTER 3

Broken mirror, broken words:
Bleak House

Is autobiography somehow always in the process of symbolically killing the mother off by telling her the lie that we have given birth to ourselves?

Barbara Johnson[1]

Our topic deals with the giving and taking away of faces, with face and deface, *figure*, figuration and disfiguration.

Paul de Man[2]

In Dickens's *Bleak House* (1852–3), generic conventions of domestic novel, detective novel, and autobiography collide in the narrative of Esther Summerson, whose quest for identity is structured through her desire to reunite with her missing, mysterious mother. In fact, Esther "loses" her mother a total of three times in the course of the novel; these "deaths" provide both the structuring principle and the central crisis of Esther's fictional autobiography. In this chapter, I will argue that each of these moments presents the conditions of "loss" in different terms, and that each time, Esther is increasingly confronted with the question of her own implication in her abandonment. The extent to which she consents to and even comes to desire loss is directly proportional to her ability to master the terms of the autobiographical narrative. In other words, Esther's ability to represent herself as a subject, as an agent, is dependent on her status as a mourner; there is a direct relationship between abandonment and articulation, and specifically, between the death of a mother and the birth of an authorial subject.

Throughout *Bleak House*, and particularly throughout the fiction of Esther's autobiography, Dickens represents maternal death as a problem of narrative, a challenge to the construction of a *Bildungsroman* or a domestic fiction. For the teleology of *Bleak House* is "Bleak House," the strangely sanitary dream world of the novel's conclusion. But this domestic dream world is an embattled construct, for the universe of the larger novel consistently destroys any pretense to conventional "family values." Esther's autobiography runs parallel in the text with the omniscient narrative of *Jarndyce v. Jarndyce*, the story of the Chancery suit which locates contention within the family even in its name, and provides the pathologized model of domesticity that pervades the densely populated world of the novel. Throughout the text, in fact, orphanage and anomie remain the status quo. The centrality of such characters as Jo and Esther, alienated from any domestic structure but virtuous nonetheless, sets the stage for the systematic dismantling of family pathologies in favor of virtue born of resistance.

Yet in a world in which children are the only true adults and in which such adults as Mr. Skimpole are guilty of the most outrageous abandonment of responsibility, it is the novel's mother-figures who receive most of its venom. Mrs. Pardiggle and Mrs. Jellyby in particular represent the clearest instances of misplaced priorities and malign neglect, as they exploit and ignore their many children in favor of "causes," feeding the children of Africa, Borrioboola-Gha, and the Tockahoopo Indians while neglecting their own. The ever-watchful Esther observes the Jellyby household:

Mrs. Jellyby, whose face reflected none of the uneasiness which we could not help showing in our own faces, as the dear child's head recorded its passage with a bump on every stair – Richard afterwards said he counted seven, besides one for the landing – received us with perfect equanimity. She was a pretty, very diminutive, plump woman, of from forty to fifty, with handsome eyes, though they had a curious habit of seeming to look a long way off. As if – I am quoting Richard again – they could see nothing nearer than Africa![3]

Mrs. Jellyby's misplaced ethic is captured in the title of the chapter in which she is introduced: "Telescopic Philanthropy." The novel is unambivalent about assigning blame specifically to her, as when her daughter Caddy plans her escape: "'If I ever blame myself, I still think it's Ma's fault. We are to be married whenever we can, and then I shall go to Pa at the office and write to Ma. It won't much agitate Ma; I am only pen and ink to *her*. One great comfort is . . . that I shall never hear of Africa after I am married'" (240).

Esther first meets her own mother in a mid-text reunion scene staged in the woods on a summer afternoon. It is at this point that Lady Dedlock reveals to Esther that she is her mother, begs forgiveness for her sins – then leaves her newfound child forever. After this scene, Esther is left with only a letter, the trace of their encounter. Esther reports, "She put into my hands a letter she had written for my reading only; and said, when I had read it, and destroyed it – but not so much for her sake, since she asked nothing, as for her husband's and my own – I must forevermore consider her as dead" (566). When Lady Dedlock offers Esther this letter, she fulfills Esther's most urgent desire: she provides her with a narrative of origins, a pre-text for her autobiography in the form of the "true" account of the events surrounding her birth. Yet when Lady Dedlock asks her to consider her dead, she asks her to repeat in fictional terms the very thing that Esther has feared as a truth throughout her life. For Esther, the letter is no replacement for the mother; it instead literalizes the fictionality of her life while it fictionalizes the "reality" of their encounter.

In her desire to reject and abandon the mother who rejects and abandons her, Esther must first confront the fact of her ambivalence; as much as she hates her mother, she loves and desires her as well. Marcia Renee Goodman writes, "Esther's sympathy for Lady Dedlock camouflages her fear of the anger at this abandoning mother."[4] In the scene of reunion, the adult Esther attempts to manage this ambivalence, to rewrite the terms of maternal loss, reversing the tale of abandonment by describing this scene self-consciously in sentimentalized rhetoric. But this rhetorical presentation strains to conceal the intensity of the power struggle taking place between mother and daughter, in which it becomes clear that the two women's lives are in question:

I raised my mother up, praying and beseeching her not to stoop before me in such affliction and humiliation. I did so in broken incoherent words; for, besides the trouble I was in, it frightened me to see her at *my* feet. I told her – or I tried to tell her – that if it were for me, her child, under any circumstances to take upon me to forgive her, I did it, and had done it, many, many years. I told her that my heart overflowed with love for her; that it was natural love, which nothing in the past had changed, or could change. That it was not for me, then resting for the first time on my mother's bosom, to take her to account for having given me life; but that my duty was to bless her and receive her, though the whole world turned from her, and that I only asked her leave to do it. I held my mother in my embrace, and she held me in hers; and among the still woods in the silence of the summer day, there seemed to be nothing but our two troubled minds that was not at peace. (565)

Ironically and significantly, what should be the most profoundly integrated moment of the novel, when Esther and her mother rest in each other's arms, is among the most disturbing. Esther is the agent in this scene, lifting her mother from the position of abject misery and embracing her with an ideal of natural maternal love. This is not a role with which she feels comfortable – "it frightened me to see her at *my* feet" – and the inversion of the parental hierarchy is the first signal of the many tensions in this tableau. Esther is theoretically an agent of forgiveness, but even in her empowerment an element of passivity remains: throughout this scene, Lady Dedlock controls both the terms and the decisions. Although Esther offers a rhetoric of forgiveness, her mother will accept only a rhetoric of disavowal. Esther is not technically rejected here – it is incumbent on her to participate in the fictionalized death of her mother – but rather she has had rejection dictated to her. In a perverse twist of logic, she has become an agent in her own abandonment; previous to this moment she was an innocent victim, but from here she is implicated in a deeply masochistic economy.

Esther reports this scene in a series of equivocal statements and qualified clauses: "if it were for me, her child, under any circumstances to take upon me to forgive her . . ."; "it was natural love, which nothing in the past had changed, or could change . . ."; "it was not for me . . . to take her to account for having given me life . . ." The fact that the reunion is described in indirect discourse underscores a narrative logic that enables Esther to construct herself as both implicated and exonerated in the emotional complexity of this transaction. The logic of the disclaimer allows her to occupy both positions at once, constructing – or perhaps deconstructing – a space between narrative representation and emotional response. Esther's rhetorical division not only represents her ambivalent response to her situation, but presents one of the many ways in which *Bleak House* is, in D. A. Miller's words, "a contradictory text."[5] Throughout Esther's narrative in particular, however, rhetorical equivocation is symptomatic of the psychodrama of her autobiography. Textual and psychological stability are for her inextricable: Esther is the putative author of this text, and in her eyes, her missing mother is the one who holds the key to both forms of stability.

Yet in the scene of reunion, Lady Dedlock provides Esther with a biographical narrative which only destroys, rather than establishes, her identity in authoritative terms: Esther, left by her mother standing on the Ghost's Walk at Chesney Wold, is at this moment established as a *ghostly* presence, a living absence, within her own autobiography. The letter describing Esther's birth, in fact, describes nothing but her death:

I clearly derived from it – and that was much then – that I had not been abandoned by my mother. Her elder and only sister, the godmother of my childhood, discovering signs of life in me when I had been laid aside as dead, had in her stern sense of duty, with no desire or willingness that I should live, reared me in rigid secrecy, and had never again beheld my mother's face from within a few hours of my birth. So strangely did I hold my place in this world, that, until within a short time back, I had never, to my own mother's knowledge, breathed – had been buried – had never been endowed with life – had never borne a name. (569)

From birth, Esther has been the unwitting participant in a fiction in which she played the role of a corpse, a dead baby, as well as an alternative fiction (the one reported in the text) in which she played an orphan. Now, at the conclusion of that fiction – the moment of her (re)birth, perhaps – she is revealed as an absent presence in this, her supposed autobiography. But the terms of the fiction have shifted: mother and daughter, dead to one another in Esther's childhood narrative, now assume the pretense of a constructed, self-conscious, fictional death. In other words, the anxieties of authorship and parentage which Esther expresses early in her narrative are literalized after she is finally, literally abandoned by her mother. What transpires is a fight for her life, an attempt to replace her death with her birth, to rewrite the biography of an animated corpse.

The questions which prevail throughout Esther's autobiography are self-reflexive to the issue of autobiography itself: she is an orphan, she knows nothing of her antecedents, nothing of her origins, nothing of her name. The narrative describes her coming into a knowledge of sorts, only to have that security removed from her immediately, a pattern that foregrounds questions of the generic construction of an autobiographical text. Is it possible for an orphan to write an autobiography? Or conversely, are all autobiographies the narratives of "orphans," insofar as they are reconstructions of the originary? Dickens's construction of Esther's autobiographical voice (or, conversely, Esther's autobiographical self-construction) consistently foregrounds its fictionality, both in terms of her attempt to write of the birth of an orphan and in terms of her acceptance of the pact to consider her mother dead. In what sense, then, is Esther Summerson's autobiography fictional? And in what sense is fictionality the predicate of autobiography?

The issues at stake here – for Esther, for Dickens – are issues of authenticity and agency. In a discussion of the relationship between fiction and autobiography, Paul de Man attempts to destabilize the assumptions that traditionally inform these generic classifications:

We assume that life *produces* the autobiography as an act produces its consequences, but can we not suggest, with equal justice, that the autobiographical
project may itself produce and determine the life and that whatever the writer
does is in fact governed by the technical demands of self-portraiture and thus
determined, in all its aspects, by the resources of his medium? And since the
mimesis here assumed to be operative is one mode of figuration among others,
does the referent determine the figure, or is it the other way round: is the
illusion of reference not a correlation of the structure of the figure, that is to say
no longer clearly and simply a referent at all but something more akin to a
fiction which then, however, in its own turn, acquires a degree of referential
productivity? (69)

De Man's analysis problematizes the discretion of the autobiographical
mode through a reversal of agency at the site of production. To privilege
a mimetic or causal relationship between experience and signification is
to do so at the expense of the narrative itself, belying its implications in
the production of experience. The extent to which the text has agency in
the production of that experience is underscored in Esther's narrative,
which is engaged, at the moment of reunion and throughout, in an
attempt to deploy this text as a means of rewriting the unsatisfactory tale
of her birth and childhood. The reversal of agency that de Man
identifies as the autobiographical trope, then, is suggestive of the real
stakes of the power-struggle between Esther and her mother, a struggle
to the death about which one of them has the agency to shape the terms
of this text. Within the scene of reunion alone, several critical reversals
of agency emerge even at the level of Esther's narration. The fact that
the terms of Lady Dedlock's rejection are presented not as "I abandon
you," but rather as "you agree to reject me," signals the real tensions of
power at the base of their encounter. The accord they reach in this
scene, in which Lady Dedlock asks permission to abandon and Esther
grants permission to be rejected, implies a relationship between the
abdication of agency and the assumption of a related form of deterministic power.

Within the context of *Bleak House*, there is a causal structure in place,
in which texts produce bodies, in which rhetorical embodiment precedes physical embodiment. Lady Dedlock, for example, is textually
manufactured as dead not just once, but twice, before she actually
appears as dead. The same is true for Esther, in the sense that she is
persistently represented as dead before she is able to articulate herself
as not only living, but powerful. Within this framework, the production
of a dead mother, the corpse of a woman, is both the logical effect of

Esther's drama of self-determination and symptomatic of the novel's anxieties about the terms of its women's power. Lady Dedlock is dangerous because she has the capacity to control both the rhetorical and the physical; as the literal "agent of production" of Esther Summerson, Lady Dedlock's function within the text as an embodied presence gives her a unique form of authority over and within Esther's autobiography. In her drive to resolve the tension between the rhetorical and the physical, Esther functionally divides the two categories, and in the process, offers the novel as a whole a new terminology for the punishment of neglectful women.

To read the mother–daughter reunion scene in the middle of *Bleak House* as both the beginning and the end of the text is, of course, to disregard the novel's formal moments of opening and closure. But this vast Victorian multiplot formally opens with the famed Megalosaurus of London and formally closes with a sentence fragment in a chapter called "Beginning the World." Resistance to formal tropes of organization is consistent throughout the logic of the novel; in a discussion of the distinctly non-teleological chaos of Chancery, D. A. Miller comments that the logic of Chancery recalls Kant's definition of the aesthetic: "The suit's effective suspension of teleology is, of course, scandalously exemplary of a whole social sphere that seems to run on the principle of a purposiveness without purpose."[6]

Significantly, then, the opening of Esther's text functions as both an originary and an historicized moment. Its title, "A Progress," refers to its own internal events, to its commencement *in medias res* in the life of Esther Summerson, and also to its position as the third chapter, not the first, of *Bleak House*. This is a moment which puts into question the status of the originary; although Esther does not respond actively to the events of the previous chapters, the opening of her story is already contingent, already inflected with the markers of an anterior presence. The condition of the narrative is equivalent to the condition of its narrator: Esther is seemingly more aware of the past than the present, attempting to read backward in these opening moments to (re)construct a personal history, but frustrated by the fact that the text of her biography is as yet a blank.

Esther's childhood narrative is constructed in the form of an apostrophe to her doll, her best friend: "And so she used to sit propped up in a great arm-chair, with her beautiful complexion and rosy lips, staring at me – or not so much at me, I think, as at nothing – while I busily stitched away, and told her every one of my secrets" (62). At this time, of course, Esther "had never, to [her] own mother's knowledge, breathed – had been buried – had never been endowed with life – had never borne a name." Esther, the dead baby, talks with this inanimate, nameless baby about her missing mother, about the mystery of her origins. In object-relations theory, Esther's doll would itself function as a substitute or median mother for her; D. W. Winnicott argues that children use transitional objects such as this doll to compensate for anxieties that accompany the process of differentiation from the mother. Transitional objects function in education about borderlines: as the child's first "not-me" possession, they provide symbolic instruction in the construction and negotiation of self–other relationships.[7] The centrality of the transitional object to Esther's early ability to articulate herself indicates why the presence of a mother, even if it is only temporary, is critical to her self-conscious construction of herself as a speaking subject. When she looks at this doll, she looks simultaneously at herself and at an Other; her ability to articulate the question of origins as a question depends on the artificial appropriation of a mother-object against which she can differentiate.

Esther's doll compensates for the multiply overdetermined markers of absence in her world. As she talks with her doll, she talks with herself, and by talking with her doll she constitutes herself; by means of apostrophe, she creates an Other, she makes an absence (at least provisionally) a presence, and manufactures the conditions for discourse. Esther's subjectivity is at this point directly dependent on her ability to construct a self by reading her reflection in the eyes of another. For it is later revealed that her father is the opium-addicted law-writer of Chancery, known only as "Nemo," which translates as "no one." With uncanny prescience, Esther foregrounds her paternal identity in her discussion with her doll; before she reveals her name, which is only the signifier of her absence, she reveals her signifier of absence: "staring at me – or not so much at me, I think, as at nothing." For an autobiographical narrator whose own mother believes her dead, the capacity for autobiographical articulation signals a form of agency: if she is capable of articulation, she is capable of existence. For when Esther speaks of herself, she animates the body of that dead baby. Returning to de Man,

The figure of prosopopeia, the fiction of an apostrophe to an absent, deceased, or voiceless entity . . . posits the possibility of the latter's reply and confers upon it the power of speech. Voice assumes mouth, eye, and finally face, a chain that is manifest in the etymology of the trope's name, *prosopon poiein*, to confer a mask or a face (*prosopon*). Prosopopeia is the trope of autobiography, by which one's name . . . is made as intelligible and memorable as a face. (75–6)

In the terms of this argument, rhetoric insistently precedes embodiment; the existence of Esther's face relies on her capacity for figuration, for the figurative construction of subjectivity maintained in her encounter with her doll–baby but disrupted in her encounter with her mother. Language is the vehicle by which Esther can create something – herself – out of nothing. In the terms of this crisis, only the physical presence of Esther's mother can possibly authorize or affirm her existence. But the body of Lady Dedlock, as we shall see, presents its own vexed issues for this text, for it is impossible to separate the maternal body from the dangerous body of the sexually transgressive woman.

It is significant, then, that Esther locates the opening scene of her narrative on her birthday; this gesture suggests a relationship between text and identity that is underscored by the generic conventions of autobiography. Yet birth in Esther's narrative is always coded as loss: she pleads with her godmother as a child, " 'O, dear godmother, tell me, pray do tell me, did mama die on my birthday?' " (64), and we learn later, of course, that Lady Dedlock believed her child was dead on arrival. "It was my birthday," Esther writes:

There were holidays at school on other birthdays – none on mine. There were rejoicings at home on other birthdays, as I knew from what I heard the girls relate to one another – there were none on mine. My birthday was the most melancholy day at home, in the whole year . . . My disposition is very affectionate; and perhaps I might still feel such a wound, if such a wound could be received more than once, with the quickness of that birthday. (64)

Esther's birthday denotes not only her physical presence, but also her difference; she is distinguished, marked, coded by a "wound" that functions primarily as the "disfiguration" about which and by which she speaks. The paradox here is that subjectivity is constituted only because it is not; Esther is distinguished because she is different, and though she desires the security and the privilege of (self-)knowledge, to know the truth implies the potential erasure of her unique subjectivity.

In her childhood narrative, however, the position of "mother" is occupied by an inadequate surrogate, "godmother." In the course of her first chapter, Esther rehearses the drama of maternal death, literalizing the tropes of loss with the death of her godmother, an event that presents the most practical implications of maternal loss devoid of emotional content. From this moment on, for the first time but once again, Esther is an orphan without a home. But this maternal death goes unmourned; the godmother has only ever offered Esther a cheerless existence. Esther pleads with her surrogate for information about her true mother: "'Oh, do pray tell me something of her. Do now, at last, dear godmother, if you please! What did I do to her? How did I lose her? Why am I so different from other children, and why is it my fault, dear godmother?'" (64). Miss Barbary replies, "'Your mother, Esther, is your disgrace, and you were hers. The time will come – and soon enough – when you will understand this better, and will feel it too, as no one save a woman can'" (65). The implication is one of shame: in her guilt and shame, Esther is like her mysterious mother. Knowledge of this particular brand of shame is the privilege of women, women who are like one another and who deserve to be punished. Recall the reversal of rhetoric in the later reunion scene: "it was not for me, then resting for the first time on my mother's bosom, to take her to account for having given me life; but that my duty was to bless her and receive her, though the whole world turned from her" (565). From the first in this text, female sexuality is suspect and dangerous. In the opening chapter of Esther's narrative, the only information she is given about her mother is that she is sexual, that her sexuality is her disgrace, and that she, Esther, is no better.[8]

Ironically, since her godmother is by no means a sympathetic figure in the text, it is her ideal of masochistic behavior that Esther follows throughout her life. "'Forget your mother and leave all other people to forget her who will do her unhappy child that greatest kindness,'" says Miss Barbary. "'Submission, self-denial, diligent work, are the preparations for a life begun with such a shadow on it'" (65). With this prescription, Miss Barbary articulates the values of the Good Esther that appear in such dramatic tension with her angry alter-ego later in the text.

Although Miss Barbary encourages Esther to forget her mother, it is in fact Miss Barbary whom she forgets. When her godmother dies, she goes unmourned, even as Esther discovers that this cold woman is actually her aunt. In fact, when her childhood home breaks up, Esther mourns only her nameless doll: "I had wrapped the dear old doll in her own shawl, and quietly laid her – I am half ashamed to tell it – in the garden-earth, under the tree that shaded my old window" (70). Unwittingly, Esther here repeats in literal form the psychological drama enacted by her own mother on her own birthday: a mother burying her dead baby. In this, the first of many burial-sequences in the text, the act of burial is both symbolic and ineffective. Esther is burying her doll–baby, her godmother, and in fact her childhood. Perhaps most importantly, however, she is doing as her godmother wished and burying her mother, for from this point on, her lost mother goes unmentioned until the actual moment of reunion. But as Lacan writes of "The Purloined Letter," "It is the realist's imbecility, which does not pause to observe that nothing, however deep in the bowels of the earth a hand may seek to ensconce it, will ever be hidden there, since another hand can always retrieve it, and that what is hidden is never but what is *missing from its place.*"[9] Esther's attempt at repression fails miserably; the gesture of burial returns on itself multiply in the form of sudden and surprising unveilings throughout the novel. She is never able to escape the ghostly interventions of dead babies and dead mothers.

Dickens turns from Esther at this point in the novel and returns to her only as an adult. Ironically, Esther's absence from the text enables her return as a figurative mother; in her assumption of the care of Ada Clare in the Jarndyce household, she begins to turn into what she is not and what she has lacked. From the first, her virtuous qualities are the wonder of all. After Esther sets the Jellyby household in order, Ada hugs her "and told me I was a quiet, dear, good creature, and had won her heart. 'You are so thoughtful, Esther,' she said, 'and yet so cheerful! and you do so much, so unpretendingly! You would make a home out of even this house'" (90). Esther is repeatedly associated with the best qualities of homeliness; throughout her residence in the Jarndyce home, she is the housekeeper, and takes great pleasure in jangling her big bunch of keys.[10] But as a matter of fact, this home is not her home, and the reasons why she is here remain unclear. Her "Progress" is a progress narrative precisely because she is unfixed and nomadic, a displaced person until the conclusion of her narrative, when the rhetoric of domesticity becomes rigidly overdetermined. But even in her role as housekeeper, Esther's identity is mythologized, multiplied; as the "good little woman of our lives," she is charged by Mr. Jarndyce with sweeping troubles "so neatly out of *our* sky, in the course of [her] housekeeping" (148). For Esther, however, "This was the beginning of my being called Old Woman, and Little Old Woman, and Cobweb, and Mrs. Shipton, and Mother Hubbard, and Dame Durden, and so many names of that sort, that my own name soon became quite lost among them" (148).

Esther is surely the uncanniest homemaker in Victorian fiction; every aspect of her identity, from name to face to family to motivation, remains unfixed and unlocatable. In his location in Esther of an ideal of domesticity, Dickens deconstructs a traditional ethic of stability and constancy. The *Unheimlich* undermines Esther even as she engages in the establishment and maintenance of a *Heim*, of a home. In a discussion of

"The Signification of the Phallus," Jane Gallop connects the home with the maternal body as she writes about the uncanny phenomenon of homesickness:

Freud says of homesickness that it can be understood psychoanalytically as a longing to return to the womb, that the lost homeland is the mother's womb. If we understand the nostalgia resulting from the discovery of the mother's castration in this way, then the discovery that the mother does not have the phallus means that the subject can never return to the womb. Somehow the fact that the mother is not phallic means that the mother as mother is lost forever, that the mother as womb, homeland, source, and grounding for the subject is irretrievably past. The subject is hence in a foreign land, alienated.[11]

In Gallop's reading, the "mother as mother" is equivalent to mother as "homeland, source, and grounding for the subject." The conditions of homesickness, alienation, and nostalgia characterize the child-subject's participation in a dyssymmetrical economy of desire, in which the mother's lack of phallus translates into the child's loss of the womb, and therefore of the mother. But Gallop's description duplicates Esther's construction of "mother" as a doubly contested ground. For the mother who may or may not have the phallus is quite different from the mother who has the womb. Gallop slides between considerations of the mother as a theoretical construct – the phallic mother – and as a physical body; there seems to be a logical progression from the mother's possession of the phallus to the child's access to the womb, and therefore the construction of the phallic mother as an inherently comforting, rather than paradoxical or threatening, being. But the inherently "castrated" condition of the psychoanalytic mother would seem to indicate that it is not possible for a mother to be both a mother and physically present: "the fact that the mother is not phallic means that the mother as mother is lost forever." The obverse of this logical construction is that the only present mother is a phallic mother, yet since she represents a condition of rhetorical impossibility, she, too, is lost. Thus within psychoanalytic logic, there is, symbolically, no such thing as a mother.

The anomic world of *Bleak House* participates in a similar logic, or, perhaps, in a similar anxiety. In this text, maternal loss is inevitable, and operates simultaneously as a source of rage, a source of nostalgia, and the central metaphor for Dickens's powerful political critique. Within Esther's narrative in particular, the paradoxical condition of the mother as both necessary and impossible is appropriated and reconfigured, achieving a sense of closure which reclaims the "home," which reclaims the "womb," which reclaims the determining psychological power of the domestic. If "homesick" or "uncanny" are appropriate adjectives to describe Esther's progress narrative, then "home" is the powerful trope of origin and destiny.

Throughout her text, however, Esther's signifiers of identity, the first person pronoun and the proper name "Esther," remain slippery. She enters a poor household on a philanthropic mission, and soon confronts the dilemma of her own significant instability. Esther and Ada attempt to help the young battered wife who sits "nursing a poor little gasping baby by the fire" (156):

We approached the woman sitting by the fire, to ask if the baby were ill . . . She only looked at it as it lay on her lap. We had observed before, that when she looked at it she covered her discoloured eye with her hand, as though she wished to separate any association with noise and violence and ill-treatment, from the poor little child . . . Ada, whose gentle heart was moved by its appearance, bent down to touch its little face. As she did so, I saw what happened and drew her back. The child died. (159–60)

This *pietà* anticipates by reversal the encounter of another "dead baby" and her mother later in the text. Among the most significant aspects of this scene, however, is its intensely visual quality. Esther and Ada watch Jenny; Jenny watches her baby with one eye, hiding the other from the infant's gaze; and finally, Esther alone bears witness to the child's death. In this most sentimentalized of scenes, Jenny attempts to edit the picture for her child, concealing from it the brutal underside of life, the violence which has brutalized this maternal body. Esther is the only one who seems to recognize the moment of the infant's death. For her, this functions as a primal scene, a phantasy of presence, of embodiment, at a moment she could not possibly have attended; instead of her conception, however, this moment is representative of her death.

As Ada, Jenny, and Jenny's companion dissolve into tears, Esther alone takes quick action: "Presently I took the light burden from her lap; did what I could to make the baby's rest the prettier and gentler; laid it on a shelf, and covered it with my handkerchief" (160). When she covers the corpse with her handkerchief, a blank white square marked, we learn much later, "Esther Summerson," she sets in motion a chain of events which results in her eventual reunion with her "dead" mother, and her ultimate discovery of her mother, dead. For with that action, Esther deploys a subtext of her own, a signifier of her presence and her identity; like Poe's purloined letter, the handkerchief assumes its own itinerary within the larger narrative, accreting significance only as its minimalist text circulates among various bearers. Once again, Esther is engaged in the act of burying a baby, but this particular act of burial, of repression, of veiling, involves the process of marking a body with a particular signifier, or signature, of identity. The cloth which veils the infant's face is marked with a name; the dead baby is quite literally labeled Esther Summerson.

This infant corpse does not work well as a decoy, however; "Esther Summerson" seems inevitably destined to find Esther Summerson. In the scene of reunion with her mother, Lady Dedlock does not announce her relationship to Esther; instead, Esther infers it from her possession of this very handkerchief. "I cannot tell in any words what the state of my mind was, when I saw in her hand my handkerchief, with which I had covered the dead baby" (565). The handkerchief bears the traces of the dead baby, bears the signifier "Esther Summerson." The text has now produced its second corpse (following Miss Barbary, the first "maternal" death), once again in a moment of uncanny repetition of an event that never took place, the death of the infant "Esther Summerson." The handkerchief *is* the autobiographical narrative of Esther Summerson, but it is a text caught in the indeterminacy of its own rhetorical slippage: what does "Esther Summerson" signify? to whom does this shroud belong?[12]

The handkerchief ultimately operates as a veil, simultaneously marking and masking the plurality of "Esther Summersons" that are loosed within this novel. From Esther's hand to the face of the dead baby, from Smallweed to Lady Dedlock to Bucket, the handkerchief represents Esther Summerson as trope, as text, unfixed from any one specific referent. Throughout Esther's narrative, then, a plurality of identities, a multiply overdetermined significance attributed to her name/nameless-ness, frustrates her ability to control the autobiographical voice, to resolve the tensions which divide "Esther Summerson"; "Esther Summerson," in fact, represents the dissemination, rather than the determination, of specific identities in *Bleak House*, and so dramatizes the problematic relationship between textuality and agency that has plagued Esther throughout the novel.

The fact that Esther's father, "Nemo," is a law-writer, present in the novel only in the character of his handwriting, underscores the novel's tropic production of the phenomenon of Esther. But in *Bleak House*, the Law of the Father is as profoundly disabled as is the legal system itself. Nemo's "law," which participates in the organic proliferation of discourse without the referent that is Chancery, represents the parasitic power of discourse, the capacity of language to destroy as well as to produce bodies. When Nemo dies of his opium addiction early in the novel, his body is discovered by Mr. Tulkinghorn, the Dedlocks' solicitor. Lady Dedlock has ordered Tulkinghorn to search for the person whose handwriting she identifies on a legal document. Handwriting is a reliable index of identity in the novel, and is perhaps even determinant of identity; the legibility of a text is evidence enough to establish a definitive link with an individual. Nemo leaves behind a packet of letters from his lover Honoria, the young Lady Dedlock, providing documentation, written proof, of the romance that produced Esther Summerson. These letters circulate throughout the novel like Esther's handkerchief, passing from Nemo to Guppy to Mr. Tulkinghorn, then to Bucket, to Sir Leicester and Mr. Jarndyce, and finally to Esther. The significance of the letters is not in their content, but rather in their existence. By evidence of handwriting alone, the detectives of *Bleak House* are able to create a parentage; like the letter at the reunion scene, this is another narrative of origins for Esther. A packet of letters comes to represent and supplement the conception of Esther; Esther Summerson is produced in this text by writing, by the commingling of the handwriting of her two parents: she is the material trace of their correspondence. The novel here reformulates its basic question about the relationship between a body and a text: if the autobiography of a subject can create that subject, then a narrative of romantic love can certainly produce an offspring. In the world of Chancery, there is no cause other than the textual, and there is no effect beyond that produced by language.

Dickens foregrounds a careful distinction, however, between the death of the father and the death of the mother. Throughout *Bleak House*, fathers and father-figures are consistently impotent, if not because they are the victims of poverty, stupidity, or addiction, then because, like Mr. Jarndyce, they are held captive by the sprawling tentacles of *Jarndyce v. Jarndyce*. But despite paternal ineptitude, the novel expends almost none of its considerable vituperative powers on them. The omniscient narrator reports Nemo's death scene in terms which invoke the desire to recuperate a long-lost mother. Nemo, the law-writer, dies alone, both alone in his room and alone in the anomic world of the Chancery narrative, in a scene that appears outside of Esther's frame of vision:

Then there is rest around the lonely figure, now laid in its last earthly habitation; and it is watched by the gaunt eyes in the shutters through some quiet hours of night. If this forlorn man could have been prophetically seen lying here, by the mother at whose breast he nestled, a little child, with eyes upraised to her loving face, and soft hand scarcely knowing how to close upon the neck to which it crept, what an impossibility the vision would have seemed! O, if, in brighter days, the now extinguished fire within him ever burned for one woman who held him in her heart, where is she, while these ashes are above the ground! (201)

The rhetorical vehicle Dickens employs to construct this loneliness makes Nemo into a lost child; a child, in other words, exactly like his child, Esther. The rhetorical energy and pathos of the death scene are generated by this description of a wrecked, alienated, abandoned man. If Nemo is to be taken seriously as the representative victim of the destructive powers of Chancery, then the hypothetical adoring mother who emerges here functions on a much larger scale than the individual. Rather, what is lost to both Nemo and to the world of this text is a utopic ideal constructed without cynicism or irony in the figure of the mother; before there existed this uncontrollable world of dissolution and dissipation, there existed a mother, a home, a protective bosom. This, not the godmother or Mrs. Jellyby, is the phantasy of origins that Esther wants to claim as her own. But it appears that the turbulent world of Chancery, like the placid world of Esther Summerson, has been constructed against the specter of maternal abandonment. The clarion cry that emerges from this description of Nemo's solitary condition – "where is she?" – reappears much later in the novel. But this time, the woman for whom the text is yearning is Lady Dedlock, Esther's lost mother and Nemo's true love. It is Detective Bucket who takes up that search:

Where is she? Living or dead, where is she? If, as he folds the handkerchief and carefully puts it up, it were able, with an enchanted power, to bring before him the place where she found it, and the night landscape near the cottage where it covered the little child, would he descry her there? On the waste, where the brick-kilns are burning with a pale blue flare; where the straw-roofs of the wretched huts in which the bricks are made, are being scattered by the wind; where the clay and water are hard frozen, and the mill in which the gaunt blind horse goes round all day, looks like an instrument of human torture; – traversing this deserted blighted spot, there is a lonely figure with the sad world to itself, pelted by the snow and driven by the wind, and cast out, it would seem, from all companionship. It is the figure of a woman, too; but it is miserably dressed, and no such clothes ever came through the hall, and out the great door, of the Dedlock mansion. (824)

The missing mother in this novel is potentially everywhere but actually nowhere. As the figure of connection and comfort and protection, she stands in sharp contrast to the neglectful mothers actually present in the text, and is therefore evocative of a greater symbolic statement. The search for her, the cry of "Where is she? Living or dead, where is she?" constitutes the detective plot of *Bleak House*, which thus functions as an attempt to find closure before the beginning of the story, to regain access to the pre-Oedipal, prelinguistic, only ever symbolic mother. As an allegory of the psychoanalytic process, the novel's attempt to find the "lost mother," whether it is represented as Bucket's literal search or as Esther's attempt to gain access to an idealized maternal object, only ever produces "mother" as grotesque and as parody. For the world of the text is so inundated with narrative, with the proliferation of the Symbolic, that its phantasies about an anterior utopia are inflected with the markers of hard-earned cynicism.

The search for the mother functions, then, as the autobiographical trope – the story of origins, beginnings, and processes of differentiation. But the implication of substitution as the basis of a self-construction remains anxiety-producing within Esther's tale; the inevitable outcome is a text and therefore a figure warped and scarred by the process of signification. In this context, then, it is revealing that Esther's first encounter with Lady Dedlock is presented in terms of a visual phenomenon. The experience is uncanny:

Shall I ever forget the rapid beating at my heart, occasioned by the look I met, as I stood up! Shall I ever forget the manner in which those handsome proud eyes seemed to spring out of their languor, and to hold mine! It was only a moment before I cast mine down – released again, if I may say so – on my book: but I knew the beautiful face quite well, in that short space of time.

And, very strangely, there was something quickened within me, associated with the lonely days at my godmother's; yes, away even to the days when I had stood on tiptoe to dress myself at my little glass after dressing my doll. And this, although I had never seen this lady's face before in all my life – I was quite sure of it – absolutely certain. (304)

The connections for Esther are eyes, books, mirrors: looking at Lady Dedlock, catching her eye, sends her back in search of a memory that is not there. Her eyes on her book, she remembers herself as a child, her mirror, her doll. Lady Dedlock is beautiful, and looking at her is like looking in a mirror. Without knowing that she is looking at her mother, Esther occupies a maternal position, seeing herself as a child dressing by herself in a very unmothered mothering moment, seeing that child playing mother to that doll, the doll who is simultaneously a mother-substitute and a dead and buried baby. Esther continues to gaze at this strangely (un)familiar woman:

It was easy to know that the ceremonious, gouty, grey-haired gentleman, the only other occupant of the great pew, was Sir Leicester Dedlock; and that the lady was Lady Dedlock. But why her face should be, in a confused way, like a broken glass to me, in which I saw scraps of old remembrances; and why I should be so fluttered and troubled (for I was still), by having casually met her eyes; I could not think.

I felt it to be an unmeaning weakness in me, and tried to overcome it by attending to the words I heard. Then, very strangely, I seemed to hear them, not in the reader's voice, but in the well-remembered voice of my godmother. That made me think, did Lady Dedlock's face accidentally resemble my godmother's? . . . And yet I – *I*, little Esther Summerson, the child who lived a life apart, and on whose birthday there was no rejoicing – seemed to arise before my own eyes, evoked out of the past by some power in this fashionable lady. (304–5)

As in a death-scene, Esther sees her whole life flash before her eyes when she sees Lady Dedlock for the first time; recalling a birth, she finds herself grasping for primal memories and primary connections. Here, yet again, Esther appears as a ghostly presence in her own narrative, past and present telescoping and conflating, this visual connection between two identical women producing the specter of the little child, Esther Summerson. We are returned to the birthday that was not, to the originary moment of this text and this person, a moment obscured from access in the autobiography. In this troubling and evocative moment in which the ghosts of her dead godmother and her dead baby self are made present through visual recognition, Esther first realizes the terrible danger of becoming at once Self and Other to herself: the vision of another version of herself acts as the dramatic representation of the destabilized narrative voice of her autobiography. Confronted with the sight of another woman who both is and is not herself, like looking into a "broken glass," Esther confronts head-on the problematic paradox of an orphan who is trying to write an autobiography, an effort destined to confront its own fictionality.

The conclusion, then, seems to rely on Esther's ability to redact this narrative. Not long before her reunion with Lady Dedlock, Esther is teaching her servant Charley (herself a substitute "mother" to her motherless siblings) to write, when Charley asks to visit the home of Jenny, mother of the dead baby. There is sickness in the house again; Jo, the orphaned tramp who had previously helped Lady Dedlock locate the grave of Nemo, has arrived with smallpox. Esther and Charley go to nurse the boy, but on the way, Esther is struck with a prophetic vision:

I had no thought, that night – none, I am quite sure – of what was soon to happen to me. But I have always remembered since, that when we had stopped at the garden-gate to look up at the sky, and when we went upon our way, I had for a moment an undefinable impression of myself as being something different from what I then was. (484–5)

Reconstructing this multiply liminal moment after the fact, knowing now what she didn't know then, Esther is struck with the perception of her own difference. This is presumably a different difference than she felt as a child, unlike all the other children, and it represents, perhaps ironically, the beginning of Esther's attempt to master her own anxieties and her own discourse by appropriating the fact of difference. The syntactical arrangement of this moment is complex: "I had for a moment an undefinable impression of myself as being something different from what I then was." Which self is she at the moment of realization? at the moment of utterance? This issue represents acutely Esther's attempt to manipulate the concept of "self" throughout her autobiography. Rather than playing victim to rhetorical instability, she now attempts to utilize that instability to differentiate herself from her own originary narrative through an act of disavowal. She turns chameleon in the drive to mastery, manipulating the tropes of fictionality in order to control the tropes of autobiography.

Through Jo and finally through Charley, Esther catches smallpox, a punishment for her philanthropy, which itself is in penance for her birth. She goes temporarily blind, but recovers completely, although she recovers *looking like* a different person. When she awakens, her friends have removed her looking-glass to protect her from shock: "'It matters very little, Charley. I hope I can do without my old face very well'" (546). Finally, early in the chapter that describes her reunion with Lady Dedlock, she looks at her own face: "I . . . went up to the glass upon the dressing-table," she writes:

There was a little muslin curtain drawn across it. I drew it back: and stood for a moment looking through such a veil of my own hair, that I could see nothing else. Then I put my hair aside, and looked at the reflection in the mirror, encouraged by seeing how placidly it looked at me. I was very much changed – O very, very much. At first, my face was so strange to me, that I think I should have put my hands before it and started back, but for the encouragement I have mentioned. Very soon it became more familiar, and then I knew the extent of the alteration in it better than I had done at first. (559)

Esther unveils the mirror and unveils her face; the gesture of revelation is the opposite of the gesture of shrouding the dead baby, but its effect is arguably the same. The baby that was Esther Summerson is gone, and the agency of Esther's ego is now quite literally situated in a fictional direction. The face of the stranger Lady Dedlock was more familiar to Esther in church than the strange visage she confronts here. Lady Dedlock was familiar because she was like Esther, Self, not Other; this face, supposedly Self, is completely Other. The sense of unfamiliar familiarity originally directed at Lady Dedlock is now directed at Esther herself at this moment of "self-recognition." The drama of self-differentiation, which was previously externalized, played out upon the missing mother, is now internalized with the division, the difference of Esther. This moment enacts a symbolic rejection of the mother who rejected, and all that that mother represents.

Esther Summerson effectively literalizes the argument Paul de Man makes in "Autobiography as Defacement": that the signifier precedes, and indeed shapes, changes, and even creates its referent. Dickens's Esther, however, constructs her autobiographical voice *by* defacement in a literalization, a physicalization of de Man's figural logic. In *Bleak House*, the signifier is fully capable of enacting figural damage on the physical body. Esther's construction of herself by and through her damage, her defacement, establishes her definitively as a character in this text because she is readable as decisively different from the (dis)embodied figure of the mother.

Throughout the novel, Esther has catalogued the narrative progression from rhetorical embodiment to the production of a physical body; Lady Dedlock's body, like Esther's, is systematically de-eroticized and ultimately destroyed over the course of the text. But the destruction of Esther's face serves a twofold practical purpose. The first assumption she makes when she steps away from the mirror is that her potential romance with Allan Woodcourt is dead: she is no longer beautiful, so she is no longer sexual or desirable. This is ironic, since she has married Allan by the time of the book's writing; however, her defacement allows her to perform more precisely the moralistic role of "Good Esther," a hard-working, non-sexual woman. A second and related advantage is that there is no longer any *visible* connection between Esther and Lady Dedlock:

when I saw her at my feet on the bare earth in her great agony of mind, I felt, through all my tumult of emotion, a burst of gratitude to the providence of God that I was so changed as that I could never disgrace her by any trace of likeness; as that nobody could ever now look at me, and look at her, and remotely think of any near tie between us. (565)

The destruction of Esther's face ensures not only that she will not disgrace her mother by announcing her illegitimate presence with her face. But now it is clear that Esther's mother will not disgrace her, either: the daughter's virtue is constructed in contrast to the counter-example of her mother, the eroticized, transgressive woman, the sinful abandoning mother begging at her feet for forgiveness.

But at the moment of reunion, Lady Dedlock knows her secret is about to be discovered and her family publicly disgraced; under these conditions, her plea to Esther to consider her dead is only a temporary fiction. The terms of Esther's second, figurative abandonment are once again, once and for all, about to become fact. Soon after the reunion scene, Lady Dedlock leaves Chesney Wold forever, leaving only Esther's handkerchief and a letter thanking Jenny for her assistance as clues for Mr. Bucket to trace. In this final episode of loss, discovery, and loss again, the paths of two mothers and two babies cross and connect powerfully; class is finally the only marker of difference in this sentimentalized tragedy. Jenny and her dead baby (Esther Summerson), Lady Dedlock and her dead baby (Esther Summerson) are two pairs constructed in a chiastic relationship to one another, in which one half of each pair survives to complement her opposite. Jenny gives Lady Dedlock her clothing, providing her with a disguise to help her to escape, in the same way that Esther is "disguised" by her defacement. With her change in costume, however, Lady Dedlock finally becomes what she thought she was for so long: the mother of the dead child. And Esther, now that doubly dead child and the ghostwriter of her autobiography, recognizes Lady Dedlock in this role. With Bucket and Woodcourt, she discovers the body: "On the step at the gate, drenched in a fearful wet of such a place, which oozed and splashed down everything, I saw, with a cry of pity and horror, a woman lying – Jenny, the mother of the dead child" (868).

The moment of discovery is a moment of recognition – or is it misrecognition? Who is dead and who is alive? Who is absent and who is present? When *Bleak House* finally becomes what it thought for so long it was, the story of a dead mother and an abandoned child, is it fiction or "autobiography"? detective novel or domestic novel? Confronted with the dead mother of the dead child, the chiastic figure marks indeterminacy as the final, tragic trope of the text, an uncanny destabilization of the authoritative, authorial, autobiographical voice. "I passed on to the gate, and stooped down," writes Esther, looking at the dead woman's body. "I lifted the heavy hand, put the long, dank hair aside, and turned the face. And it was my mother, cold and dead" (869). With the final act of unveiling, the production of the dead mother's body, the text comes full circle, arriving at the *literal* representation of Esther's instantiating crisis and the tragic culmination of all her fears and desires. But even as it comes full circle, the text also confronts the possibility that it has gone nowhere, that Esther is still the vulnerable orphan, or worse, the dead baby; or even worse, that when she pushes aside the hair and looks at that face, she sees herself, as in a broken glass.

For the empire of the domestic under the reign of Esther inevitably maintains a tenuous hold over the teeming elements of Chancery and London that it so dearly desires to contain. The queen of this empire has been defaced in the battle toward her dominion, and the rhetorical function of this defacement implies, not the domestic dream world described in contrast to Nemo's dissolute deathbed, but rather, a more cynical, certainly a more parodic attitude toward the world it claims to endorse. The final, broken line of the novel underscores the terms of the contest at its conclusion, terms under which Esther still struggles to manipulate the terminology of "defacement" tropologically. The novel's final question comes from Esther's husband Allan, who implies if not a literal, then a figurative return of the repressed in the guise of female sexuality: "'And don't you know that you are prettier than you ever were?'" (935). Allan's question is an extremely dangerous one for the text. Esther's response represents a return to the familiar logic of disavowal and displacement:

I did not know that; I am not certain that I know it now. But I know that my dearest little pets are very pretty, and that my darling is very beautiful, and that my husband is very handsome, and that my guardian has the brightest and most benevolent face that ever was seen; and that they can very well do without much beauty in me – even supposing –. (935)

Bleak House and "Bleak House" conclude in a moment of rhetorical indeterminacy, in which the subject, Esther Summerson, is quite literally effaced by the imposition of the textual frame. The question of agency returns in this final moment; if "Esther" is the putative subject here, then the novel ends on a note of bald manipulation in the guise of false modesty, for as one 1867 conduct book suggests of female diplomacy, "Whether it is artifice or tact is one of those nice questions which is perhaps not consistent with the rules of gallantry to examine too closely."[13] If it is "Dickens" who controls the end, however, the novel concludes with a commentary on, and thus an appropriation of, the terms of Esther's empowerment as a narrator. Either way, the narrative itself functions here as the "broken glass," the figurative representation of Esther's battle to contain herself, to create herself in one particular image, as one particular subject, through the vehicle of an autobiography. To conclude with a rupture is only appropriate, for at this point the narrative only duplicates the terms of victory even as it models the conditions challenging its maintenance.

I was engaged to attend a young married lady in West Smithfield, who was expected to be confined of her first child, the first or second week in January. She went into the immediate neighbourhood of her own house, to join a party of friends on the evening of New-Year's-Day, being at that time apparently in perfect health; and after she had been among them a few hours, in full enjoyment of the hilarity of the evening, she suddenly complained of being very ill. With great difficulty she was got up-stairs, and was seated in an easy nursing chair; but presently she fell lifeless on the floor!! The people about her supposed her to be in a fainting-fit; a neighbouring medical-man was called, who, in the first instance, thought the lady in a state of syncope; but he presently pronounced her to be dead!! Some time was lost in the confusion which prevailed in the house; but by-and-by a messenger was dispatched for my attendance. I arrived at the house a little after midnight; at that time, the lady had been lifeless at least an hour. Notwithstanding, I would gladly have removed the child by the caesarean section, but her friends would not consent to that operation.

John Ramsbotham, M.D., *Practical Observations in Midwifery, with Cases in Illustration* (2nd edition, revised, in one volume) (London: S. Highley, 32, Fleet Street; John Churchill, Princes Street, Soho, 1842), 495.

CHAPTER 4

Wilkie Collins and the secret of the mother's plot

What is peculiar to modern societies, in fact, is not that they consigned sex to a shadow existence, but that they dedicated themselves to speaking of it *ad infinitum* while exploiting it as *the* secret.

Michel Foucault[1]

It seemed almost like a monomania to be tracing back everything strange that happened, everything unexpected that was said, always to the same hidden source and the same sinister influence.

Wilkie Collins[2]

Walter Hartright, the protagonist, principal narrator, and "editor" of Wilkie Collins's *The Woman in White* (1859–60), returns from the jungles of Central America in the middle of the novel's action, only to learn of the recent death of Laura Fairlie, the love of his life first made inaccessible through her arranged marriage to the sinister Sir Percival Glyde. Unable to recover from the blow of Laura's new, more permanent inaccessibility, Walter decides to visit her grave, hoping to forsake his ideal woman once and for all. The opposite occurs. He stands by the tombstone, watching as two women walk toward him, one mysteriously veiled:

The veiled woman had possession of me, body and soul. She stopped on one side of the grave. We stood face to face with the tombstone between us. She was close to the inscription on the side of the pedestal. Her gown touched the black letters.

The voice came nearer, and rose and rose more passionately still. "Hide your face! don't look at her! Oh, for God's sake, spare him –"

The woman lifted her veil.

"Sacred to the Memory of Laura, Lady Glyde –"

107

Laura, Lady Glyde, was standing by the inscription, and was looking at me over the grave. (431)

In a moment of irreducible uncanniness for Walter and for the novel, the sight of Laura, Lady Glyde, living, next to her tombstone, at once demands and resists empirical explanation. Medusa *and* virgin bride, Laura lifts her veil to gaze into Walter's eyes on the consecrated ground of the burial-plot that contains not only her body, but the body of her mother as well. Resisting the shrieked warnings of Laura's half-sister Marian, Walter sees the face behind the veil; apprehending this specter of the physically impossible, Walter is thus thrust into a "burial-plot" of his own.

That burial-plot, on its most literal level, involves the exposure of Sir Percival Glyde's scheme to bury the identical Anne Catherick in place of Laura, thereby enabling Sir Percival to inherit Laura's fortune. But Walter's obsession with this plot, originating here in the graveyard at a moment of uncanny "truth," gestures as well to a more persistently sublimated set of preoccupations. The discrepancy of the living Laura, Lady Glyde, and a tombstone memorializing her dead body not only precipitates the drive to discovery that is the novel's detective plot; it also foregrounds a tension between the physical and the rhetorical that poses as realistic something at once uncanny and empirically provable, impossible, yet true. Which tells the true story, the body or the text? If the woman standing before Walter is Laura, then whose body is buried in the ground below? If she is not Laura, then who is she? And what are the implications of Walter's insistent attribution of Laura's identity to someone else altogether?

The "plot" at the center of this book is, significantly, not only the plot of "Laura"; it is also the plot of Laura's mother, Mrs. Fairlie. This incidental detail becomes important to a larger consideration of the ethics, morality, and rhetoric of "truth" in the text. The mother, missing, is the site of *rhetorical* "truth" and "virtue" here, and the persistent undermining of such rhetoric indicates a larger crisis of biographical knowability. *The Woman in White* is about the determining power of mothers in the construction of identity; for mothers, throughout the mystery genre, are the shaping figures behind both social class and the construction of desire, and mid-Victorian detective fictions are obsessed with such questions. From Dickens onward, the genre consolidates itself in the sensation novels of the 1860s in an efficient and titillating mix of domestic and detective plots. As Todorov has suggested, the detective plot enacts a critical temporal reversal that distinguishes it from conventional narrative: by definition, the detective plot reaches backward in an analysis and explication of the historical past, in contrast, for example, to the forward-looking temporal structure of the *Bildungsroman*.[3] Domestic detective fictions, then, return to the site of previous generations, their desire to affix contemporary mysteries of identity completely dependent on their ability to interpret accurately events of personal history. Mothers, within this framework, are critical guarantors of identity, and in the context of the paternal mystery, maternal virtue emerges as a source of anxiety: not only name, but also inheritance and class depend on the mother as a reliable source of truth, and as a conformist within cultural definitions of her sexuality. Returning again and again to the inscrutable specter of the dead mother, Victorian detectives attempt to locate her within the narrow parameters of middle-class sexual virtue; again and again, however, that attempt fails, prompting the paranoiac destabilization of identity. An endogamous crisis – If I can't trust my mother, who can I trust? If I don't know my mother, who do I know? If my mother doesn't know me, who am I? – is turned outward to become the exogamous logic of social disarray.

As modeled in *Bleak House*, the dead mother is the figure for the generic crisis that produces detective fiction: her absence suggests a crisis in the world of the present, while in her absence, she remains an abstract ideal that can be invoked as the signifier of order and reason in an entropic world; only dead can she enable such a split purpose. It is my argument in this chapter that in *The Woman in White*, that central crisis concerns legitimacy; it is implicated in "telling the difference" between legitimate and illegitimate children (and thus guaranteeing the proper disposal of real property), and telling that difference, as well, in the context of potentially unreliable textual and physical evidence. In the context of paternity anxiety, the mother is the *sujet supposé savoir*, the only figure whose testimony can validate legitimacy; thus the desire to contain female sexuality retrospectively collides with empirical evidence of maternal transgression.[4] The overdetermined language of the maternal ideal thus emerges to distract from – and to compensate for – the massively disruptive potential of such testimonial power. *The Woman in White*, in its concluding claims of truth and justice, capitalizes on a theory of maternal moral influence, yet the mother in question is necessarily dead – and it is her very absence from the world of the text that enables an ideology of "truth" to be constructed. For the living mothers represented in the novel insistently belie the ideal of maternal

virtue: time and again, Collins's characters trace to the mother the
origin of criminality, falsehood, and transgression. In fact, mothers are
the immediate source of every problem in the world of the well-
intentioned Walter Hartright, and it is the containment of what these
bad mothers represent toward which the novel moves in its assertion of
truth grounded in motherly virtue.

Seeking to inscribe the "truth," not on the tomb of Laura but on that
of her dead mother, Walter yearns after a scenario which proves that
Laura's is not the body buried in this plot. He explains to the family
solicitor:

She has been cast out as a stranger from the house in which she was born – a lie
which records her death has been written on her mother's tomb – and there are
two men, alive and unpunished, who are responsible for it. That house shall
open again to receive her in the presence of every soul who followed the false
funeral to the grave – that lie shall be publicly erased from the tombstone by the
authority of the head of the family, and those two men shall answer for their
crime to ME, though the justice that sits in tribunals is powerless to pursue them.
I have given my life to that purpose, and, alone as I stand, if God spares me, I
will accomplish it. (465–6)

Walter's melancholic inability to forsake Laura as his love-object is only
facilitated by his response to the woman who appears before him at
Laura's grave; indeed, the mission of the novel as a whole is to construct
a plausible framework for Laura as a living person, its polemic to
convince the reader, in lieu of a court of law, that she lives on, married to
Walter. His mission makes clear that this novel exists in its entirety as a
tour de force of melancholia, as a gesture to a phantasy of the historical
past that secures the permanence of an unambivalently ideal love-object
in the historical present. Reflected throughout the novel in its preoccupation with securing that which is uncanny, preserving as pure that
which is sullied by time, Walter's melancholic impulse foregrounds the
novel's investment in a phantasy of sanitized anteriority.

The novel's primary characters, Marian and Laura, Anne Catherick
and Walter, return no less than five times in the novel to this apparently
incidental place, the gravesite of the dead mother, "the white marble
cross that distinguished Mrs. Fairlie's grave from the humbler monu-
ments scattered about it" (113). Mrs. Fairlie's cross is at once a meeting-
place and a cross-road; the site of physical reunion, it is also the site of
dissolution and departure. Marian in particular constructs the memory
of her mother in the (theoretically) unambiguous terms of the domestic
ideal; she says to the village schoolteacher, "'If there are people in this

village, Mr. Dempster, who have forgotten the respect and gratitude due from every soul in it to my mother's memory, I will find them out; and, if I have any influence with Mr. Fairlie, they shall suffer for it'" (111). Through its revealing defensiveness, Marian's statement figures the novel's primary desire, to defend a good and virtuous woman against ingratitude and disrespect. However, Marian's intervention is significantly belated: that aspersions may already have been cast upon the good name of the dead mother suggests that something rotten in the past rears its head in the present. The dead mother embodies the unreadable and disturbing center of the novel's detective plot. The logic of maternal virtue and the physical evidence of maternal lives are at cross-purposes to one another; Mrs. Fairlie's cross, as a cross, emblematizes that tension even as it is persistently misread as an icon of the ideal.

Mrs. Fairlie's gravesite first appears in the text in the punitive context suggested by Marian's desire to make heretics against her mother's memory suffer. Walter and Marian visit a school founded by the late Mrs. Fairlie, and walk in on the punishment of young Jacob Postlethwaite, who persists in claiming to have seen "'T'ghaist of Mistress Fairlie'" (111) in the graveyard: "'He saw, or thought he saw, a woman in white, yesterday evening, as he was passing the churchyard; and the figure, real or fancied, was standing by the marble cross, which he and everyone else in Limmeridge knows to be the monument over Mrs. Fairlie's grave. These two circumstances are surely sufficient to have suggested to the boy himself the answer which has so naturally shocked you?'" (111). Walter's immediate conclusion, which he confides to Marian after they leave the school, is that this ghost is in truth a ghost-writer: Laura has recently received a letter warning her away from her impending marriage to Sir Percival Glyde. "'The belief is strong in me, at this moment,'" Walter says and later writes, "'that the fancied ghost in the churchyard, and the writer of the anonymous letter, are one and the same person'" (112). The subtle implication here is that "T'ghaist of Mistress Fairlie" actually produced a letter of warning to her youngest daughter. The text underscores this impression in several different ways. First of all, to have her mother as an ally in her suspicions of Sir Percival Glyde would be Marian's greatest desire, for Laura is engaged to this man only to fulfill her father's dying wish, against the intuition of every living advocate she has; her mother's allegiance would provide Marian with the authority to block the marriage, and both daughters really *need* a mother at this moment of crisis.

Further, we have just seen evidence of Mrs. Fairlie's letter-writing activities: during Walter's first night at Limmeridge House, he tells Marian of his mysterious encounter with a woman in white, who mysteriously knows Limmeridge and its occupants. Marian delves into her mother's correspondence with her father in order to produce a name and an identity for Walter's spectral friend – the name Anne Catherick.

Mrs. Fairlie is, in fact, the figure in the novel who *manufactures* the woman in white, who produces her – as a story and as a dramatic figure – within the bounds of the larger text. Marian reads a letter written by her mother years before, channeling, as others will also, her mother's voice:

"This poor little Anne Catherick is a sweet, affectionate, grateful girl; and says the quaintest, prettiest things (as you shall judge by an instance), in the most oddly-sudden, surprised, half-frightened way. Although she is dressed very neatly, her clothes show a sad want of taste in colour and pattern. So I arranged, yesterday, that some of our darling Laura's old white frocks and white hats should be altered for Anne Catherick; explaining to her that little girls of her complexion looked neater and better in all white than in anything else. She hesitated and seemed puzzled for a minute; then flushed up, and appeared to understand. Her little hand clasped mine, suddenly. She kissed it, Philip; and said (oh, so earnestly!), 'I will always wear white as long as I live. It will help me to remember you, ma'am, and to think that I am pleasing you still, when I go away and see you no more.' This is only one specimen of the quaint things she says so prettily. Poor little soul! She shall have a stock of white frocks, made with good deep tucks, to let out for her as she grows –" (84–5)

This quotation reveals the fact that Mrs. Fairlie "produces" the woman in white in more than one sense. Not only does Mrs. Fairlie's letter attach a name – Anne Catherick – to the mysterious figure, but Mrs. Fairlie herself was the person who put the woman in white in the first place. As author and agent, Mrs. Fairlie's significance as a symbolic as well as literal mother is doubly determined: the origin of the woman in white herself, she is also the origin of information about Anne.

From the beginning of the novel, Mrs. Fairlie is the source of the logic behind the text's apparently inexplicable events, and like her, other mothers, too, will occupy this role, not only informing but authoritatively confirming otherwise uncanny plot-twists. Surrogate mother to a foundling mysteriously identical to her own child, Mrs. Fairlie is linked to the mother whose *failure* to mother necessitates her virtuous intervention. Anne's mother, Mrs. Catherick, is still alive in the historical present of the text, and the information she possesses will ultimately prove as fatal to her child as it is instructive to the rest of the novel. The only living mother in this text, Mrs. Catherick is the only source of information about the historical past, information that is at once authorizing and menacing; uncaring and even brutal to her child, associated with extramarital sexuality, deceit, violence, extortion, and hypocrisy, she is a figure of vice who belies the rhetoric of maternal virtue embodied in Mrs. Fairlie. She is, in other words, the novel's worst nightmare, precisely the kind of authorizing, illegitimizing, destabilizing mother the entire narrative anxiously attempts to rewrite.

Anne Catherick's bizarre appearance as "the woman in white" thus refers to the symmetrical equation of bad mother and good mother, of the vicious woman who abandoned her and the woman whose kindness and pity she memorializes in her dress. For Anne's lifetime fixation on the color white represents the compulsion to repeat the transaction in which she repudiates the bad mother in exchange for the good: "'I will always wear white as long as I live. It will help me to remember you.'" Embodied as a walking tombstone, the woman in white herself, like *The Woman in White* itself, is a signifier whose referent is the benign figure of anterior authority, the overdetermined good mother whose aggressive recapitulation as "good" belies the symbolic power of the vicious and living Mrs. Catherick. The doctor who has predicted young Anne's stubbornness in forming and keeping a certain idea – "'her unusual slowness in acquiring ideas implies an unusual tenacity in keeping them, once they are received into her mind'" (84) – also predicts her melancholia. Representing herself as "the woman in white," Anne refers to an ideal of Mrs. Fairlie's virtue that is symptomatic of the entire novel's melancholic attachment to a maternal ideal constructed in the context of violent and passionate ambivalence toward the dangerous, bad mother. Anne is an emblem of the novel's impulse to import a historical figure, the mother, into the present day as a means of securing stability; when Anne Catherick writes the anonymous letter warning Laura of Sir Percival Glyde, she does so through the invocation of maternal authority, constructing herself as the living mouthpiece of the dead mother. Anne further memorializes Mrs. Fairlie by representing herself as the vehicle through which the long-dead mother reaches out from the grave into the lives of her living daughters, constructing her agency as only an extension of that of the dead mother.

The search for the ghost/writer leads Walter and Marian directly to the tombstone, where they encounter not only the marker of Mrs.

Fairlie's life and death, but also the marker of Anne Catherick's visitation. They find the headstone mysteriously half-scrubbed; someone or something has clearly been there before them, and their search for the writer of the letter and for the ghost is now compounded to include the agent who has left such a visible trace on the marble:

The natural whiteness of the cross was a little clouded here and there, by weather stains; and rather more than one half of the square block beneath it, on the side which bore the inscription, was in the same condition. The other half, however, attracted my attention at once by its singular freedom from stain or impurity of any kind. I looked closer, and saw that it had been cleaned – recently cleaned, in a downward direction from top to bottom. The boundary line between the part that had been cleaned and the part that had not, was traceable wherever the inscription left a blank space in the marble – sharply traceable as a line that had been produced by artificial means. Who had begun the cleansing of the marble, and who had left it unfinished? (113–14)

The tombstone's peculiar pattern of soiling, leaving "a blank space in the marble," is clearly an unnatural phenomenon, and Walter's interpretation of this phenomenon acquires a moral valence: the discourse of "stain and impurity" signifies a statement of greater moral complexity than a simple observation of physical fact. To find *any* soil on the tombstone of the mother is surprising, however, considering the hyperbolic rhetoric with which her daughters have described her life and with which they represent their ongoing dedication to her. (Mrs. Fairlie's daughters are far less perturbed than Anne Catherick, we later learn, by witnessing the grave's neglect – they simply don't care that much.) To the extent that Mrs. Fairlie is "embodied" as and by her tombstone, she is therefore, now and throughout the rest of the novel, represented in the simultaneity of virtue and vice, half "cleansed," half "stain or impurity." Rather than the locus of unambiguous purity, Mrs. Fairlie remains the most persistent signifier of doubleness within the text; her tombstone itself reads as a mixture of pure and impure, stained and clean, the line dividing the two readable in and as a blank space.

The critical verb in the drawing-master's analysis of the tombstone is the verb "to trace": his description of the boundary line as something "traceable," "sharply traceable," is awkward enough to call attention to itself. To say that this line is "traceable" implies a physical, not merely a visual, connection between the observer and the headstone: as an act of repetition, the act of tracing is at once mimetic and tactile. But to trace this line is not possible, in the sense that the line is not a line at all, but merely the difference between dirty and clean, or pure and impure; to be on this borderline is to be at once both and neither. Ultimately, the headstone, invoked as the novel's locus of purity and originality (and purity as originality), is only another sign, not unified but dialectical, not singular but divided and doubled, not one but two. Like the dark and fair daughters of the late Mrs. Fairlie, the two halves of her headstone are related versions of the same mold, characterized more accurately in terms of difference than in terms of sameness.

The word "trace" is both noun and verb. Under the dictionary heading of noun, definitions include: "a mark or line left by something that has passed"; "a path beaten by or as if by feet"; "a sign or evidence of some past thing"; "something (as a line) traced or drawn"; "a minute and often barely detectable amount or indication; esp.: an amount of a chemical constituent not quantitatively determined because of minuteness."[5] These definitions suggest that the "trace" exists as the material residue of events that have occurred in the past. In addition, however, a "trace" element signifies the corruption of chemical purity brought about by that material residue. Dictionary definitions of the verb "to trace" proceed as follows: "to drag, draw"; "to form (as letters or figures) carefully or painstakingly"; "to copy (as a drawing) by following the lines or letters as seen through a transparent superimposed sheet"; "to follow the footprints, track, or trail of"; "to follow or study out in detail or step by going backward over the evidence step by step." The verb "to trace" makes explicit the role of the detective plot's pursuit of the noun, the "trace": the activity of pursuit is at once fueled and frustrated by a desire for the "original," which is only visible by means of its corruption, the "trace" of prior evidence.

In what sense, then, is the figure of this dead mother related to the act of "tracing"? The relationship between maternity and the trace in *The Woman in White* explicitly links a question of narrative strategy with a question of individual – and cultural – morality. This detective plot, and, I would argue, detective plots more generally, rely on fixed notions of "truth," "identity," and "knowability" grounded both symbolically and ideologically in the mother. Should that mother, the source of the individual and the anchor of the domestic unit, threaten nonconformity with this structure, then the entire social order predicated on her containability is threatened. That the grave of the mother is the locus of difference emblematizes the major anxiety of the novel: the replacement of the family tree with the signifying chain, or rather, the replacement of an orderly pattern of genetic and thus social order with a proliferation of tangled bloodlines that need to be traced to their corrupt sources. Mrs.

Fairlie's cross, *as* a cross, emblematizes the novel's connection of narrative and individual instability; in terms of that narrative and its principal
narrators, there remains an investment in securing the mother as the
origin of its structures of cause and effect. U. C. Knoepflmacher argues
that "*The Woman in White* depicts a collision between a lawful order in
which identities are fixed and an anarchic lawlessness in which these
social identities can be erased and destroyed."[6] The location of this
"collision" in the disembodied figure of the mother underscores the
narrative and psychological tensions at stake in an effective reconciliation. The phantasy of the novel's narrators and participants is the
production of "truth" through the process of narration. Their anxiety is
"anarchic lawlessness," and the replacement of "truth" with indeterminacy.

As a means of articulating this investment, Walter Hartright and his
myriad narrators invoke the "trace" throughout the novel, as both a
noun and a verb, in order to perpetuate the work of the tombstone's
mysterious cleansing agent. At the outset of his first narrative, for
example, Hartright claims that the object of this text is "to trace the
course of one complete series of events" (33). In the first of several
searches for Anne Catherick and her companion Mrs. Clemens, Walter's agent reports: "'I am sorry to say I could find no further trace of
them'" (144), and Sir Percival Glyde puts a moral spin on this effort: "'It
is a duty we all owe to the poor creature herself to trace her'" (157).

Here, in the order of their appearance, is a sampling of other "traces"
in the text. Soon after Sir Percival's first appearance, the Fairlie family
solicitor detects the sign of duplicity in him: "The only trace of [Sir
Percival's] former self that I could detect, reappeared, every now and
then, in his manner toward Miss Fairlie" (159). As a physical signifier,
the "trace" turns the body into a text, betraying the outward manifestation of hidden emotions: "The glimmer of the night-light showed me
that [Laura's] eyes were only partially closed: the traces of tears glis-
tened between her eyelids" (216). The trace functions as the means by
which people locate other people, by which people are kept safely within
the bounds of visibility: "Since that time, civilisation has lost all trace of
[Walter]" (221). "No mark of [Laura's] presence appeared inside the
building; but I found traces of her outside it, in footsteps on the sand"
(312). "The sandy ground showed no further trace of them. Feeling that
the persons whose course I was tracking, must necessarily have entered
the plantation at this point, I entered it, too. At first, I could find no path
– but I discovered one, afterwards, just faintly traced among the trees;

and followed it" (313). The act of writing itself is implicated in the doubleness of the trace; like tears, writing betrays its existence by leaving a residue: "Some sheets of blotting paper, . . . had the impression on them of the closing lines of my writing in these pages traced during the past night" (325). And finally, the trace emerges from the unconscious mind, reminding the dreamer, in this case Laura, of events repressed from conscious memory: "At times, dreams of the terrible past still disconnectedly recalled to her, in the mystery of sleep, the events of which her waking memory had lost all trace" (583).

To trace, the trace: the function of the trace in this narrative reveals the simultaneity of revelation and concealment, the connection between writing and searching, between physicality and textuality, between event and memory. As residue or intrusion – footprints in the sand, vestiges of Sir Percival's former self – the trace privileges a structural logic of displacement; this novel, because it is a detective novel, is concerned not with that which is present, but with that which is absent but still detectable in absence. The novel's larger narrative structure is implicated in this displacement, for as it describes the act of pursuit it inscribes the record of that pursuit, offering to the reader the material trace of the act of tracing. For Collins's detectives, and particularly for Walter and Marian, the material fact of the trace underscores a persistent faith in both originality and readability. The act of pursuit itself – of tracing the line – presupposes the existence of an answer and access to a destination. When the questions are those of identity, of legacy, as they are in *The Woman in White*, the construction of an answer presupposes the legibility of an ancestry; Collins, in other words, establishes the second generation as the trace of its predecessor, implying a cause–effect relationship across generational lines, in which children are the effects and parents the cause.

However, within the novel's larger structure of generational relationship, the logic implicit in this causality is problematic: no attempt in *The Woman in White* to idealize the past is effective, and this fact is particularly significant when a parental generation is nonconformist by current standards. Walter writes early in the novel:

I have observed, not only in my sister's case, but in the instances of others, that we of the younger generation are nothing like so hearty and so impulsive as some of our elders. I constantly see old people flushed and excited by the prospect of some anticipated pleasure which altogether fails to ruffle the tranquillity of their serene grandchildren. Are we, I wonder, quite such genuine boys and girls now as our seniors were in their time? Has the great advance in education taken rather too long a stride; and are we, in these modern days, just the least trifle in the world too well brought up? (38)

Locating not the ideal of the "well brought up" in the parental generation, but rather the affects of heartiness, impulsiveness, flushed excitation, and implied immaturity, Walter's incidental contrast of his mother and sister, minor characters, foregrounds a major conundrum for the novel as a whole. His detective plot represents a movement toward the imposition of a conservative ideal of behavior *retrospectively* on the unruly, unfortunate generation past. In other words, Walter works to "legitimate" himself and those around him through the revision of family histories that allude to past transgressions, constructing, effectively, the detective narrative as wish-fulfillment.

The significance of the trace in *The Woman in White* returns us again to the problematics of originality: Walter Hartright, detective, exploits evidence in order to construct narratives of containment after the fact, constructing individuals' originary histories as legitimate or illegitimate, depending on their relationship to his agenda. When Derrida speaks of the trace, he does so, as well, in terms of origins – in this case, of the original in perpetual regression: "The trace is not only the disappearance of origin – within the discourse that we sustain and according to the path that we follow it means that the origin did not even disappear, that it was never constituted except reciprocally by a nonorigin, the trace, which thus becomes the origin of the origin."[7] Derrida makes explicit the implications of the dictionary definitions of "trace" as noun and verb: the act of tracing an "origin" only ever occurs in the context of the trace, of the material evidence of prior corruption; no origin ever exists, he argues, except as it is later perceptible. The sign of otherness within a structure of presence, Derrida's trace functions as the link in the chain of signification, the marker of simultaneous connection and difference, like the line/non-line in the marble of Mrs. Fairlie's tombstone. Within the structure of the sign itself, however, the trace is the index of the difference within; again, as in the case of the headstone, legibility is constituted in terms of contrast. Derrida writes several pages later:

These chains and systems cannot be outlined except in the fabric of this trace or imprint. The unheard difference between the appearing and the appearance [*l'apparaissant et l'apparaître*] (between the "world" and "lived experience") is the condition of all other differences, of all other traces, and *it is already a trace*. This last concept is thus absolutely and by rights "anterior" to all *physiological* problematics concerning the nature of the *engramme* [the unit of engraving], or *metaphysical* problematics concerning the meaning of absolute presence whose trace is thus opened to deciphering. *The trace is in fact the absolute origin of sense in general. Which amounts to saying once again that there is no absolute origin of sense in general. The trace is the différance which opens appearance [l'apparaître] and signification.*[8]

Derrida argues that the physical representation or "engraving" of a logic of "originality" is always implicated in its own self-subversion. He argues, therefore, that "there is no absolute origin of sense in general"; that the trace exists as différance suggests that "originality" is always already a secondary logic, chasing its own tail in pursuit of a beginning. Derrida's trace is at once spectral and functional, providing a logic of anteriority and displacement to structures of immediacy and presence, to structures of meaning. Certainly within the parameters of *The Woman in White*, there is a tension between the act of tracing – of reading events and circumstances backwards – and the material signifier of "the trace." What Derrida's paradigm makes explicit, however, is the inextricable interrelationship of difference and signification, the inevitability of the ruptures, gaps, and breaks that Collins's empirically driven Hartright – and, indeed, the genre of detective fiction as a whole – resists. In terms of the gravestone itself, for example, quite literally *une engramme*, absence and presence combined signify even before Walter and Marian arrive to read its mysterious traces. As the marker of a presence that is disembodied, a presence that is by definition an absence, a placeholder for loss, the gravestone is a melancholic structure emblematic of the structure of the sign. And as the trace and the act of tracing converge on a place marked "mother," it is the figure of that mother as an absent presence that focuses the narrative's instantiating and ultimate crises.

In contrast to the activity of tracing, *the* trace in *The Woman in White* comes into being as the difference between desire and satisfaction: the detective plot is constituted in the difference, as the difference, between the question asked and the answer given. As Lacan writes with reference to the phallic mother in "The Signification of the Phallus," "Demand in itself bears on something other than the satisfactions it calls for. It is demand of a presence or of an absence – which is what is manifested in primordial relation to the mother, pregnant with that Other to be situated *within* the needs that it can satisfy."[9] For Lacan, desire originates in the failure of a phantasy of the phallic mother, the figure who promises that ultimate security, complete fulfillment; like the detective plot bracketed by the structures of question and answer, the paradigm of Lacanian desire is bracketed by the figure of the phallic mother, the point of *jouissance* at which signifier and referent coincide. The detective plot, the logic of the trace, the logic of desire itself, for that matter, exist in the arc of indeterminacy, in the space between. Throughout *The Woman in White*, the trace is a problematic residue, signaling a question asked but not an answer given, a desire but not a fulfillment: "Who had begun the cleansing of the marble, and who had left it unfinished?" And throughout *The Woman in White*, the answer, the space of knowing that is both origin and terminus, is the province of the mother. The detective, Walter Hartright, thus faces in the dead mother his primary competition as he attempts to establish himself as the *sujet supposé savoir*.

Derrida's concepts of "origin" and "trace" are quite necessarily elusive, a metalanguage describable only in terms of an alternative metalanguage. But even, or perhaps predictably, within such an endlessly self-referential structure, the mother as a figure recast for the trace lurks around the edges of his description, suggesting a shared fixation, or at least figuration, between *The Woman in White* and *Of Grammatology*. Alice Jardine suggests that Derrida's metalinguistic discourses are readable in terms of an encoded structure of gender. In her discussion of the "early," Americanized Derrida, Jardine reads the gender politics of *Of Grammatology*:

The distinctions between Nature and Culture propagated by anthropology and philosophy can only "stand up" if the dissimilation of writing is ignored. Derrida's own style goes to work on the myth of the natural; for as a myth of pure maternal presence, and voice as pure virginity before writing, it is a male myth . . . The trace, nonexistent, invisible, and overwhelmingly passive, marks the spot – of future feminine connotations.[10]

Jardine is speaking both of Derrida's work in years to come and of structures he invokes still later in the same text. For in fact, throughout his reading of Rousseau's *Confessions* later in *Of Grammatology*, Derrida both critiques and exploits Rousseau's construction of "mother" as the site of unfulfilled desire, the mark of anteriority, the supplement: "Thus presence, always natural, which for Rousseau more than for others means maternal, *ought to be* self-sufficient. Its *essence*, another name for presence, may be read through the grid of this ought to be [*ce conditionnel*]. Like Nature's love, 'there is no substitute for a mother's love,' says Emile."[11] Rousseau's autobiography is preoccupied with maternal death, taking its primary configurations of identity and sexuality from the fact of his mother's death following his birth: "I was born . . . a poor and sickly child, and cost my mother her life. So my birth was the first of my misfortunes."[12] Derrida's text is similarly readable through the lens of the "ought to be," within the context of Rousseau's preoccupation with his "first misfortune." For Derrida, the metalanguage of trace and origin is enmeshed in a psychoanalytic discourse that maps structures of signification onto the grid of displacement and desire configured first in the endogamous structure of the family. Derrida's appropriation of the mother as a figure, as the signifier of absent presence, reinscribes the equation of signification and maternal absence represented by Freud in his description of the *fort-da* game. As Gayatri Chakravorty Spivak suggests in her translator's introduction to *Of Grammatology*, "Freud's psychoanalysis, to some extent in spite of itself, recognizes the structure of experience itself to be a trace-, not a presence-structure."[13]

That the origin is a trace and that the trace is an origin is a familiar construct in psychoanalytic discourse. The conflation of mother and origin, and the division of mother from signification, are contiguous, mutually interdependent events: the mother is a necessary placeholder within the structure of the sign, but one that is inevitably in a relationship of alterity to the process of signification. In Lacan's "Mirror Stage," to offer one small example among many, the infant achieves triumphant subjectivity by capitalizing on this structure of context without implication:

Unable as yet to walk, or even to stand up, and held tightly as he is by some support, human or artificial (what, in France, we call a "*trotte-bébé*"), he nevertheless overcomes, in a flutter of jubilant activity, the obstructions of his support and, fixing his attitude in a slightly leaning-forward position, in order to hold it in his gaze, brings back an instantaneous aspect of the image.[14]

As a necessary but unassimilated textual presence, the absent mother – the prosthetic *trotte-bébé* – figures a crisis of generic signification for this novel, the potentially disruptive signifier of absence within the empirically driven culture of detective fiction. While the characters of *The Woman in White*, like the child of Freud's *fort-da* game, want to acquire mastery over the signifier through the maintenance of maternal absence, as Lacan reminds us, mastery is continually implicated in its opposite, alienation.[15]

As the figure for disrupted signification, then, the dead mother becomes the central site of resistance to the drive to "truth" engaging the detective–narrators of this text. For although the trace is, to use Jardine's description, "nonexistent, invisible, and overwhelmingly passive" like the dead mother in Collins's novel, again like the dead mother in *The Woman in White*, it is also deterministic and oddly powerful.

Ideologically, the dead mother is the phallic mother – judge, jury, and jailer alike; the fact that she is endlessly displaced from the world of the text, visible only as a trace and through the failings of bad mothers, is a convenience displaying an entrenched ambivalence about her powerful role.

In the texts of both Collins and Derrida, then, the mother must be absent *because* she is a phallic mother, embodying a condition of sheer impossibility: the guarantor of anterior events, she must remain an abstraction in order to provide the context in which the plot can unfold. In *The Woman in White*, the mother is the figure in possession of know-ledge, the one who holds the key to the "Secret"; she assures a principle of truth, justice, and virtue that is the required episteme of the detective plot. As the origin, she is thus also the novel's terminus, that from which it is generated and ultimately that to which it returns to fulfill the promise of its mystery narrative.

What, then, does this return to the maternal plot portend? The question of the "plot" of *The Woman in White* has, from the time of its first critical reception, been inextricable from the issue of the "unsayable," and ultimately from the issue of transgressive female sexuality. The mother is, quite literally, that which has been excluded from the novel's plot: contained in her cemetery plot, she is marginalized, stripped of agency even as she is invoked insistently as the icon motivating virtuous action. As a figure excluded, she is intimately related to the novel's larger teleology of exclusion. The genre of mid-Victorian mystery fic-tion is inherently conservative in the closure it constructs, and *The Woman in White* is no exception to this rule: as D. A. Miller has argued, although detective fiction serves as a means of displaying scenarios of sensationalistic, titillating transgression, it is precisely these scenarios that the detective plot itself seeks to occlude, overwriting subversion with the security of structure.[16]

In the preface to the first single-volume publication of *The Woman in White* in 1860, Wilkie Collins includes a request in anticipation of the novel's reviews, a request that repeats and projects the text's internal anxiety about the "unsayable" and the status of its narrative processes:

In the event of the book being reviewed, I venture to ask whether it is possible to praise the writer, or to blame him, without opening the proceedings by telling his story at second-hand? As the story is written by me – with the inevitable suppressions which the periodical system of publication forces on the novelist – the telling it fills more than a thousand closely printed pages. No small portion of this space is occupied by hundreds of little "connecting links," of trifling value in themselves, but of the utmost importance in maintaining the smoothness, the reality, and the probability of the entire narrative. If the critic tells the story *with* these, can he do it in his allotted page, or column, as the case may be? If he tells it *without* these, is he doing a fellow-labourer in another form of Art, the justice which writers owe to one another? And lastly, if he tells it at all, in any way whatever, is he doing service to the reader, by destroying, beforehand, two main elements in the attraction of all stories – the interest of curiosity and the excitement of surprise?[17]

Here Collins implies that it is impossible for critics to talk about the narrative without reproducing it in its entirety, foregrounding the problematics of "story" and "wholeness" in *The Woman in White*. The text emerges as a whole for which there is no metonym; "the interest of curiosity" and "the excitement of surprise" depend on the maintenance of virginity, the novel's deliverance to the reader intact. Yet Collins's attempt to construct his audience – in this case, critics – as a single entity, sworn to secrecy for the benefit of readerly titillation, places that audience in a peculiar position with regard to the novel's internal discourse of intactness. This peculiarity is manifest even within the language of his request: the whole text of the novel is written by Collins "with the inevitable suppressions which the periodical system of publication forces on the novelist." This novel, delivered by the author directly to the reader, presupposes that the reader overlook "inevitable suppressions" in favor of "whole truth." In a very direct sense, Mrs. Fairlie's half-cleaned tombstone operates as a figure for the text as a whole: on her tombstone, the "boundary line" is "traceable wherever the inscription left a blank space in the marble." An allusion to the tension challenging the novel's empirical mission, the fact that borderlines emerge only in contrast to "blank space" suggests the epistemological centrality of lack, or "inevitable suppression," within the rhetoric of the whole. In a discussion of the problematic yet inevitable discovery of maternal castration – and thus the fall of the twin empires of belief and certainty – Barbara Johnson writes: "The theory seems to imply that at some point in human sexuality, a referential moment is unbypassable: the observation that the mother does not have a penis is necessary . . . To borrow a joke from Geoffrey Hartman's discussion of certain solutionless detective stories, . . . 'instead of a whodunit we get a whodonut, a story with a hole in it.'"[18]

Collins constructs himself, and later his surrogate author-figure Walter Hartright, as master-narrators with deterministic power over both "suppressions" and "connecting links." Through this consolidation of narrative and authorial power, Collins claims the role assigned to the abstract "mother" in the novel itself, protector of the innocent and preserver of the truth. As Anne Catherick, through the invocation of maternal authority, attempts to protect the unsuspecting Laura from the evils of Sir Percival Glyde, Collins, too, attempts to protect the unsuspecting reader from the evils of critical usurpation. But while Anne seeks to preserve Laura's innocent virtue in the name of the mother, Collins emerges here as the protector of the "interest of curiosity" and the "excitement of surprise" – in defense of sensation, titillation, and arousal. The novel's internal discourse of virtue would appear to be in some tension with its larger marketing plan.

Predictably, Collins's directive prompted an irritated response from his contemporary reviewers. The otherwise sympathetic reviewer in *The Times* writes:

We therefore think that so good a story-teller as Mr. Collins might have been a little less peremptory in forbidding us to handle his tale. We might ask in return, has he so little faith in his own powers as to imagine that if the secret is once out his novel will lose its fascination, and have nothing else to recommend it to the reader? In a more savage mood, which no one will be inclined to indulge towards an author who has contributed so much to our amusement, we might put the question differently, and ask – if we are not to touch the story, what else is there to touch?[19]

In another unsigned review, this one in the *Dublin University Magazine*, a critic writes:

A good story with any life in it will lose nothing by our previous knowledge of the plot . . . A novel that cannot bear a slight rehearsal must either be wholly unreadable, or, at best, belong to a low type of literary art whose whole merit lies in the production of clever puzzles and startling metamorphoses. To which of these classes *The Woman in White* may be assigned we shall leave for others to settle for themselves, only asking, for our own part, how it is possible to criticize a book of this sort without a continual reference to the plot. Take that away, and there is nothing left to examine.[20]

"If we are not to touch the story, what else is there to touch?" . . . "Take that away, and there is nothing left to examine." The language of physical contact persistently appears in critical discourses around *The Woman in White*, from D. A. Miller's analysis of the novel's literal "sensation" elements to these critics' antagonized resistance to Collins's request for forbearance.[21] Emerging suggestively in the wake of that request, the issue of the body in critical treatments of *The Woman in White* is symptomatic of anxieties regarding the body – and particularly the eroticized female body – within the novel. In other words, the desire to "touch the text" on the part of critics mirrors the desire, expressed within the novel, to "touch the text," "traceable, sharply traceable"; and in the absence of text – in the absence of the legal documentation of legitimate bloodline – the ideological structure of the culture Collins constructs at the end of the novel is sorely undermined. At stake in the question of legitimacy are issues of class, inheritance, and family structure, and perhaps most compellingly within the psychodrama of *The Woman in White*, the question of the integrity of the female, and more specifically the maternal, body. For the mother is the guarantor of legitimacy, her honesty and willingness to abide by the marriage contract the insurance of bloodlines; the potential for forbidden forms of touching is a powerful anxiety within the world of this text, and thus requires close containment and regulation.

Throughout the novel and critical responses to it, the necessary containment of the female body is figured through a number of ingenious tropes, from cemetery plots to marriage registers. To quote the *Times* reviewer once again:

[We] are commanded to be silent, lest we should let the cat out of the bag. The cat out of the bag! There are in this novel about a hundred cats contained in a hundred bags, all screaming and mewing to be let out. Every new chapter contains a new cat. When we come to the end of it out goes the animal, and there is a new bag put into our hands which it is the object of the subsequent chapter to open. We are very willing to stroke some of these numerous cats, but it is not possible to do it without letting them out.[22]

Although this novel is replete with secrets, surprises, and twists (many of its contemporary critics draw the analogy to a puzzle[23]), the *Times* critic's distinctly overdetermined response calls to mind another feline moment, in which cats appear unexpectedly in defense of a descriptive strategy. In his study of Dora, *Fragment of An Analysis of a Case of Hysteria*, yet another text delivered fractured, fragmented to the reader, Freud assures his readers that he is perfectly "dry and direct" with his young patient about matters sexual: "*J'appelle un chat un chat.*"[24] But as Jane Gallop writes,

At the very moment [Freud] defines nonprurient language as direct and noneuphemistic, he takes a French detour into a figurative expression. By his terms, this French sentence would seem to be titillating, coy, flirtatious. And to make matters more juicy (less "dry"), *chat* or *chatte* can be used as vulgar (vulvar) slang for the female genitalia. So in this gynecological context, where he founds his innocence upon the direct use of terms, he takes a French detour and calls a pussy a pussy.[25]

When he is confronted with the need to describe what he has been prohibited from describing, Collins's critic, like Freud, takes recourse in the discourse of the feline; the implication of Gallop's reading of such a detour is to link the taboo of the "unsayable" with a displaced but nevertheless clear anxiety about female sexuality. The detective plot of *The Woman in White* is formulated as a double search: Hartright and his allies desire to understand the origins of two individuals, Anne Catherick and Sir Percival Glyde. This inquiry leads back to the mother of each of these people, and to the circumstances of each conception and birth. The novel consistently conflates the anxiety of physical reproduction – of the origins of the individual – with that of textual reproduction – of the origins of the written word. The relationship, then, between the novel's spectral mother, Mrs. Fairlie, and the processes of narrative focuses on the novel's tortuous plot and its similarly complex narrative modes. What is the difference, then, between stroking these cats and letting them out?

The novel's crisis of articulation is inextricable from its crisis about the terms and configurations of sexual desire. And as Gallop's analysis of Freud indicates, the "detective plot" of desire and discourse inevitably finds its answer in the figure of the mother: "The riddle is solved: the mother is 'the source' of sexuality, of perversion, of neurosis. The detective work is completed."[26] Yet within *The Woman in White*, the project of locating the mother after she has been reliably identified as "the source" is problematic and unstable. Gallop proceeds to critique Freud's inevitable conclusion, that the mother is a reliable source; she suggests, in fact, that it would be more productive to interrogate the mother's role as the source of anxiety rather than stability.[27] Certainly within the context of *The Woman in White*, the characters' reliance on maternal stability is betrayed by the mother's implication in the very events she is symbolically constructed to condemn. Thus the detective plot, which moves to foreclose on those transgressive events through its "solution," must confront the ambivalent distinction between the idealized virtuous mother and the transgressive embodied mother. If Collins's novel is in search of a phallic mother, of a totalizing presence that enables the unproblematic construction of borderlines, bloodlines, and identities, then its ambivalence both toward that figure and toward any understanding of an all-encompassing narrative only reinscribes its instantiating questions. In the detective plot, however, the mother is at once central and long since dead, the constructed site of narrative stability and also the exact place in which the inherent fragility of the myth is exposed. As the "answer" to the novel's detective work, the mother only ever functions as the source of the question in the first place; it is resistance to her text that dictates the terms of the novel's compulsion to repeat. Within the quest for origins that principally structures the genre of Victorian detective fiction, the mother-as-origin functions as a *mise en abîme*; she is ideologically central so necessarily unlocatable, and thus fictions of this period insistently project themselves toward their mother-ideal while simultaneously constructing the conditions that enable her retreat.

For it is not clear what the effects of storytelling will be, nor what the relationships between narration and originality have been; the text's narrative consists of the experiential affidavits of a series of "witnesses" to its central events, including, significantly, Mrs. Fairlie's tombstone. This fragmented mass is edited and organized by Walter Hartright, who is also a narrator, a structure that suggests hidden agendas and problems of credibility. In its detective narrative, then, as well as its thematic and temporal structures, the central logic of *The Woman in White* is the trope of reversal, and specifically, of the inversion of cause and effect. Within this novel, according to Sir Percival's disparaged "bit of copy-book morality," "'Crimes cause their own detection'" (255): in the logic of this text, effect determines cause, just as the trace implies and describes its causal origin. Again, the tombstone is an emblem here, for the novel as a whole as for the mother-figure, enabling the articulation of "difference" only through the invocation of loss, of the "blank space." Returning to the acute tension between "the trace" and "to trace," the progression of the narrative through an uncanny wilderness of indeterminacy raises the question of causality. Which comes first, the activity of tracing or the material spectacle of the trace itself? And if, in fact, the action determines the effect of its own pursuit, what are the implications of this reversal for a novel, especially for a detective novel, so concerned with the processes of its narration? If crimes in fact cause their own *narration*, what does it mean to "tell the story"? or perhaps more importantly, what does it mean not to?

The fact that it is nearly impossible to distinguish between the physical appearance of Laura Fairlie, later Lady Glyde, and that of Anne Catherick, allows Sir Percival Glyde to inherit his wife's fortune by declaring the one who is actually Anne Catherick dead and by incarcerating his real wife, Laura, in an asylum. But the question that goes unasked for most of the novel is *how* Anne and Laura, strangers to one another, come to look identical; the cause of this particularly bewildering effect remains in the past, uninterrogated. Even Laura's half-sister, Marian Halcombe, looks nothing like her at all; connected through the mother, these two women have almost nothing else in common. Marian explains the circumstances to Walter Hartright in their first meeting:

> "My mother was twice married: the first time to Mr. Halcombe, my father; the second time to Mr. Fairlie, my half-sister's father. Except that we are both orphans, we are in every respect as unlike each other as possible. My father was a poor man, and Miss Fairlie's father was a rich man. I have got nothing, and she is an heiress. I am dark and ugly, and she is fair and pretty. Everybody thinks me crabbed and odd (with perfect justice); and everybody thinks her sweet-tempered and charming (with more justice still). In short, she is an angel; and I am – " (60–1)

Reminiscent of the concluding line of *Bleak House*, this is only the first of several "broken" moments in the text. Like Esther, Marian deploys ellipses as a means of describing herself; the graphic representation of Marian's speech effectively renders her a "blank," an occluded presence if a presence at all. As Miller argues, Marian functions within the text as the primary site of gender indeterminacy; Hartright has just finished describing the disconcerting combination in her of beautiful form and swarthy, mustached, apelike face. Through the rest of the novel, Marian is praised for her virtues, her wisdom, energy, resourcefulness, and most of all, her intelligence, in sharp contrast to her half-sister, who is more often than not the unwitting pawn in a high-stakes game controlled by others. The mother who connects Marian and Laura is a cipher in the terms of Marian's description: the two daughters whom she produced would seem to embody – physically, emotionally, psychologically, and sexually – pure difference, and in the material determination of social rank, Laura and Marian acquire class distinctions that are dictated solely on the basis of their paternity.

The third member of the family triangle is Anne Catherick, who looks nothing like Marian and exactly like Laura. Only at the end of the novel, and only by implication, is Anne's paternity ascertained. Walter writes of this event in a typically elliptical fashion:

> Knowing now, that Mr. Philip Fairlie had been at Varneck Hall in the autumn of eighteen hundred and twenty-six, and that Mrs. Catherick had been living there in service at the same time, we knew also – first, that Anne had been born in June,

eighteen hundred and twenty-seven; secondly, that she had always presented an extraordinary personal resemblance to Laura; and, thirdly, that Laura herself was strikingly like her father. Mr. Philip Fairlie had been one of the notoriously handsome men of his time. In disposition entirely unlike his brother Frederick, he was the spoilt darling of society, especially of the women – an easy, light-hearted, impulsive, affectionate man; generous to a fault; constitutionally lax in his principles, and notoriously thoughtless of moral obligations where women were concerned. Such were the facts we knew; such was the character of the man. Surely, the plain inference that follows needs no pointing out? (574)

Hartright's narrative only reenacts the novel's resistance to discussions of Anne Catherick's personal history; in the phrase "the plain inference that follows needs no pointing out," Anne simply remains by the process of narrative elision the unacknowledged daughter. Never in Walter's reports – otherwise so scrupulous in questions of legacy and fairness – is there an implication that Anne Catherick had a financial claim on the Fairlie family, nor is her death mourned in the text; instead, the fact of her passing is completely subsumed into the celebration of the "proof" it ensures of Laura's life.[28] Anne, in her psychological dependence on Mrs. Fairlie, in her uncanny resemblance to Laura, in her mysterious and ultimately illegitimate birth, is a symptom of every form of anxiety set loose in this novel: whether the anxieties touch on the determining power of mothers, the impossibility of "telling the difference," or the transgression of extramarital eroticism, they are embodied in Anne Catherick, and with the containment of Anne's body, they are contained (theoretically) for the novel more generally. The construction of Anne as Laura's doppelganger enables the segregation of characteristics, the splitting of the erotic – embodied in the madwoman Anne – from the asexual angelic – embodied in the childlike Laura. That the novel forcefully moves to "prove" Anne's death and Laura's survival signals its desire to repress the whore and resurrect the angel; that this "proof" remains only tenuously convincing undermines the overdetermined language of domestic bliss asserted at the novel's end.

Within *The Woman in White*, a text eternally conscious of the problematics, if not the failures, of its narrative efforts, how, then, does the dead mother signify? In the triangle of "sisters," Marian and Anne each have in common, through the mother and through the father, half of Laura; Laura, like the line traced on her mother's tombstone, is at once the site of connection and divergence. The significance of Marian, Laura, and Anne in this text is constituted in their status as children, as daughters. By establishing a certain truth about Laura, Hartright hopes that the generation of children can effectively contain and rewrite the activities of its parents. The figure through which this anxiety is contained – theoretically – is the figure of the idealized, angelic, asexual mother. But that mother-image is increasingly problematic for the novel, as mothers are revealed to be, more often than not, the source of transgression rather than passive ideal; hence the persistent *absence* of mothers – whether through death, desertion, or containment within a vague abstraction – for in their absence, they can be constructed retrospectively as virtuous. The characters' constant return to the gravesite of Mrs. Fairlie gradually begins to detach itself from an express concern with the mother. As "The Narrative of the Tombstone," the burial-plot is imported into the later stages of the text, but the "narrative's" ostensible referent is not the mother, it is "Laura," or the body currently occupying Laura's place. Hartright reproduces, as a freestanding chapter and therefore as an autonomous "voice" within the text, the fictional inscription that apparently misreads Anne as Laura:

Sacred
TO THE MEMORY OF
LAURA,
LADY GLYDE,
WIFE OF SIR PERCIVAL GLYDE, BART.,
OF BLACKWATER PARK, HAMPSHIRE;
AND
DAUGHTER OF THE LATE PHILIP FAIRLIE, ESQ.
OF LIMMERIDGE HOUSE, IN THIS PARISH.
BORN, MARCH 27TH, 1829.
MARRIED, DECEMBER 22ND, 1849.
DIED, JULY 25TH, 1850.[29]

The authenticating proximity of Mrs. Fairlie's body has a double-edged effect with respect to the revelation that this inscription is a fake. When the tombstone speaks in this novel, it lies; when the mother speaks, she lies.

This is a logic that reflects on the novel's prior construction of maternal originality even as it places the tombstone within the web of implication that includes Walter, Marian, and the many other narrators. When Walter and Marian take as their mission the revision of the false pretenses of its narrative, imposing a distinction between fiction and non-fiction, they deploy the badge of Mrs. Fairlie's honor as a means of justifying their activities, even as their actions have the effect, quite literally, of imposing a revisionary narrative over the inscription of origins. The goal of the project is erasure in the name of "truth," the suppression of "The Narrative of the Tombstone," with all its ambiguity, for a fully-cleansed version of the story. Walter writes at the novel's end, "My last labour, as the evening approached, was to obtain 'The Narrative of the Tombstone,' by taking a copy of the false inscription on the grave, before it was erased" (637). Once again, however, Walter's preservation and reproduction of "false" evidence privileges the indeterminate even in the midst of a claim to justice; manipulating the reader for the sake of narrative suspense, Walter allows "The Narrative of the Tombstone" to exist as truth for over two hundred pages before revealing that he, like Sir Percival Glyde, has deliberately perpetuated a falsehood. Thus the empirical project of a detective plot is subordinated to the titillating project of a sensation narrative, and Walter exposes his manipulations of "truth" for the sake of a personal agenda. That agenda is to effect a rereading of the tombstone narrative that is tantamount to a rewriting, a reinterpretation that produces a difference in the source-text itself, akin to the revisionary histories projected upon the ancestors of the present generation, in which crimes, unfortunately, cause their own detection.

Walter's task is predicated on the belief that the embodied Laura, the one standing in front of him, is the "true" Laura, against the widespread belief that she is an impostor. "Telling the difference" is at once a description of the narrative goal of this novel and a description of the narrative itself. The structures through which Walter is able to articulate "difference" between two ostensibly identical women are structures that implicate his own desire to make what he sees coincide with an inscribed "truth." But as Walter and Marian try in vain to convince Laura's friends that this woman is actually Laura, they confront the resistance born of the textual determination of identity: a proliferation of signifiers declares the difference between Laura and Anne, the death certificate and the tombstone on one hand labeling Anne Catherick Lady Glyde, the labels on the underclothes worn by Lady Glyde signifying her identity as Anne Catherick. How, then, is the difference between these two women constituted?

When Walter first meets Laura, early in his narrative, he is struck not by her resemblance to the woman in white, Anne Catherick, whom he has so recently encountered, but by something more elusive. He describes it as follows:

Mingling with the vivid impression produced by the charm of her fair face and head, her sweet expression, and her winning simplicity of manner, was another impression, which, in a shadowy way, suggested to me the idea of something wanting. At one time it seemed like something wanting in *her*; at another, like something wanting in myself, which hindered me from understanding her as I ought. The impression was always strongest, in the most contradictory manner, when she looked at me; or, in other words, when I was conscious of the harmony and charm of her face, and yet, at the same time, most troubled by the sense of an incompleteness which it was impossible to discover. Something wanting, something wanting – and where it was, and what it was, I could not say. (76–7)

Hartright's peculiar characterization of Laura's lack, or of Laura *as* lack, assumes the structure of a projection in the context of his expressed love for her; "something wanting, something wanting" turns quickly into "wanting something, wanting something." What Walter wants from Laura is confounded by his confusion about the other woman, the mysterious woman in white he had met on the road to London two days earlier, who had expressed an unaccountable affection for Limmeridge House, the home in which he finds himself now. To clear up the mystery, Marian turns to her mother, or rather, turns to the vestige of maternal representation, her mother's letters. It is only in this context that Laura's "lack" coheres. Through the vehicle of Marian, Mrs. Fairlie tells her husband of her affection for Anne Catherick eleven years ago. The sentence is, as usual, fractured: " 'My dear Philip, although she is not half so pretty, she is, nevertheless, by one of those extraordinary caprices of accidental resemblance which one sometimes sees, the living likeness, in her hair, her complexion, the colour of her eyes, and the shape of her face – ' " (86). As Marian's voice, her mother's words, break off, Laura's body intrudes on a textual description in a direct anticipation of the scene at the tombstone. The imposition of Laura literalizes for Walter the equation Mrs. Fairlie was about to make when she was "broken off." Walter describes his response:

There stood Miss Fairlie, a white figure, alone in the moonlight; in her attitude, in the turn of her head, in her complexion, in the shape of her face, the living image, in that distance and under those circumstances, of the woman in white! The doubt which had troubled my mind for hours and hours past, flashed into conviction in an instant. That "something wanting" was my own recognition of the ominous likeness between the fugitive from the asylum and my pupil at Limmeridge House. (86)

The location of "something wanting," of lack, shifts from the fulsome beauty of Laura's face to Hartright's own mind, to his inability to make the connection between two identical women.

To ask the question again, then, how does the dead mother signify in *The Woman in White*? What is the "difference" between Laura Fairlie and Anne Catherick? The answer is, of course, the mother; as Barbara Fass Leavy writes, "had Anne had Laura's mother, then she would in effect be Laura."[30] Laura and Anne have paternity in common and maternity in difference; Marian, as Anne's foil, shares the mother with Laura. In the algebra of this novel, maternal difference is precisely what propels Anne into the lives of Laura and Marian; her desire to recover, to have, to *be* their mother, Mrs. Fairlie, is the desire that ultimately costs her her life. Desire for that mother is, in fact, the prevailing structure of desire in *The Woman in White*, the "something wanting" for both Anne Catherick and the melancholic novel as a whole. But what is the nature of this desire? Less a structure of mourning for a beloved mother lost, the "something wanting" in this text signifies the desire for the security of an ideal of female decorum that operates as the linchpin of world order; along the lines of the angelic mother bodied forth only in memory throughout *Oliver Twist*, *Bleak House*, and *Dombey and Son*, this mother emblematizes the reassertion of sentimental, secular family values as a means of foreclosing the entropic disarray of the prevailing social order. Safely dead and contained beneath her tombstone-cross, "Mrs. Fairlie" is a blank space upon which a new order can be inscribed, over whom a new "narrative" can be engraved. Equated at once with the ideology of virtue that Walter so desires to appropriate, and with the potential for sexual transgression that threatens to undermine the family tree he is so deeply invested in constructing, the burial-plot of the dead mother operates as the site of containment in this novel, but a site of containment so overdetermined that it consistently signals its subversive intent.

When Anne intervenes in Laura's marriage, it is Mrs. Fairlie, rather than Laura herself, who is the object of Anne's desire, whose approval Anne desires. In other words, Anne acts out an impulse of mimetic desire based on her perception of what Mrs. Fairlie would want, if Mrs. Fairlie herself were only there to act. The equation of Anne's difference with "something wanting" underscores the terms by which Walter and his fellow narrators construct structures of substitution that are structures of pleasure. Walter looks on as Anne speaks to the headstone: "'Oh, if I could die, and be hidden and at rest with *you!*' Her lips murmured the words close on the grave-stone; murmured them in tones of passionate endearment, to the dead remains beneath. '*You* know how I love your child, for your sake! Oh, Mrs. Fairlie! Mrs. Fairlie! tell me how to save her. Be my darling and my mother once more, and tell me what to do for the best!' " (127). Mrs. Fairlie's cross, where death and kisses, ritual purification and "passionate endearments" converge, is Anne's – and the novel's – fetish, a site of pleasure that is also a site of displacement. And Anne, of course, gets her wish: the novel concludes with the reinscription of this stone to commemorate her ultimate communion with Mrs. Fairlie. But in the meantime, she positions herself prosthetically within the text, acting out the mother-function in order to achieve relations with that mother. The ideology of maternal care represented through Anne's performance is thus consolidated as an explicitly eroticized, explicitly melancholic desire for the dead mother.

Anne and Walter alike act on erotic impulses that are mimetic, triangulated, and traceable, sharply traceable, to the vestigial mother. Triangulated desire is, in fact, the paradigm of both love and narration for Collins's novel. The ultimate "love triangle," the triadic marriage of Walter, Laura, and Marian, acts out the configuration introduced through Anne's relationship with the dead mother. Walter's proposal to Laura is actually a proposal to *Marian*, who then relays the message to Laura, who comes back with an acceptance. The fact that it takes three to tango allows the "unsaid" – in this case, the proposal – to remain implicit, a logic that returns to the novel's reliance on the potency of the absent, of the "something wanting." René Girard's rereading of the Oedipal paradigm to account for narrative desire focuses ultimately on the relationship between the two desiring subjects, on the mimetic relationship, as ultimately more significant than the object of desire itself:

In all the varieties of desire examined by us, we have encountered not only a subject and an object but a third presence as well: the rival. It is the rival who should be accorded the dominant role. We must take care, however, to identify him correctly; not to say, with Freud, that he is the father; or, in the case of the tragedies, that he is the brother. Our first task is to define the rival's position within the system to which he belongs, in relation to both subject and object. The rival desires the same object as the subject, and to assert the primacy of the rival can only lead to one conclusion. Rivalry does not arise because of the fortuitous convergence of two desires on a single object; rather, *the subject desires the object because the rival desires it.*[31]

Girard operates under the assumption, however, that the two rivalrous subjects are males who pretend to desire a female subject. Eve Kosofsky Sedgwick reads this triangular structure as a vehicle for male homosocial desire, as it constructs a relationship between men under the cover story of desire for the female.[32] But significantly for *The Woman in*

White, I believe, Toril Moi argues that the "extraneous female object" in Girard's theory of mimetic desire is the missing mother, who in this case so centrally structures the novel's patterns of figuration. In "The Missing Mother: The Oedipal Rivalries of René Girard," Moi argues that the missing mother is a powerfully disruptive presence for Girard, for within Freud, "original desire" is always desire for the mother. She writes, "If Girard's mimetic theory is applied to the preoedipal stage, one is obliged to posit the woman's desire as original, the mother's desire becomes paradigmatic of all desire."[33] With this in mind, I would argue that all patterns of desire in *The Woman in White* subtend toward an absent but powerful mother; although structures of erotic desire are elaborately arranged to supplement her absence, the product of these structures is the inevitable exposure of original, formative loss.

Anne Catherick's own mother, described in one review as "the paragon of she-devils,"[34] is lacking precisely the ideal of maternal affection that Anne discovers in her surrogate, Mrs. Fairlie. But Mrs. Catherick *is* the novel's maternal "voice," both as the only mother who speaks, and as the narrator who confirms – by the authority of her proximity in time and place – historical events of sexual transgression, deceit, and crime that have produced the contemporary mysteries that preoccupy the novel's protagonists. Anne's only legacy from her mother is the "Secret" of Sir Percival Glyde, which in turn refers back to Sir Percival's own mother; but Anne knows only that a secret exists – although she does not know its particulars, this is threatening enough to Sir Percival to prove fatal to Anne.

As Laurie Langbauer points out, Mrs. Catherick alone knows the details of the "Secret" that is Sir Percival's Achilles' heel and therefore central to his motivations:

Walter Hartright makes no headway in restoring Laura's identity and fortune, and his novel's plot remains tangled, as long as he suspects that "the way to the Secret lay through the mystery, hitherto impenetrable to all of us, of the woman in white." Only when he realizes that Anne knows nothing, that it is her mother, Mrs. Catherick, who alone is "in possession of the Secret," can his search and the novel begin to wind up.[35]

The "Secret" is the property of Mrs. Catherick, and the income extorted from Sir Percival Glyde to guarantee its preservation enables Mrs. Catherick's facile mimicry of virtuous, middle-class respectability before her church and town. Walter Hartright observes her behavior just moments after learning of her daughter's sudden death:

Not all the strength of all the terrible passions I had roused in that woman's heart, could loosen her desperate hold on the one fragment of social consideration which years of resolute effort had just dragged within her grasp. There she was again, not a minute after I had left her, placed purposely in a position which made it a matter of common courtesy on the part of the clergyman to bow to her for a second time. He raised his hat once more. I saw the hard ghastly face behind the window soften, and light up with gratified pride – I saw the head with the grim black cap bend ceremoniously in return. The clergyman had bowed to her, and in my presence, twice in one day! (511)

Mrs. Catherick performs a parody of domestic respectability funded by the wages of crime and sin. She is the novel's only living mother, a mother in name only who from the first abandoned her daughter to the kindness of strangers. Her performance only underscores the problematic fact that far from innate or morally determined, in the world of this novel, bourgeois respectability is a commodity to be purchased on the open market. Not coincidentally, this is a lesson from which Walter Hartright himself ultimately profits as well.

Mrs. Catherick and the mother of Sir Percival Glyde have in common illegitimate children: Anne, born of Mrs. Catherick's encounter with Mr. Fairlie, and Sir Percival, the offspring of a relationship never certified with a marriage ceremony. The implications of Sir Percival's illegitimacy are precisely that he is not Sir Percival at all: he is not entitled to his title, his fortune, or his land. The "Secret" discovered by Walter Hartright and confirmed by Mrs. Catherick is illegitimacy; at stake in the revisionary containment of female sexual activity is the paternal legacy of class. The question of birth, and specifically, anxiety about legitimacy, underpins every twist of the tortuous plot of *The Woman in White*. The act of tracing the origins of a person is coincident with the act of reading, but only legitimate birth leaves a paper trail in the form of marriage certificates and wills. The extramarital is extratextual, and to be an illegitimate child is to be a character without a narrative. With the noteworthy exception of Laura, Sir Percival and Anne are the novel's only major figures, including the tombstone, who lack narratives of their own. And, again with the possible exception of Laura, they are alone in not surviving the events of the text.

In her anonymous letter to Laura, Anne has described a dream of Laura's wedding to Sir Percival: "'And the clergyman looked for the marriage-service in vain: it was gone out of the book, and he shut up the leaves, and put it from him in despair'" (104). Much later, in search of Sir Percival's "Secret," Walter consults the register of the country church in order to confirm the marriage of his parents. While the church copy of the register bears the record of a union, the safe-deposit copy shows only a blank:

No! not a doubt. The marriage was not there. The entries on the copy occupied exactly the same places on the page as the entries on the original. The last entry on one page recorded the marriage of the man with my Christian name. Below it, there was a blank space – a space evidently left because it was too narrow to contain the entry of the marriages of . . . two brothers, which in the copy, as in the original, occupied the top of the next page. That space told the whole story! (529)

Here, in anecdotes about two missing marriage ceremonies traceable to two illegitimate characters, it is clear that the signifying power of absence determines identity. The "blank space" in the marriage register is a far more powerful signifier than any entry Hartright might find; silence speaks louder than words, for in this marriage register, it is the *absence* of text, not its presence, that is graphically significant. Propelling the novel backward to other sites of contested female virtue, the blank space in the marriage register is equivalent to the blank space on the pure/impure tombstone of Mrs. Fairlie, the blank space of Laura's face, "something wanting." Sir Percival Glyde and Walter Hartright, the two husbands of Laura Fairlie, alike attempt to inscribe over the blank space of the feminine a narrative of legitimacy guaranteeing inheritance, fortune, and class. In an effort to provide himself with a legitimizing narrative, Sir Percival perpetrates a criminal act of *fiction*, forging textual evidence of a marriage ceremony in the blank space of the church register.

Like the missing mother, powerful because inscrutable, the readable blankness of the "space" is key. Sir Percival dies in his attempt to conceal the forgery that reveals his birth, and therefore his inheritance, as fiction. Meanwhile, however, in his attempt to acquire Laura's fortune and the trappings of legitimacy, he has ensured the death of the novel's other illegitimate child, Anne. The signifier of Sir Percival's illegitimacy appears in the distinction between the "original" of the marriage register and its copy; the distinction between original and copy, legitimate and illegitimate, exists in the plot of Sir Percival Glyde as it does in the relationship of Laura Fairlie and Anne Catherick. Mrs. Catherick describes the process of the forgery: "He was some time getting the ink the right colour (mixing it over and over again in pots and bottles of mine), and some time, afterwards, in practising the handwriting. But he succeeded in the end – and made an honest woman of his mother, after she was dead in her grave!" (552). Once again, the rhetorical convention invoked in this episode refers back to the mother. Like Mrs. Fairlie's headstone, Lady Glyde's "text" – the absent presence of her marriage – proves resistant to proximate fictionalities: neither Anne's false inscription nor Sir Percival's faked certification survive, and neither do Anne and Sir Percival.

Anxieties about legitimacy, inheritance, and class in *The Woman in White* focus on the relative containability of female sexuality. But the centrality of the dead mother within this novel undermines the characters' desires to read their mothers as stable and safely contained. The gravestone of Mrs. Fairlie, as a trace and as the object of a trace, is implicated in the mimetic project that it sets in motion: to find the mother is never more than coextensive with the act of searching itself. Mrs. Fairlie's plot is at once the beginning, the means to an end, and an end in itself. As the narrative's most consistent – and consistently elusive – emblem of the historical past, Mrs. Fairlie herself represents the disruptive potential of originality and difference in the discourse of mastery. In *The Woman in White*, the virtuous mother who secures legacy by securing paternity is at all times a back-formation, a retrospective, belated construct. Yet she also represents the ideology on which the novel's detective plot predicates itself; thus the maternal ideal is at every turn, in *The Woman in White* as in mid-Victorian culture more generally, personated in the figure of a *dead* mother, against the living example of a figure such as Mrs. Catherick. For the detective plot, in its tenuous construction of "truth" and "justice" over the figure of the dead mother, exposes maternal virtue as much more than a cultural ideal; it demonstrates that it is a cultural necessity, overdetermined in its significance, and embattled in its ideology.

The intersection of detective and domestic narrative structures in *The Woman in White*, characteristic in the world of mid-Victorian fiction, enables both titillation and the rearticulation of conservative, conventional structures of family. The novel concludes with the birth of yet another generation, represented in the new heir of Limmeridge, young Walter Hartright. In this child's birth, the generational lines of the novel are transposed: the generation of Walter, Marian, and Laura is newly constructed as "parental," and happily for the novel's larger deterministic teleology, their identities have by this time been safely fixed and stabilized. In addition, however, the novel's conclusion demonstrates the selective nature of its investment in the historical stability of class:

master-narrator Walter Hartright, who begins the story an impoverished tutor of drawing, ends it the lord of the manor. The novel's final
tableau instantiates a purified and asexualized "mother" image, constructing in Marian a truly marian notion of virgin birth and redemptive
future: calling on Walter to look to the future with optimism, "She rose
and held up the child kicking and crowing in her arms. 'Do you know
who this is, Walter?' she asked, with bright tears of happiness gathering
in her eyes" (646). Although Laura is ostensibly the mother of this child,
the novel's final triangle explicitly excludes her, constructing itself
around the fraternal relationship between Walter and Marian, and
what appears to be their son.

While this triangle recurs to the novel's persistent anxiety about
maternal eroticism by successfully splitting the maternal and the erotic
in the construction of the spinster aunt as mother, it also recurs to the
awesome power of that eroticized mother as the source of paternity
anxiety. For Marian's apparently rhetorical question – "'Do you know
who this is, Walter?'" – is greeted with a typically elliptical and symptomatically erroneous reply: "'Even *my* bewilderment has its limits,'
[Walter] replied. 'I think I can still answer for knowing my own child'"
(646). Marian hastens to correct this assertion: "'Do you talk in that
familiar manner to one of the landed gentry of England? Are you aware,
when I present this illustrious baby to your notice, in whose presence
you stand? Evidently not! Let me make two eminent personages known
to one another: Mr Walter Hartright – the Heir of Limmeridge'" (646).
Introduced to the son who may or may not be his own, who may or may
not share his name, but who is guaranteed to live his life in a different
class than his father, Walter's "pen falters in [his] hand," and his final
gesture is toward Marian, "the good angel of our lives – let Marian end
our Story" (646).

Thus ends the story; it is not Marian's ending, it is Walter's ending
masquerading as Marian's. And it is Walter's final, strained attempt at
the containment of what Marian now might represent, constructed as
she has been as the deterministic mother after the model of her own
mother. For as Mrs. Fairlie had the power to create "the woman in
white," so Marian has the power to create "the Heir of Limmeridge."

Convulsions; Death before Delivery; Twins. – No. 26. February 7, 1858. – A German Jewess, primipara; about eight months and a half gone. Seen by a midwife at 1:30 A.M., when waters broke; head presented; pains very feeble; no progress; convulsions appearing; at 8:30 A.M., she sent for me; messenger failed to find my house, and called in a German physician, who saw patient about 9, and ordered laudanum draughts. Convulsions and exhaustion, however, increased; Mr. Blackman and myself arriving soon after 10, found her dead. The head was entering pelvis, very movable. I laid open the uterus; the placenta was spread all over the anterior aspect of the uterus, stretching to fundus, & round to the right side. The foetus which presented being removed, I found another in an unbroken amnion; both girls; the placenta was single. This removed, I inverted the uterus for thorough examination; no laceration; pelvis not contracted. I learned that this poor woman had been much prostrated by misery and want of food. This had probably induced a degree of uterine inertia; but another circumstance contributed to retard delivery; the discharge of the amniotic fluid of one sac, and retention of the fluid of the other sac broke the contractile power, and frustrated the effort of nature to expel the first child. The feeble contraction could impart no expulsive action on the presenting child, because the force had to be transmitted through the fluid medium of the unbroken sac. It was left to regret that forced delivery had not been performed at 9 o'clock, or earlier.

Robert Barnes, M.D., "Clinical History of the Eastern Division of the Royal Maternity Charity, During the Year Ending September 30, 1858," *Dublin Quarterly Journal of Medical Science* 28 (1859), 118.

CHAPTER 5

Denial, displacement, Deronda

Early in George Eliot's *Daniel Deronda* (1876), the narrator describes a scene from Daniel's adolescence:

Deronda's circumstances, indeed, had been exceptional. One moment had been burnt into his life as its chief epoch – a moment full of July sunshine and large pink roses shedding their last petals on a grassy court enclosed on three sides by a Gothic cloister. Imagine him in such a scene: a boy of thirteen, stretched prone on the grass where it was in shadow, his curly head propped on his arms over a book, while his tutor, also reading, sat on a camp-stool under shelter.[1]

In a scene of barely repressed decadence worthy of Oscar Wilde, a pubescent boy sprawls on a bed of dead rose-petals in a defunct Gothic cloister. Still the innocent in his bed of flowers, Daniel asks his tutor a question, the answer to which represents his intellectual defloration: "'Mr. Fraser, how was it that popes and cardinals always had so many nephews?'" The reply gives Daniel his first lesson in the euphemisms that politely disguise both sexual and religious transgressions: "'It was just for the propriety of the thing; because, as you know very well, priests don't marry, and the children were illegitimate'" (203).

In her location of this scene within the architectural frame of a Gothic cloister, George Eliot foregrounds a structure that subtends the novel as a whole, for *Daniel Deronda* depends not only on the conventions of Gothic architecture, but also on those of Gothic fiction for its indictment of social and moral hypocrisy and its psychodramatic tension. As Judith Wilt argues, the "machinery of the Gothic" functions as a strategy of exposure throughout Eliot's fiction: "In George Eliot's . . . spacious worlds the sublime thrusts constantly at the common, breaking dynamically through those wadded layers of 'stupidity' and chatter with which humans protect themselves."[2] With its emphases on the uncanny, the liminal, and the sexually transgressive, the Gothic destabilizes the realistic narrative world of *Daniel Deronda* in the stories of both protagonists, Daniel Deronda and Gwendolen Harleth. Undermining the reliable structures of realism, offering a vocabulary for the fact of sexual transgression, Eliot deploys Gothic tropes to problematize conventional borderlines of gender identity and desire. This pattern culminates in her representation of Daniel's mother, the Princess Leonora Halm-Eberstein, known worldwide as the singer "Alcharisi," who abandoned him in infancy. When Alcharisi invades the world of the novel, she tears down the idealized mother-image Daniel has constructed in her absence. Her attack on this abstract ideal exposes the damaging potential of conventional gender roles and the implications of the often competing desires of men and women. For male and female characters in *Daniel Deronda* cross and oppose one another in a chiastic pattern: the women embrace Gothic horror as portending the truth of their domestic lives, while the men attempt to domesticate the Gothic, containing horror and uncanniness within the parameters of a domestic ideal.

Claire Kahane has argued that the missing mother is a central trope within Gothic fiction, and in *Daniel Deronda*, through Daniel's preoccupation with his missing mother and Gwendolen's fascination with the mystery of this woman, Eliot exploits the psychodramatic implications of maternal loss. Kahane writes, "What I see repeatedly locked into the forbidden center of the Gothic which draws me inward is the spectral presence of a dead–undead mother, archaic and all-encompassing, a ghost signifying the problematics of femininity which the heroine must confront."[3] Within Kahane's argument, the absent presence of a mother represents the imminent potential of feminine desire to act as a disruptive force within conventional narrative. The "undead" mother is at once disruptive to the progress of the narrative and instructive to the young female heroine. The novel's "maternal space" is a proving ground for the terrors and pleasures of the feminine. Gwendolen Harleth is particularly fascinated by the imaginative implications of Daniel's motherlessness, for Daniel but even more for herself as a young woman dreading marriage; her own mother is all too present and imperfect, and the existence of Daniel's missing mother offers Gwendolen a glimpse of the temptations of an alternative pathway.

Daniel's significantly "undead" mother is pivotal to the novel's larger deconstruction of gender conventions, although the Princess Leonora Halm-Eberstein appears only briefly, in two short scenes of reunion with her grown son at the end of the novel. In total violation of every Victorian ideal of motherhood and womanliness, the Princess confesses to the abandonment of her son in his early childhood, the rejection of her father and his faith, and perhaps most stunningly of all, her unwillingness to express shame about any of these acts. Alcharisi's explicit – and unsentimental – rejection of the cultural ideal of femininity disrupts notions of femininity and masculinity alike throughout the world of this text. For her presence as an unrepentant, unmotherly woman offers an implicit standard of identification for Gwendolen and an explicit standard of rejection for Daniel. Thus through Gwendolen's incipient vocational ambitions and accompanying disinterest in marriage, and through Daniel's failure to locate, rescue, and embrace the missing mother of his dreams, the novel's two primary characters enact fundamental ambivalence about conventions of "masculinity" and "femininity." The novel's women, who are almost universally resistant to cultural expectations that include their subjection in marriage, emerge as characters through that resistance; but in a vicious cycle, the novel's men, frustrated by its women, seek a notion of identity predicated on women's objectification.

DANIEL AND THE FRUSTRATION OF NARCISSISM

Halfway through the novel, Daniel returns to the Gothic cloister where, as Eliot writes, "among the falling rose-petals thirteen years before, we saw a boy becoming acquainted with his first sorrow" (475). Here Daniel first articulates the aesthetic of Platonic idealism that will underwrite every pattern of his life:

"I wonder whether one oftener learns to love real objects through their representations, or the representations through the real objects," he said, after pointing out a lovely capital made by the curled leaves of greens, showing their reticulated under-side with the firm gradual swell of its central rib. "When I was a little fellow these capitals taught me to observe, and delight in, the structure of leaves." (476)

Daniel's is an aesthetic that proceeds from the representational to the actual, from the carved-stone artifact to the organic leaf, from the mother idealized in her absence to the flesh-and-blood woman he meets, only to find disappointment and rejection, later in the text. Throughout the novel, Eliot exposes the shortcomings of such idealism by confronting Daniel with the flip side of the "Gothic cloister," threatening direct exposure to horror, abjection, and resistance. While Daniel reads the Gothic cloister as an aesthetic abstraction, the novel's women insist on a more material confrontation with the real, on an interrogation of the horrific implications of Gothic portents.

The only information Daniel Deronda has about himself is that, since the age of two, he has been the ward of Sir Hugo Mallinger. Daniel is widely assumed to be Sir Hugo's illegitimate child, and perhaps, in the absence of legitimate sons, his heir.

[Daniel] had always called Sir Hugo Mallinger his uncle, and when it once occurred to him to ask about his father and mother, the baronet had answered, "You lost your father and mother when you were quite a little one; that is why I take care of you." Daniel then straining to discern something in the early twilight, had a dim sense of having been kissed very much, and surrounded by thin, cloudy, scented drapery, till his fingers caught in something hard, which hurt him, and he began to cry. (203)

Sir Hugo's response to the boy's predicament remains both euphemistic and ambiguous: the idea that Daniel "lost" his father and mother implies that they might possibly, even probably, be found again. However, when Daniel racks his memory, archaic recollections offer him only the juxtaposition of idyll and pain. Reflecting the polarized conditions of connection and loss, the contiguity of the "sense of having been kissed very much" with "something hard, which hurt him," proves a pattern prophetic for the rest of his narrative. For throughout the rest of the novel, Daniel's ambivalent recollection of "early twilight" directly predicts the fate of all idyllic phantasies of origin. While he desires a fairy-tale reunion, what he seems destined to find is "something hard, which hurt[s] him."

Predicting by half a century the discourse of psychoanalytic object-relations theory, Eliot constructs Daniel's single historical recollection in terms of a display of ambivalence, a complex balancing-act between harmony and catastrophe, love and pain. In 1935, Melanie Klein will describe the infantile "depressive position" in terms of a mastery of the phenomenon of "splitting"; in normal child development, she will argue, a child will establish a critical relationship of ambivalence toward his or her mother. As I have discussed earlier, that ambivalence is characterized by the dialectic of dependency surrounding the issue of feeding: the mother, as the first source of nutrition, is capable of providing or withholding "satisfaction" from the infant. As a defense mechanism against the "bad mother" who withholds her breast from the child, forcing him or her to go hungry, the child is forced to become an independent agent, exercising sadistic, aggressive impulses against the mother. But this aggression is also potentially suicidal, for the mother is as bad and dangerous as she is good and necessary. The child's ability to articulate him or herself as an independent subject, then, depends on the successful resolution of competing impulses found in the depressive dialectic; establishing an identity against the specter of the good mother / bad mother split, the subject is socialized between the mediating poles of kindness and aggression.[4]

Klein's theory of the depressive position begins to suggest several issues at stake for Daniel in his desire for the recovery of his mother. Because he was *literally* abandoned, placed in the infant's most anxious predicament, what Klein would describe as his infantile phantasies of aggression against the mother have come true; his pervasive feelings of culpability prompt the desire, articulated time and again throughout the text, for reparation. In the absence of reunion with the missing mother, however, Daniel constructs himself as the rescuer of other, substitute women, most literally Mirah, and most problematically Gwendolen. Robbed of the opportunity to love or hate with impunity, Daniel, in his guilt, can recall only a negative progression, in which physical pleasure turns to pain, then to tears. Disempowered by ambivalence, he is caught between feelings of guilt and anger at his abandonment. He is not capable of fully articulating that still-hazy memory (what was the "hard" thing catching at the fingers of the innocent child? why was he not better protected?) or of resolving his relationship to the figure kissing him, surrounding him with "thin, cloudy, scented drapery." Without the facts to flesh out this story, *his* story, Daniel must necessarily remain in the middle, paralyzed in an indeterminate emotional state between the psychological poles that are constitutive of identity.

Daniel's recollection of archaic pain figures not only a structure of loss, but also a structure of desire that indicates once again the generic conflation of *Bildungsroman* and mystery narrative. His incipient desire is formulated on several levels at once. First and most immediate is his desire to know the whole story of his past and its destruction. Frustrated by the fact that, try as he may to clear it, his memory seems destined to remain "misty," enigmatic, inaccessible, Daniel realizes that as long as his autobiography remains a mystery, he remains a mystery to himself. Quickly conflated, however, with his curiosity about this intellectual and emotional mystery is a sense of budding eroticism; his body is multiply implicated, in the brief scene he remembers, in its positive response to the sensual stimuli of kisses, perfume, and draperies, as well as in its negative recoiling from pain. The connection, then, of narrative and physical desire provides the motivating impulse behind Daniel's activities throughout the text; as he searches for the key to a personal mythology, he searches for a love-object; as he engages in courtship, he seeks in the faces of his loved ones his origin.

The family romance that Daniel constructs represents, therefore, his attempt to compensate for the anxiety-producing implications of mysterious abandonments and potential illegitimacy. Importing the informing concepts behind Klein's depressive position, he phantasizes himself into a scene in which moral certitude emerges from the phenomenon of "splitting." Within his phantasy, however, polarization results in the demonization of the male and the canonization of the female. This phantasy allows Daniel to retain the mythic, undead mother as the object of desire and the receptacle of potential salvation:

> The ardour which he had given to the imaginary world in his books suddenly rushed towards his own history and spent its pictorial energy there, explaining what he knew, representing the unknown. The uncle whom he loved very dearly took the aspect of a father who held secrets about him – who had done him a wrong – yes, a wrong: and what had become of his mother, from whom he must have been taken away? – Secrets about which he, Daniel, could never inquire; for to speak or be spoken to about these new thoughts seemed like falling flakes of fire to his imagination. Those who have known an impassioned childhood will understand this dread of utterance about any shame connected with their parents. The impetuous advent of new images took possession of him with the force of fact for the first time told, and left him no immediate power for the reflection that he might be trembling at a fiction of his own. (206)

Well schooled in the "imaginary world" of his books, Daniel enters into a phantasy world in which he and his mother alike are constructed as the victims of his father's – his uncle Mallinger's – malignancy. The silence the uncle has imposed on his curiosity confirms for Daniel the suspicions associated with his birth. It is the narrator, then, who supplies the passage's central emotional word, "shame," the term missing in the elliptical gap between being "taken away" and "Secrets"; "shame" is unnamed by Daniel in this passage as it is unspeakable in his life. Although it is both terrifying and dangerous, the stigma of shame overshadows his mission, the dangerous project of ascertaining the circumstances of his birth, of coming to terms with "a fiction of his own": his desire to know is mediated by the anxiety of shameful discovery. Deronda is as yet paralyzed by the internalized polarities of desire and shame, love and pain.

Desire, shame, love, guilt, pain, an abandoned boy-child, a good mother, an evil father; Eliot's construction of Daniel's adolescent mystery operates as a pre-Freudian recasting of the Oedipal narrative. Writing in 1900 in *The Interpretation of Dreams*, Freud speaks of the etiology of psychoneurotics, whose passions differ from those of the normally neurotic not in kind, but only in degree: "Being in love with the one parent and hating the other are among the essential constituents of the stock of psychical impulses."[5] Accordingly, in the absence of actual parental figures, Daniel is empowered by his phantasy of a drama in which he can gain revenge against the powerful father-figure and love for the wounded mother, resolving both positions of psychological need. But implicit within Freud's presentation of the Oedipal drama is the child's overwhelming awareness of guilt:

The action of the play consists in nothing other than the process of revealing, with cunning delays and ever-mounting excitement – a process that can be likened to the work of a psycho-analysis – that Oedipus himself is the murderer of Laïus, but further that he is the son of the murdered man and of Jocasta. Appalled at the abomination which he has unwittingly perpetrated, Oedipus blinds himself and forsakes his home. The oracle has been fulfilled.[6]

Freud's analysis reveals the danger at the heart of revelation: when Oedipus' story is told, what is revealed is regicide, father-slaying, incest – the literalization of the child's whole repertoire of deeply felt wishes. Likewise for Daniel, bound by the specter of shame, to face the truth of his life story is potentially to face the truth of culpability. So while he is initially comforted by the control this phantasy offers, the scapegoating of the father-figure remains only a temporary solution to the displacement of guilt.

For Daniel as for Freud's Oedipal child, there emerges a problem of relationship between desire and identification: erotic desire is created aversively, through competition with the father for the protection, the possession, of the mother. But Freud's Oedipal drama relies not only on the secure presence of a nuclear family, but also on its recognizability; unlike Daniel or Socrates' Oedipus, Freud's Oedipal child operates within closely regulated boundaries. For Daniel and Oedipus Rex, however, the people who are meant to occupy maternal and paternal positions, and therefore the morally absolute status of "good" and "bad," are insistently in the wrong place at the wrong time; for them as abandoned children, the drama of knowability and the reliable orientation of sexual desire are destined to remain indeterminate. Daniel's agency and masculinity are constituted through his desire to vindicate the mother and gain revenge upon the father. The sentimentalized topos of a bereaved mother is the paradigmatic object of desire for him; seeking to imagine his way into a domestic novel, he is frustrated by the "secrets" and "concealments" of his more Gothic plot.

The Freudian Oedipal scheme presumes an ultimate resolution, for the normative male heterosexual subject, of identification with the empowered father-figure and desire – displaced, of course – for the mother; the Oedipal drama is meant to teach the young boy a pattern of sadistic behavior, coded as "masculine" and directed toward the masochistically oriented "feminine" person who is his erotic object. But Daniel's peculiar position in the world compromises the simple binary relationships of identification and desire, sadism and masochism, activity and passivity. For Daniel perceives himself, from the moment of this primal memory, as a victim of his father's actions, identifying primarily with his mother, aligned with his phantasy of her against the spectral malignant father. George Eliot's narrator only underscores this distinction by repeatedly emphasizing the fact that Daniel does not look like his "uncle," or like any other father-figure, for that matter. Growing into adulthood, Daniel scans every face he sees on the street, in portraits in his home, searching for that visible sense of "likeness," for the *mother*, not the father, whom he is sure he will know by seeing his own face in hers. Like Narcissus achieving erotic and epistemological wholeness through the visual apprehension of sameness, Daniel's "desire" – the erotic and the epistemological now twinned – faces at once inward and outward. And the logic of that desire duplicates the logic of his aesthetic education; the boy who learns to appreciate the structure of leaves through the observation of sculpture desires first an idealized abstraction, only later to encounter the organic, the actual, the real.

Daniel's search for "likeness" produces, in true Lacanian fashion, only disjunction and disappointment. In the hall of his own home, he compares his face to the portraits of the Mallinger ancestors: "But in the nephew Daniel Deronda the family faces of various types, seen on the walls of the gallery, found no reflex" (205). Eliot's narrator elaborates on only one of these portraits, and she uses this to indicate the primary site of difference, both literally and symbolically, between the "nephew" and the "uncle":

In Sir Hugo's youthful portrait with rolled collar and high cravat, Sir Thomas Lawrence had done justice to the agreeable alacrity of expression and sanguine temperament still to be seen in the original, but had done something more than justice in slightly lengthening the nose, which was in reality shorter than might have been expected in a Mallinger. Happily the appropriate nose of the family reappeared in his younger brother, and was to be seen in all its refined regularity in his nephew [and Gwendolen's husband] Mallinger Grandcourt.

In contrast, however, Daniel is represented as promising even more distinction than the noble Mallinger line:

Still he was handsomer than any of them, and when he was thirteen might have served as model for any painter who wanted to image the most memorable of boys: you could hardly have seen his face thoroughly meeting yours without believing that human creatures had done nobly in times past, and might do more nobly in time to come. The finest childlike faces have this consecrating power, and make us shudder anew at all the grossness and basely-wrought griefs of the world, lest they should enter here and defile. (205)

Nobler than nobility, Daniel's face is an index of moral good, past, present, and future, that transcends the established social status of even the Mallinger men. Although he is the "most memorable of boys," however, Eliot paints his portrait in largely symbolic terms, still a boy, as yet unshaped, in a gallery of men.

Eliot draws a clear comparison here between the disparate visages of Daniel and Sir Hugo Mallinger, quite obviously *not* father and son. She elaborates this distinction most notably through the discourses of nobility and noses; while Daniel is unusually good-looking, Sir Hugo possesses an unnaturally foreshortened nose. Sir Hugo's nose, prosthetically augmented in his picture through the good offices of Sir Thomas Lawrence, symbolically underscores his other problematic characteristic, one not unrelated to his adoption of Deronda: although wealthy and entitled, Sir Hugo has only thus far produced daughters, and has failed at the task of directly perpetuating the Mallinger line. Daniel, therefore, is assumed publicly to be his heir. Through the displacement upward of phallic inadequacy, Sir Hugo's nose distinguishes him from his more generously endowed ancestors.

In Victorian England, however, the iconographic interchangeability of nose and penis carried another connotation. As Sander Gilman explains in *The Jew's Body,* Jewish males were conventionally represented as men with long noses and, chiastically, circumcised and thus foreshortened penises. Gilman writes: "the 'nose' is the iconic representation of the Jew's phallus throughout the nineteenth century . . . the nose is the displaced locus of anxiety associated with the marking of the male Jew's body through circumcision – an anxiety which was fueled by the late nineteenth-century debate about the 'primitive' nature of circumcision and its reflection on the acculturation of the Western Jew."[7] Arguing that Jewish males were feminized in the conventions of representational media, Gilman reads the iconography of long nose and compensatory foreshortened penis as markers of sexual difference.

In its innocence, purity, and goodness, Daniel's face is determinedly feminized; in the gallery of Mallinger ancestors, Daniel stands a mere boy among men. Later revealed as a Jew, Daniel's "difference," at this point in time, is visible only in his face. Critical implication has suggested, however, that Daniel is biographically readable by the status of his penis, that his penis is in fact a phallus, a signifier; Steven Marcus, writing, "In order for the plot of *Daniel Deronda* to work, Deronda's circumcised penis must be invisible, or nonexistent," suggests that Daniel would be able to locate his place in the world by simply looking down.[8] Thus, Marcus's comment implies, Daniel's circumcised penis remains at the center of the plot, unseen; to see it would be to read it, and to read it would be to have the answer to Daniel's mystery of identity. The text would foreclose prematurely on its central narrative tension, as Daniel would have a predetermined set of affiliations to call his own.

However, Marcus's assumption, that for Daniel to see his own penis is immediately to comprehend its difference from a "normal" British penis, presupposes Daniel's access to comparative context. Yet the narrator reports that Daniel "had not lived with other boys, and his mind showed the same blending of child's ignorance with surprising knowledge which is oftener seen in bright girls" (205). Like the little boy in Freud's "On Fetishism," horrified by his first glimpse of female genitals, Daniel would naturally require a number of contrasting examples in order to understand his own phallic difference. So if he were to look down and understand the significance of his own body, would he read maleness, femaleness, or indeterminacy? "Jewishness" or "Englishness"? excess or lack? My point here is to suggest that Daniel's phallus, with its overdetermined indeterminacy, is implicated not only in the negotiation of his identity as a Jew, but also in his identity as a male. Inexorably, the novel moves toward the reunion of Daniel and his mother, and through this reunion, as critics have argued, his Jewishness is confirmed; also at stake in this transaction, however, are negotiations of power and desire that ultimately work to manufacture Daniel, as unlikely as the prospect may at certain points seem, as a normatively heterosexual male adult.

When Daniel looks in the mirror, he sees someone whom he knows must resemble someone else, but someone else not known to him. His face is a signifier without a referent: his "own face in the glass had during many years been associated for him with thoughts of some one whom he must be like – one about whose character and lot he had continually wondered, and never dared to ask" (226). In fact, when Daniel first sees his future wife Mirah, literally catching her at the moment before her suicide, he is occupied with the business of analyzing ways he can mend this disjunction:

He was forgetting everything else in a half-speculative, half-involuntary identification of himself with the objects he was looking at, thinking how far it might be possible habitually to shift his centre till his own personality would be no less outside him than the landscape, – when the sense of something moving on the bank opposite him where it was bordered by a line of willow-bushes, made him turn his glance thitherward. (229–30)

Staring into space, Daniel attempts, half-consciously, to lose himself in the surrounding landscape; literalizing the implications of object-relations theory, his attempt to identify "himself with the objects he was looking at" underscores his strong psychological need for a reliable context, to be able to use his environment – for Klein's infant, the mother, for Daniel, the landscape – to secure a sense of identity. Significantly, then, Mirah emerges from the camouflage of this tangled bank. Predicting the pattern of resistance found in many of the novel's female characters, Mirah is at first a statue, part of Daniel's passively compliant horizon, then she proves the disruptive element that destroys his reverie. While Daniel has nearly constructed the perfectly contained dyadic communion of wholeness comforting to every Oedipal child, Mirah, rupturing his solipsistic communion, is the problematic triangulating factor. Intruding like the vengeful father into the mother–child dyad, she startles him into acting out his phantasies of retribution. Spurred into saving her from suicide by drowning, Daniel exonerates himself from his failure to rescue his own mother during her phantasized despair years before. Mirah is the victim who enables Daniel to play the saviour, and so her position shifts from that of intrusive father to that of good, passive mother. And indeed, Daniel is quick to make the connection explicit: "The agitating impression this forsaken girl was making on him stirred a fibre that lay close to his deepest interest in the fates of women – 'perhaps my mother was like this one'" (231). Daniel identifies Mirah as a mother-figure, which stirs his deepest passions. Mirah becomes the source of narcissistic gratification, enabling him to perform feats of chivalric assistance and thus to construct his "masculinity" aggressively against the passive background of her exhausted need.

Interestingly, however, Daniel's response to Mirah's "immovable, statue-like despair" soon shifts from the impulse to chivalry to the impulse to identification. For her story appeals to his lust for an originary Oedipal narrative implicating a guilty father and an innocent, victimized mother. Unlike Daniel, who has only phantasized this scenario for himself, Mirah was *really* stolen from a beloved and gentle mother by a profligate, immoral father. Mirah's story *is* Daniel's story, offering him a real mother to avenge, a real father to blame. She recalls her mother in choric language that reinforces his tendency to idealize:

I think my life began with waking up and loving my mother's face: it was so near to me, and her arms were round me, and she sang to me. One hymn she sang so often, so often: and then she taught me to sing it with her: it was the first I ever sang. They were always Hebrew hymns she sang; and because I never knew the meaning of the words they seemed full of nothing but our love and happiness. When I lay in my little bed and it was all white above me, she used to bend over between me and the white, and sing in a sweet low voice. I can dream myself back into that time when I am awake, and often it comes back to me in my sleep – my hand is very little, I put it up to her face and she kisses it. Sometimes in my dream I begin to tremble and think that we are both dead; but then I wake up and my hand lies like this, and for a moment I hardly know myself. But if I could see my mother again, I should know her. (250)

Mirah, whose very name foregrounds the centrality of the visual, articulates her own sense of self in terms of visual continuity. When she tells the story of the beginning of her life, she describes a scenario of strong identification with a good object: "waking up and loving [her] mother's face," as D. W. Winnicott would suggest, offers Mirah a secure, positive reflection of herself and of the world at large, components of continuity notably missing from Daniel's infantile recollections. Mirah's mother's songs signify "love and happiness," an emotional connection that is made physical through the contact of hand, lip, face, now accessible to the young woman only in her dreams. For Mirah, stolen and exploited by her father, longs to recuperate, like Daniel, the security of the maternal connection prior to the paternal intervention; Mirah and Daniel alike desire access to the world of dreams, of memory, of phantasy, a world they recall only through the hazy filter of the unconscious.

While Mirah's archaic memory is almost identical to Daniel's, it lacks the immediate imposition of physical pain. For although Mirah was later kidnapped by her father and violently separated from the mother she so adored, her memory, in its purity and its wholeness, is the stuff of Daniel's family romance: she is secure in identifying her father as villain, her mother as victim. Her experience offers Daniel both a vocabulary for revenge and a mission of reparation, literalizing his own story and giving him an identifiable enemy. Under the guise of rescuing Mirah, Daniel assumes agency: he is acting as her agent *and* he is finally unparalyzed, able to seek out the mother who is missing.

Mirah's father changes their names and travels with his daughter through Europe and America, singing in music-halls for a living. The exploitation of her singing abilities, a skill associated specifically with her mother, is anathema to the daughter who honors her memory. In Mirah's story, it is clear that pain and violence extend from the father, and that the mother, even in her absence, occupies the privileged position of innocence. Through these circumstances, Mirah fulfills two roles for Daniel. In her status as a victim, she resembles her own mother, and therefore the mother that Daniel desires to have for himself. In turn, her memory of her mother recalls the memory Daniel wants to have had. Through this pattern of identification, displacement, and substitution, Daniel conflates his search for the mother with his search for a lover. But as he adopts Mirah's mission, he also adopts her subject-position, for to conduct her search is, in some sense, to offer himself to the world as a substitute for her. "Something in his own experience caused Mirah's search after her mother to lay hold with peculiar force on his imagination" (245). As in the case of the mother whom he wants not only to have but to be, Daniel doesn't want to have Mirah as much as he wants to *be* her, to possess the certitude of her victimization, the reality of her memories.

Daniel not only takes on the task of locating Mirah's mother; he also vows to find her missing brother, Ezra Cohen. The boundaries between Mirah and Daniel, between mother, lover, and brother, between masculine and feminine, are confounded through this search; Daniel is impelled by a free-floating desire for reparation, for revenge. Knowing that Mirah is a Jew, he plunges into the communities and public spaces of London's East End in search of a man named Ezra Cohen, a man who has a lost sister. Because this search is Mirah's, it is at once less dangerous and more accessible to Daniel's conscious powers of analysis; through the mechanism of displacement, he is in complete control over this scenario: "The desire to know his own mother, or to know about her, was constantly haunted with dread; and in imagining what might befall Mirah it quickly occurred to him that finding the mother and brother from whom she had been parted when she was a little one might turn out to be a calamity" (246). Nonetheless, of course, Deronda plunges ahead.

Operating from Mirah's position, from the position of the abandoned daughter, Daniel's search only produces a new, doubly complex dilemma. After a series of wild coincidences, in which Daniel himself is identified in connection with his own mother (although he doesn't know it), and in which he finds the wrong Ezra Cohen who turns out to be the right Ezra Cohen, he befriends Ezra Mordecai Cohen, Mirah's brother, and learns of the death of the mother. The much glorified mother, whom Mirah has so deeply desired for so long, passes almost without notice in Mirah's – and Daniel's – excitement to get to the brother. Instead of finding a mother for Mirah or even a mother for himself, Daniel has found a brother for Mirah and, finally, an erotic object for himself. Daniel identifies with Mirah as a victim, and accordingly, his erotic interest is directed toward the object found in the course of the search for the missing mother; that the erotic object is therefore Mordecai only underscores the text's fluid patterns of sexual desire.

In an essay about the replacement of the erotic with the fraternal, Marianne Hirsch argues that "Mirah is indeed better off with a dead mother," for in the absence of the structure that mother would have supplied, Mirah can do as Daniel has done (even against his will) and determine her own identity.[9] I would supplement this assertion by arguing that *Daniel* is better off with Mirah's mother dead: in the macrostructure of the novel, his search for Mirah's mother always had more to do with him than it did with Mirah. And Mordecai offers Daniel the immersion into Jewish traditions that fully foregrounds the connection that the Princess Alcharisi later confirms, namely, the connection between Daniel and his Jewish grandfather, who so strongly desired a grandson to follow in his faith. The Princess, the woman who acts as the conduit between Daniel and his grandfather, reports, "'I have after all been the instrument my father wanted.' – 'I desire a grandson who shall have a true Jewish heart. Every Jew should rear his family as if he hoped that a Deliverer might spring from it'" (726). In this quotation, Daniel's grandfather ventriloquizes Daniel's mother to offer a message – and a heritage – to Daniel. The Princess's complaint is precisely that her father ventriloquized her still more perniciously in his assumption that she would marry her cousin and bear the children who would perpetuate his patriarchal vision. The Princess and Mirah are in an analogous position, for each provides the important but extraneous connection between two men – in the case of the Princess, between Daniel and his grandfather, and in the case of Mirah, between Daniel and Mordecai. Just as Daniel and Mirah are so quickly willing to forget Mirah's dead mother when they meet Mordecai, Daniel's disappointment after his reunion with the Princess is mediated by the critical importance of his new relationship to the long-lost grandfather.[10]

But it is not completely clear that, in finding Mordecai, Daniel has failed to find the missing mother. For Mordecai, with his perpetual consumption and his multiple eccentricities, is perhaps the most consistently feminized, even maternalized, "male" character in the novel. In his nurturing relationship with young Jacob Cohen, for example, Mordecai *is* the mother: "Jacob lifted up his small patriarchal countenance and wept aloud. This sign of childish grief at once recalled Mordecai to his usual gentle self: he was not able to speak again at present, but with a maternal action he drew the curly head towards him and pressed it tenderly against his breast" (535). Mordecai acts here as the mother-figure idealized by Daniel's late grandfather; nursing the young patriarch is precisely what Alcharisi refuses to do, to the frustration of her father's agenda. In his gentleness and in his soothing physicality, Eliot represents Mordecai, far more insistently than Mirah, as the nurturing, self-sacrificial embodiment of maternal virtue.

It is not at all surprising, then, that Daniel finds himself attracted to this figure, who represents, more than anyone else in the novel, the potential fulfillment of his eroticized phantasy of maternal reunion. Thus the connection between Daniel and Mordecai is described in terms of a metaphysical and choric melting-away of borders, distinctions, and troubles:

Obstacles, incongruities, all melted into the sense of completion with which his soul was flooded by this outward satisfaction of his longing. His exultation was not widely different from that of the experimenter, bending over the first stirrings of change that correspond to what in the fervour of concentrated prevision his thought has foreshadowed. The prefigured friend had come from the golden background, and had signalled to him: this actually was: the rest was to be. (550)

For Daniel, this relationship realizes both the terms of his archaic memory and his desire, expressed most explicitly in the moments before his discovery of Mirah, to merge inside and outside, self and

other. Daniel's soul, "flooded by this outward satisfaction of his longing," finds itself as one with Mordecai; "this actually was: the rest was
to be."

The nature of the "to be," of the future, for Daniel and Mordecai is
the expression of intellectual passion mediated through the related
intensity of physical and emotional union. The language Eliot uses to
describe this complex passion is far more explicit, and far less ambivalent, than her usual, more cynical approach to love relationships:

> In ten minutes the two men, with as intense a consciousness as if they had been
> two undeclared lovers, felt themselves alone in the small gas-lit book-shop and
> turned face to face, each baring his head from an instinctive feeling that they
> wished to see each other fully. Mordecai came forward to lean his back against
> the little counter, while Deronda stood against the opposite wall hardly more
> than four feet off. I wish I could perpetuate those two faces, as Titian's "Tribute
> Money" has perpetuated two types presenting another sort of contrast. Imag-
> ine – as we all of us can – the pathetic stamp of consumption with its brilliancy
> of glance to which the sharply-defined structure of features, reminding one of a
> forsaken temple, give already a far-off look as of one getting unwillingly out of
> reach; and imagine it on a Jewish face naturally accentuated for the expression
> of an eager mind – the face of a man little above thirty, but with that age upon it
> which belongs to time lengthened by suffering, the hair and beard still black
> throwing out the yellow pallor of the skin, the difficult breathing giving more
> decided marking to the mobile nostril, the wasted yellow hands conspicuous on
> the folded arms: then give to the yearning consumptive glance something of the
> slowly dying mother's look when her one loved son visits her bedside, and the
> flickering power of gladness leaps out as she says, "My boy!" – for the sense of
> spiritual perpetuation in another resembles that maternal transference of self.
> (552–3)

"With as intense a consciousness as if they had been two undeclared
lovers," the men, heads bared, face one another in a closed shop. But for
the presence of the narrator, this is one of the most singularly private
moments in the novel: Daniel and Mordecai find themselves in perfect
complementarity, perfect union, despite their physical differences. Indeed, the physical distinctions that Eliot elaborates here present a sharp
contrast between the healthy youth and the consumptive older man.
Eliot's narrator reads the "stamp of consumption" as the stamp of the
maternal; in fact, the symbolic mother produced through the course of
the passage functions as the primary connecting metaphor between the
two men. Their encounter described in terms of a son's attendance at
the maternal deathbed, Daniel and Mordecai are linked metaphorically
and symbolically in a transaction that approaches the transcendent: "for

the sense of spiritual perpetuation in another resembles that maternal transference of self."

Linked to Judaism through their mothers, Mordecai and Daniel become linked with one another through the metaphoricity of mothers. And as Joanne Long Demaria points out, given the novel's investment in Judaism, Eliot's recourse to the maternal has its practical as well as its symbolic function: "Judaism is centrally important to the novel precisely because through it Eliot defines familial and racial connectedness in feminine terms."[11] As the two men stand together, face to face, Mordecai is at once the mother who guarantees Daniel's Jewishness, the grandfather who planned for Daniel to be the vessel perpetuating his faith, and the passionate lover. Although Eliot's narrator has promised us the description of "two types presenting another sort of contrast," the difference between Mordecai's "type," that of the consumptive, and Daniel's, the noble young man, is effectively effaced by "the sense of spiritual perpetuation in another" that "resembles that maternal transference of self." The passage that begins by drawing the distinction of difference rises to its crescendo through a reconfiguration of the terms of "likeness"; rather than relying on the merely visible, Daniel learns to calculate connection metaphysically. Thus a specifically maternal form of relating emerges in the novel, a form characterized less by its literal reliance on the visible than through its allusion to the metaphysical, the affective, and the psychological. Effecting a "maternal transference of self" without the hindrance of actual maternal presence, the relationship of Daniel and Mordecai is at once erotic and parental, intensely physical yet sublime, even as the material horror of Mordecai's rapidly decaying body is displaced onto the ephemeral realms of the spiritual and the intellectual.

From Mordecai's point of view, finding Daniel is an equally momentous event, the culmination of a quest even more intense and anguished than Daniel's mimetic search for lost parents. "For many winters," writes Eliot's narrator, "while [Mordecai] had been conscious of an ebbing physical life, and a widening spiritual loneliness, all his passionate desire had concentrated itself in the yearning for some young ear into which he could pour his mind as a testament, some soul kindred enough to accept the spiritual product of his own brief, painful life, as a mission to be executed" (528). Mordecai's "yearning for transmission" requires the location of the ideal vessel, and it is this young man for whom he has searched all over the world. Like Daniel, Mordecai has learned from the Gothic trope that connects portrait and person:

"Sensitive to physical characteristics, he had, both abroad and in England, looked at pictures as well as men, and in a vacant hour he had sometimes lingered in the National Gallery in search of paintings which might feed his hopefulness with grave and noble types of the human form, such as might well belong to men of his own race" (529). In contrast to Hans Meyrick, Daniel's painter friend who seeks his ideal model in the world, Mordecai seeks his ideal in art, yearning precisely for Daniel. Through Daniel, Mordecai conflates objects of aesthetic and nationalistic desire through the metaphor of the ideal: Deronda embodies a type for him, the living perfection of an aesthetic capable of realizing Mordecai's still more abstract nationalistic ideal of a Jewish state. Working from the Caballa, Mordecai argues for the cyclical and gradual evolution to perfection of the soul:

Souls are born again and again in new bodies till they are perfected and purified, and a soul liberated from a worn-out body may join the fellow-soul that needs it, that they may be perfected together, and their earthly work accomplished. Then they will depart from the mortal region, and leave place for new souls to be born out of the store in the eternal bosom. It is the lingering imperfection of the souls already born into the mortal region that hinders the birth of new souls and the preparation of the Messianic time: – thus the mind has given shape to what is hidden, as the shadow of what is known, and has spoken truth, though it were only in parable. (599–600)

Mordecai's description of the displacement of – and the impulse toward – perfection verges on an aesthetic theory in its emphasis on the relationship of mimesis and ideal. For Mordecai, the foundation of a Jewish nation state becomes the displaced ideal toward which he himself, and Daniel as his surrogate, must strive. In their affinity for a model of displacement, and for the ensuing quest, Daniel and Mordecai alike share an impulse outward toward a Platonic, phantastic ideal, configured variously as beautiful boy, victimized mother, and utopic Israel. This impulse conditions attitudes toward immediate life circumstances, making relatively unimportant Mordecai's imminent physical death, as well as other materialistic concerns. Their gazes firmly fixed on the horizon, the aesthetic, the erotic, and the physical are but means to a loftier end.

In the essay "The Decomposition of Elephants: Double-Reading *Daniel Deronda*," Cynthia Chase suggests that the events of Daniel's narrative, and in particular the central event of his relationship with Mordecai, work as a means of producing his mother's announcement of his Jewishness: "The account of Deronda's situation has made it increasingly obvious to the reader that the progression of the hero's destiny – or, that is to say, the progression of the story – positively requires a revelation that he is of Jewish birth."[12] But, Chase argues, in order to facilitate this narrative progression, Daniel must undergo a "conversion" at the hands of Mordecai, a conversion that is actually *not*, in the sense that Daniel's Jewishness is an always-already fact, a fact predetermined by genetic heritage, the trace of physical evidence of that fact is also the site of the text's most consistent aversion. Working from Marcus's observation about the text's unwillingness or inability to "look" at Deronda's phallus, Chase writes:

The text's insistent reference leads relentlessly to the referent – to *la chose,* in fact: the hero's phallus, which must have been circumcised, given what we are told of his history. In the period in which Deronda's story takes place, male babies were not routinely circumcised. Circumcision was a ritual procedure practiced by Jews, so that evidence of circumcision amounted to evidence of Jewish origin. For Deronda not to have known he was Jewish until his mother told him means, in these terms, "that he never looked down," an idea that exceeds, as much as does magical metamorphosis, the generous limits of realism. Deronda must have known, but he did not: otherwise, of course, there could be no story. The plot can function only if *la chose,* Deronda's circumcised penis, is disregarded; yet the novel's realism and referentiality function precisely to draw attention to it.[13]

Chase's theory of the referential structure of the phallus – or perhaps more precisely, of the phallus as referent, as *la chose* – suggests the analogy of phallus and mother, both figures toward which the novel tends, yet which remain unincorporated within its larger economies. Chase continues:

Circumcision stands as an emblem for the fact or act that is at once the proof that the text requires and the referent that it excludes . . . As a mark that tells too much of the conditions of history or too much of the limits cutting off significa- tion or storytelling, circumcision is a sign that the story must evade or exclude or cut out: narrative must cut out or cut around the cutting short of the cutting off of narrative.[14]

Whether *la chose* is the phallus or the mother, or whether the two are in some sense identical for Deronda, Chase's persuasive emphasis on the ethics of excision underscores a major omission from her analysis. In the history of *Daniel Deronda* criticism, the burden of "double reading" is most notably articulated as the burden of reconciling the apparently discordant plots of Daniel and Gwendolen; F. R. Leavis, for example, symptomatically suggests republishing the novel's aesthetically worthy half under the title *Gwendolen Harleth*, and as for Daniel Deronda's much disparaged plot, "there *is* nothing to do but cut it away."[5] Given Chase's concern with the unreadability of castration anxiety in *Daniel Deronda*, what is the implication of the fact that her "double reading" attends to only half the plot, "cutting out" Gwendolen altogether?[16] How is *Gwendolen* implicated in the novel's overdetermined phallic economy? And of what is Chase's analysis, so peculiarly cut in half, symptomatic?

GWENDOLEN AND THE NARCISSISM OF FRUSTRATION

In yet another incursion of the Gothic into *Daniel Deronda*, Gwendolen Harleth's younger sister accidentally exposes a horrific sight when she opens a hinged panel in the drawing-room of their new home, Offendene.

Everyone, Gwendolen first, went to look. The opened panel had disclosed the picture of an upturned dead face, from which an obscure figure seemed to be fleeing with outstretched arms . . . "How dare you open things which were meant to be shut up, you perverse little creature?" said Gwendolen, in her angriest tone. Then snatching the panel out of the hand of the culprit, she closed it hastily, saying, "There is a lock – where is the key? Let the key be found, or else let one be made, and let nobody open it again; or rather, let the key be brought to me." (56)

Gwendolen's attempt to repress this terrifying sight is both literally and figuratively doomed to failure; among other things, the panel prefigures the events surrounding the death of Gwendolen's husband Grandcourt in Genoa later in the novel. In that scene, following Grandcourt's drowning (and the fulfillment of her deepest and most transgressive wish) and Gwendolen's attempt to save his life, she flees "with outstretched arms" into the safe harbor of Daniel Deronda's arms; Daniel, in fact, has just similarly fled from the side of his equally horrifying mother. "'His face will not be seen above the water again,'" says Gwendolen, "'Not by any one else – only by me – a dead face – I shall never get away from it'" (753). In this instance, Daniel has succeeded where Gwendolen has failed, by saving a spouse – or future spouse – from drowning. But the tableau of fleeing from the scene of the crime has great symbolic resonance, both within Gwendolen's narrative and within Daniel's. The pivotal encounter between Daniel and Gwendolen at this moment marks the major reversal in condition for each character, and effectively represents an exchange of subject-positions. Within the novel as a whole, the scene of *divergence* is the primary configuration of heterosexual and heterosocial relationships; men and women in this text generally flee the Gothic spectacle of the other with their arms outstretched.

From the novel's earliest moment, male and female characters have engaged in a dance of attraction and repulsion. In the opening scene, the eyes of both Daniel and the narrator focus on Gwendolen (as Daniel will later focus on Mirah), and this gaze produces a string of questions:

Was she beautiful or not beautiful? and what was the secret of form or expression which gave the dynamic quality to her glance? Was the good or evil genius dominant in those beams? Probably the evil; else why was the effect that of unrest rather than that of undisturbed charm? Why was the wish to look again felt as coercion and not as a longing in which the whole being consents? (35)

As the progressive movement of these questions would indicate, it is, it would appear, dangerous even to look at Gwendolen: the questions evolve from a simple evaluation of her beauty to an analysis of the "unrest" she seems to cause, in which the onlooker is implicated against his will in the gaze of desire. But regardless of its power dynamics, this seduction achieves only the tension of ambivalence, peaking with curiosity about indeterminacy rather than any great consuming passion. Gwendolen's response to Daniel is similarly curious and similarly implicated in the dynamics of power: she wonders about the identity of this mysterious stranger whose gaze turns into the "evil eye" that ruins her run of luck at the roulette wheel.

In a fictional world in which "power" is constituted as wealth, and in which men control that wealth, Gwendolen's financial investment in her success at the gambling table represents an attempt to appropriate the terms of that power as her own. In this context, Daniel's "evil eye" acquires significance as an attempt to thwart that appropriation of power, to stifle Gwendolen. It is critical, then, that the first "direct" encounter between the two protagonists occurs around Gwendolen's attempt to give away the family jewels and Daniel's successful intervention to preserve them intact: desperate for money after her losses, Gwendolen pawns a necklace belonging to her late father. Shortly thereafter, however, she receives a package:

Something – she never quite knew what – revealed to her before she opened the packet that it contained the necklace she had just parted with. Underneath the paper it was wrapt in a cambric handkerchief, and within this was a scrap of torn-off note paper, on which was written with a pencil in clear but rapid handwriting – "*A stranger who has found Miss Harleth's necklace returns it to her with the hope that she will not again risk the loss of it.*" (48–9, italics in original)

Daniel, a stranger, replaces the lost jewels of Gwendolen's father. As a phallic signifier and as the return of the repressed, this necklace, only the novel's first icon of bondage, haunts, troubles, and oppresses Gwendolen. In fact, she wears this very necklace as a bracelet on New Year's Eve to signal Daniel into a secret meeting in which she plans to tell him the horror story of her marriage. When Grandcourt witnesses this meeting, the chain functions as the material evidence of transgression, for which he punishes Gwendolen by taking her out on his yacht. This is the trip that results in Grandcourt's death.

Although the chain of events set in motion through the vehicle of the necklace ultimately results in a form of "freedom" from patriarchal constraint for Gwendolen, it is not freedom without implication. For it is the connection of jewels and money – and the exchange of jewels and money – that most directly oppresses her. When she chooses to marry Grandcourt, despite her awareness that he has a mistress and family to whom she has made a pledge, she chooses to do so because her mother is in desperate need of money. The material emblem of her "sale," her prostitution, is Grandcourt's set of diamonds, sent to her with a horrifying note from his mistress, Mrs. Glasher. When Daniel returns her father's necklace, Gwendolen gets to keep both the jewels and the money she received at the pawnshop. Through her marriage with Grandcourt, she once again gets to keep the money and the diamonds; she does so, however, at the expense of another woman.

Female characters in *Daniel Deronda* have a great deal in common; Eliot represents the coherence of female community in her portrayal of the Meyrick household, which consists of a mother and her enterprising and intelligent daughters, and to a lesser extent, in her representation of the more dysfunctional Davilow household of mother and daughters. The most profound links among women, however, are articulated in the common concerns of the novel's most prominent female characters, Gwendolen, Mirah, and the Princess, even though the three never meet one another. These three women are all singers of varying strength and ability, and they are all figures desirable to Daniel. Eliot's portrayal of these strong women relies on dual gestures of resistance and continuity: each of these women describes herself explicitly in terms of resistance to fathers or figures of paternalistic authority, and Eliot represents each of them in relationships of sympathy, identification, and continuity with other women, even with women who are complete strangers. The rejection of the father is in each case accompanied by the woman's attempt to appropriate the tokens of phallic power – worldliness, independence, agency, and ethical enfranchisement – for herself. Simultaneously, the prospect of domesticized femininity is figured as a terrifying spectacle of bondage and captivity. The horror of this spectacle is expressed through a common disregard for marriage and children, as well as through the consistent and revealing description of women, particularly Gwendolen and Mirah, as metaphorical statues. And in the imagery of statues, these women have two choices: to be uncanny and horrifying, or to be disempowered by their embodiment of an aesthetic ideal, frozen in time.

During a presentation by Gwendolen and her friends of a *tableau vivant* from *The Winter's Tale*, Gwendolen is confronted for the second time by the painting in which one figure flees, arms outstretched, from another. As the panel hiding this terrifying and mysterious scene spontaneously pops open, Gwendolen responds to the horror by enacting the very drama of aesthetic entrapment that she so fears might be her fate in life. She is playing the role of Shakespeare's Hermione, and the scene is the last in *The Winter's Tale*, in which King Leontes weeps before the statue of his dead Queen Hermione. When he cries out in grief and repentance, the statue is animated and revealed as the living Queen.

Eliot's rendition of this scene, however, recasts the comic conclusion of *The Winter's Tale*, illustrating not the moment of a woman's triumph over the arbitrary violence of patriarchal power, but rather the menacing future in store for Gwendolen, who finds herself, for the first time ever, unable to perform:

Herr Klesmer, who had been good-natured enough to seat himself at the piano, struck a thunderous chord – but in the same instant, and before Hermione had put forth her foot, the movable panel, which was on a line with the piano, flew open on the right opposite the stage and disclosed the picture of the dead face and the fleeing figure, brought out in pale definiteness by the position of the wax-lights. Everyone was startled, but all eyes in the act of turning towards the opened panel were recalled by a piercing cry from Gwendolen, who stood without change of attitude, but with a change of expression that was terrifying in its terror. She looked like a statue into which a soul of Fear had entered: her pallid lips were parted; her eyes, usually narrowed under their long lashes, were dilated and fixed. Her mother, less surprised than alarmed, rushed towards her, and Rex too could not help going to her side. But the touch of her mother's arm had the effect of an electric charge; Gwendolen fell on her knees and put her hands before her face. (91–2)

The picture of the dead face intrudes on this dramatic performance, the panel popping open when Herr Klesmer strikes a "thunderous chord." The immediate effect of this revelation is to make Gwendolen into an actual statue, paralyzed by the Gothic spectacle in front of her in an uncanny twist on a scene that already depends on the uncanniness of statues for its effect. The moment of Hermione's reemergence into life is suspended by Gwendolen's confrontation of this horrifying spectacle, confirming "Hermione," or Gwendolen, in the condition of wifely and maternal captivity. The animating influence of Gwendolen's own mother predicts her liberating role later in the novel, when Gwendolen returns to her a widow, shattered by her nightmare marriage, determined to resurrect herself. Returning once again to the framing structure of the Gothic, Eliot invokes the generic convention of the hidden picture to expose, again, a moment of psychological truth: the Gothic panel is the materialization of Gwendolen's anxiety and her fate, a frighteningly accurate representation of her predicament.

Rosemarie Bodenheimer comments, "Gwendolen reveals herself as the antithesis of Hermione's redemptive womanhood; at the moment when Hermione melts into love, she freezes into fear."[17] Eliot's invocation and reversal of Hermione's narrative, in combination with the spectral force of the "dead face," suggests that women who are wives and mothers are turned into statues, objects, things for the functional use of their husbands and children. The implications of "thingness" for women in this novel are at once spectacular and theatrical; Eliot's female characters are forced to resist the terrifying implications of objectification. Writing in the discourse of feminist film theory, Laura Mulvey argues, "Woman . . . stands in patriarchal culture as signifier for the male other, bound by a symbolic order in which man can live out his phantasies and obsessions through linguistic command by imposing them on the silent image of woman still tied to her place as bearer of meaning, not maker of meaning."[18] The distinction that Mulvey draws here describes the issues at stake for Gwendolen, Alcharisi, and to a lesser extent, Mirah as mimetic artists: far from aspiring to passive objectification, each of these women desires to generate meaning herself, to construct her identity, her world, her vocation. The structure that Eliot's women, particularly Gwendolen and Alcharisi, must work so hard to resist, is the structure that will, half a century later, preoccupy psychoanalytic object-relations theory, which argues that subjectivity, sexuality, and epistemology progress in an orderly fashion from the objectification of the mother. Daniel, in his desire not only to produce his mother, but to produce the mother of his phantasies, is implicated in the creation of the maternal "statue."

For it is precisely the mother-as-thing that structures Daniel's economy of desire. A true child of object-relations, Daniel seeks a "good object," a beneficent mother like Mirah's, from whom he can construct an identity. But the threat of objectification is the greatest dread of Gwendolen and the Princess, and Daniel's drive to self-construction entails the objectification of women. Daniel's desire to merge with a "thing" is clearly articulated throughout the initial stages of his discovery of loss; once again, the focus of his daydreams just before meeting Mirah makes this explicit: "He was forgetting everything else in a half-speculative, half-involuntary identification of himself with the objects he was looking at, thinking how far it might be possible habitually to shift his centre till his own personality would be no less outside him than the landscape" (229). That landscape is still, at this point in Daniel's development, the mother with whom he longs to identify. But for Gwendolen and the Princess, the threat of objectification is a menace; the fact that each of these women possesses a strong desire to perform and to sing underscores the need to control the terms of self-representation, and this entails resistance to those structures of objectification and identification – most perniciously here marriage and motherhood – that society would have them occupy. Recall that in Daniel's daydream, Mirah, even though she is the least willing performer of the three women, is the source of the disruptive movement that ruptures his idyll: " – when the sense of something moving on the bank opposite him where it was bordered by a line of willow-bushes, made him turn his glance thitherward" (229–30). Although Mirah is an attraction, she is also a distraction, not yet assimilated into Daniel's structure of relations; through her assimilation, through his "rescue," he appropriates the terms of her search and her identity for his own.

The issue at stake for Eliot's women is a sense of self in the face of a culture's annihilating expectations. Although Gwendolen's marriage-plot is conventional in its expectations, it is only ever constituted in terms of resistance, compromise, and failure. For Gwendolen, it appears, is ambivalent about the notion of marriage altogether:

That she was to be married some time or other she would have felt obliged to admit . . . But her thoughts never dwelt on marriage as the fulfillment of her ambition; the dramas in which she imagined herself a heroine were not wrought up to that close. To be very much sued or hopelessly sighed for as a bride was indeed an indispensable and agreeable guarantee of womanly power;

but to become a wife and wear all the domestic fetters of that condition, was on the whole a vexatious necessity. Her observation of matrimony had inclined her to think it a rather dreary state, in which a woman could not do what she liked, had more children than were desirable, was consequently dull, and became irrevocably immersed in humdrum. Of course marriage was a social promotion; she could not look forward to a single life; but promotions have sometimes to be taken with bitter herbs – a peerage will not quite do instead of leadership to the man who meant to lead; and this delicate-limbed sylph of twenty meant to lead. (68–9)

"Leadership," in Gwendolen's book, means self-determination and agency unimpeded. When circumstances conspire to force her to support her family, she longs to be able to succeed vocationally (as a singer) on her own terms. In contrast to such a protagonist as Emma Wood-house, Gwendolen's distinction between the terms ambition and marriage represents a major departure; Emma's ambitions, of course, involve not only her own marriage, but also the marriages of every other single party of her acquaintance. But in contrast to the predicament of a similar protagonist such as Margaret Oliphant's Lucilla Marjoribanks, Gwendolen's predicament is dangerous; while Lucilla quite successfully filters vocational ambition through the useful vehicle of marriage, Gwendolen seems to be on a crash course with the "domestic fetters" of wedlock. Her dreams are characterized by desire, not by consummation, and her role in the matriarchy of her home is that of Princess, functional "husband" to her mother, calling the shots and controlling the domestic scene. The achievement of "womanly power" requires that marriage remain in the subjunctive state of future possibility.

Unfortunately, however, Gwendolen suspects that her fate might be predicted in the figure of Lydia Glasher, the woman who has given up all to be Grandcourt's mistress and to have his children, the woman for whom Gwendolen vows to give up Grandcourt. Mrs. Glasher, formerly beautiful, forges a relationship of empathy through common fear with Gwendolen when she secretly meets with her to claim what is rightfully hers, marriage with Grandcourt and legitimacy for her children.

"You are very attractive, Miss Harleth. But when he first knew me, I too was young. Since then my life has been broken up and embittered. It is not fair that he should be happy and I miserable, and my boy thrust out of sight for another." . . . These words were uttered with a biting accent, but with a determined abstinence from anything violent in tone or manner. Gwendolen, watching Mrs. Glasher's face while she spoke, felt a sort of terror: it was as if some ghastly vision had come to her in a dream and said, "I am a woman's life."

Like the painted panel that shows a figure fleeing from a dead face, Gwendolen remains haunted, not only by the specter of Mrs. Glasher, but also by the specter of what Mrs. Glasher might signify for her. When Lydia Glasher left her husband and child in Ireland to roam Europe with the dashing young Grandcourt, she did so because she was being suffocated and restricted by marriage; but it is much worse, she tells Gwendolen, to be both bound to a man *and* vulnerable to his whims. Mrs. Glasher implies that the claustration of marriage holds the sole advantage of social acceptability over the ostensible "freedom" of sexual liberation. Burdened with her offspring, the result of her willing transgression, Mrs. Glasher seems destined to live out her life a social pariah, damaged not only by her actions, but also by their consequences. Lydia Glasher haunts the world of *Daniel Deronda* as an extreme example, the limit-case, along with Alcharisi, of the double bind that exists for women who act on their status as desiring subjects. The novel concludes with a gesture of reparation to Mrs. Glasher, reparation from Gwendolen, who always feels that she betrayed this woman when she married Grandcourt; because Gwendolen chooses not to challenge a will that favors Mrs. Glasher and her children, and in accepting a modest settlement, Gwendolen and Mrs. Glasher both get what they need: money, legitimacy, security, and independence, and a life unfettered by the demands and petty cruelties of Grandcourt.

The life-stories of the central female characters in this novel are variations on a single theme: the frustrating constraints of "a woman's life" for women with some performative talent in a rigidly phallocentric society. When she hears that Deronda might be Sir Hugo's illegitimate son, and therefore in a structurally identical position to Grandcourt's illegitimate boy, Gwendolen conflates the specter of Mrs. Glasher with the mystery of Daniel's missing mother: "An image which had immediately arisen in Gwendolen's mind was that of the unknown mother – no doubt a dark-eyed woman – probably sad. Hardly any face could be less like Deronda's than that represented as Sir Hugo's in a crayon portrait at Diplow. A dark-eyed beautiful woman, no longer young, had become 'stuff o' the conscience' to Gwendolen" (378–9). In her imaginary construction of a relationship with the mother of Daniel's dreams, Gwendolen perceives herself in a position of contiguity with two women ultimately victimized through their sexuality. But it is Daniel himself who is Gwendolen's nightmare-child: he is equated with her husband's illegitimate son, who might well have been Gwendolen's son. This logic is supported in the novel's temporal structure, in which Gwendolen's

courtship with Grandcourt is structurally parallel to the narrative of
Daniel's childhood and youth. In this regard, Eliot constructs these two
narratives as symbolically, if not actually, sequential. When they encounter one another directly, Daniel and Gwendolen are of the same
generation. However, within the novel's larger structure, which casts
itself back to Daniel's childhood and early adolescence, but travels only
a few months into the history of Gwendolen's life, Gwendolen is suggestively older than Daniel. Although he assumes the role of her rescuer
from the first, the psychodramatic nature of their relationship suggests a
duplication of the mother–son dialectic that ultimately proves so horrifying to both, and for Gwendolen, of the twin predicaments of Leonora Halm-Eberstein and Lydia Glasher.

If Daniel's erotic impulse toward the mother-figure is informed by a
desire to be like her, then Gwendolen's is informed with the sad
recognition of inevitable sameness. While Daniel's "femininity" is constituted by this impulse to continuity, Gwendolen's "femininity" is
constituted in terms of the continuity of predicament, and for Gwendolen and the Princess, this predicament entails a fight. Gwendolen
pawns the family jewels, Leonora Halm-Eberstein chooses her art over
the expectations of a father, and even Mirah escapes the grip of paternal
exploitation; these three singers manipulate the terms of self-display in
order to survive intact, in order to construct survival in terms of a
separatist vision based on resistance.

The site of the novel's most radical agenda is also, perhaps not
surprisingly, the site of its most problematic cross-currents of desire.
During the two chapters in which Daniel confronts his mother, he learns
that Alcharisi had, quite willingly, given him up as a small child,
rejecting not only him, but also her father, her husband, and the whole
series of ideological standards by which Daniel has been formulating his
code of conduct. In fact, the Princess Leonora Halm-Eberstein
threatens to deconstruct all cultural assumptions that inform classifications of proper femininity:

"Every woman is supposed to have the same set of motives, or else to be a
monster. I am not a monster, but I have not felt exactly what other women feel
– or say they feel, for fear of being thought unlike others. When you reproach
me in your heart for sending you away from me, you mean that I ought to say I
felt about you as other women say they feel about their children. I did *not* feel
that. I was glad to be freed from you." (691)

With this statement, the Princess effectively indicts the mythos of the
"Angel in the House" as rhetorical and hypocritical. Setting herself

apart from "other women," she actively resists capitulating into the role of the "good-enough" mother, the figure who, D. W. Winnicott will later suggest, is instrumental in her child's development, the masochistic woman willing to sustain pain and rejection in order to facilitate her *baby's* ability to hurt and reject with impunity. Resisting an ideal, the Princess lays claim to agency, and therefore to her career and her independence. She offers Daniel a choice of whether to comprehend her activities or to blame her (692); although he tries to understand, the Princess's complete rejection of his offerings of love and succor result in an unstated but implicit rage.

Catherine Belsey writes of the generic irregularity of Alcharisi's emergence: "a feminist reading of the text necessarily attends to Deronda's final encounter with his mother. The normal pattern of classic realism does not strictly endorse the introduction of a character who appears so briefly towards the end of the novel, and the interest of the narrative would permit Daniel's discovery of the 'truth' of his birth in any number of ways."[19] Belsey's implicit question seems to address Alcharisi's aggressive rejection of both her son and social standards. Refusing to provide a perfectly conventional teleological resolution, such as that of *Tom Jones* or *Oliver Twist*, in which the hero's "identity" is seamlessly revealed, this enigmatic, veiled woman insists on radically disrupting the world of her son *and* formal conventions of contemporary fiction. Presenting a mother who aggressively lays claim to her subjectivity, Eliot exposes the extent to which conventional structures of desire and even genre depend upon a pernicious ideal of femininity. Alcharisi's rejection of this formulation constitutes for *Daniel Deronda* the reconfiguration of structures of gender, desire, and power, and the indictment of paternalistic assumptions about the roles of women. Warping generic conventions as she warps gender conventions, Eliot exploits the mid-Victorian trope of sentimentalized maternal loss as the means of altering decisively the ideological and formal assumptions of nineteenth-century fiction.

For the anger expressed by the Princess in her two meetings with her son is only a more fully articulated version of the anger expressed by Gwendolen and almost every other woman in the novel. For Gwendolen and others, the Princess is a central and critical presence in the text: as the most significant site of resistance and as the most significant site of desire, she is the linchpin among the novel's various plots. The spider at the center of the web of narrative, the Princess begins to embody the phallic mother as a powerful presence.[20] The text needs her in order to demonstrate the implications of maternity for the lives of women and the function of maternity in the construction of adult male subjectivity. The Princess also succeeds in demonstrating, however, that the full realization of both masculine and feminine desire threatens to remain a mutually exclusive proposition.

His "mother" arguably remains missing for Daniel even in the moments of his most direct contact with her. As an actress, the "real" Princess is elusive to him:

> The varied transitions of tone with which this speech was delivered were as perfect as the most accomplished actress could have made them. The speech was in fact a piece of what may be called sincere acting: this woman's nature was one in which all feeling – and all the more when it was tragic as well as real – immediately became matter of conscious representation: experience immediately passed into drama, and she acted her own emotions. In a minor degree this is nothing uncommon, but in the Princess the acting had a rare perfection of physiognomy, voice, and gesture. It would not be true to say that she felt less because of this double consciousness: she felt – that is, her mind went through – all the more, but with a difference: each nucleus of pain or pleasure had a deep atmosphere of the excitement or spiritual intoxication which at once exalts and deadens. (691–2)

Eliot's narrator "looks" at the Princess and finds a polymorphous vision, a "double consciousness." "Acting" and "feeling" converge in the figure of this woman, producing a highly self-conscious representation, on the part of Eliot as well as Alcharisi, of what it means to be unique, to be her own agent. For Daniel to be "like" this woman is impossible, for as a completely "representational" individual, she is not even "like" herself. Yet the Princess's multiplicity is at once her salvation and her downfall; she says to Daniel, "'You are not a woman. You may try – but you can never imagine what it is to have a man's force of genius in you, and yet to suffer the slavery of being a girl'" (694). In *A Room of One's Own*, Virginia Woolf writes of the brief life and early death of Judith Shakespeare: "who shall measure the heat and violence of the poet's heart when caught and tangled in a woman's body?" Woolf's conclusion, like the Princess's, is that all too often, a woman's mind and body are sacrificed to a culture which stifles the impulse of genius.[21] In her representation of a series of female artists of varying strength and ability in *Daniel Deronda*, Eliot constructs a universal among women, at least among the women in the novel: a legacy of frustration and division that provides the grounding of her female characters' potent cultural, political, and aesthetic critique.

And for Daniel, coming face to face with his mother only confirms the larger sense of disjunction and lack for which she was formerly the compensatory phantasy: "He had often pictured her face in his imagination as one which had a likeness to his own: he saw some of the likeness now, but amidst more striking differences" (687). As is the case for Gwendolen, who focuses on desire rather than on consummation, when Daniel's phantasy is consummated, he is greeted only with disappointment. When the ephemeral becomes material, he is forced to confront the shortcomings in his imaginative construction:

> The words of his mother's letter implied that his filial relation was not to be freed from painful conditions; indeed, singularly enough that letter which had brought his mother nearer as a living reality had thrown her into more remoteness for his affections. The tender yearning after a being whose life might have been the worse for not having his care and love, the image of a mother who had not had all her dues whether of reverence or compassion, had long been secretly present with him in his observation of all the women he had come near. But it seemed now that his picturing of his mother might fit the facts no better than his former conceptions about Sir Hugo. He wondered to find that when this mother's very handwriting had come to him with words shrunk holding her actual feeling, his affections had suddenly shrunk into a state of comparative neutrality towards her. A veiled figure with enigmatic speech had thrust away that image which, in spite of uncertainty, his clinging thought had gradually modelled and made the possessor of his tenderness and duteous longing. (681)

Daniel has constituted his identity in terms of a phantasized relationship with a phantasmagoric mother: she exists, she *must* exist, as the receptacle of his love, as the object of his affections; she must have suffered at the loss of his company as he has suffered at the loss of hers. Like Esther Summerson, Daniel finds his family romance shattered by means of a letter that proclaims the terms of his mother's agency rather than his ideal. When his mother becomes graphic, represented in her handwriting, rather than phantastic, the intrusion of reality shatters the idol he has worshiped since adolescence.

What are the implications, then, of this encounter with the mother who unveils herself, and reveals herself to be not like a "mother" at all, who tells him, "'I am not like what you thought I was'" (687)? As has so often been the case, Daniel occupies the "feminine" position in this scene, and becomes himself the "mother" figure in his last attempt to forge a relationship based on likeness and affinity:

But to Deronda's nature the moment was cruel: it made the filial yearning of his life a disappointed pilgrimage to a shrine where there were no longer the symbols of sacredness. It seemed that all the woman lacking in her was present in him as he said, with some tremor in his voice – "Then we are to part, and I never be anything to you?" (724)

In her power to make him "nothing," the Princess strips Daniel of the terms of his identification with the "objects in the landscape" around him. In her power to castrate him, to make him once and for all a "woman," she acts the role of the terrible phallic father. And in the logic of her abandonment of him, she exposes the extent to which she is in actuality exactly as he had imagined her; as the phallic mother, however, she is decidedly phallic and only incidentally a mother. These are not tenable terms for Daniel. His "pilgrimage" produces, through alienation, a conversion, not to Judaism, but *from* identification with the mother to identification with a heritage of patriarchal continuity handed down from his grandfather.

The shrine of idealized maternity shattered, the mother demystified and newly demonized, Daniel is equipped for adulthood, as adult subjectivity, in the psychoanalytic sense, requires for its commencement the signal failure of that first love-object; Neil Hertz astutely comments: "[Daniel's] interview with his mother seals his identity as a Jew and a proto-Zionist, and allows him to move from a 'suspended' state into what the novel claims is genuine activity. In psychoanalytic terms, Daniel puts the pre-Oedipal mother aside when he enters the symbolic order and takes his place under the sign of his Jewish grandfather."[22] Daniel marries Mirah, and much more importantly, he inherits Mordecai's proto-Zionist mission, constructing through a fusion of hetero-sexual and homosocial impulses the contracts of relationship that consti-tute patriarchal masculinity. Gwendolen, on the other hand, returns to Offendene and a life with her mother and stepsisters. As Daniel turns toward a worldly–domestic space with his vision of a Jewish homeland, Gwendolen returns to a domestic space that was for her, in the not too distant past, a worldly space of sorts, giving her a measure of autonomy and self-determination that was notably lacking in her marriage; it would oversimplify the novel's real valuation of such crowded feminine spheres as Offendene and the Meyrick home to read Gwendolen's return as a defeat.

George Eliot's *Daniel Deronda* offers an object-lesson to the psychoanalytic reader through its representation of the mutually im-plicated, mutually competing fates of Daniel and Gwendolen. Worldly heterosexual masculinity, Eliot suggests, exists as normative at the expense of female potential. For to be a desiring subject in the world of this text is to desire, in some identifiable way, the missing mother. For Daniel Deronda, that mother represents the familiar Victorian ideal, while for Gwendolen Harleth, her absence signifies the certainty of options alternative to the claustrophobic economic and sexual roles available to women. Eliot's novel explores the implications of the tension between desire for the mother and maternal desire, between the mother as object or template and the mother who conceives of her identity in more broadly based terms. When that mother speaks up, she announces her final departure from the stage of Victorian fiction, not in yet another long-suffering death, but in a rejection of the lexicon of feminine convention. Constructing a melancholic novel in which the designated object disavows object status, Eliot reveals a set of ideological assumptions informing the search for the missing mother in Victorian fiction. For although the ideal of Victorian maternity looms large over the world of *Daniel Deronda*, it is not an ideal divorced completely from the implications of its logical effect in the lives of women.

Anne Douglass was admitted into Hospital, March 19th, in labour of her 13th child. She was not delivered for 20 hours, during the greater part of which time her pains were very severe; her child was born alive. Fifteen or twenty minutes after, suddenly, a dash of blood took place from the uterus, not however to any unusual extent. We were sent for, and in less than five minutes reached the ward; she was very much debilitated; her pulse only to be felt at intervals, her countenance ghastly, her body and extremities quite cold, accompanied with a state of great restlessness and anxiety. After having admitted some stimulants, the hand was passed into the uterus, which was found considerably distended and filled with clotted blood; part of the placenta was adherent to the fundus; it was easily separated; the uterus acted well, expelling both hand and placenta into the vagina, from which they were slowly withdrawn. The patient from this time lost *no blood*; the uterus remained firmly contracted; the pulse continued weak and fluttering, often imperceptible, particularly after vomiting; which is not usually the case with patients reduced by haemorrhage after delivery; as this occurrence seems rather to rouse the patient and improve the pulse. She gradually became more exhausted, her respiration difficult, the power of swallowing almost lost, and frequently so restless, as to be with difficulty kept more than a minute or two in the same position; which in all cases of uterine haemorrhage, is one of the very worst symptoms.

From the time of the removal of the afterbirth, which was at 1 o'clock P.M., till 11 P.M. she was watched by myself and Assistants, Drs. Nicholson and Darley, with the closest attention, and was liberally supplied with cordials; having in the course of ten hours taken at intervals not less than two thirds of a bottle of spirit, burned, and mixed with a little water and sugar, besides more than a pint of port wine. All the possible means were used to restore heat to the body and extremities, as warmer flannels, jars filled with boiling water, hot bricks, hot stupes, &c, but in vain; at length finding our efforts to produce any rally ineffectual, we determined on trying the effect of transfusion.

Having heated Read's apparatus, by injecting through it water at the temperature of 98°, it was filled with blood which was made to flow through the pipe previous to its being inserted into the patient's vein, in order, as much as possible, to exclude all air from the instrument. The blood flowed copiously from a healthy young woman, whom we selected for the operation, and was easily thrown into the median vein of the patient's right arm. It did not seem to have any more marked effect than that of causing the woman to mutter indistinctly; the circulation was not improved, though we injected about ten ounces of blood. She expired in a few minutes after the operation.

This woman's death seemed to have been principally owing to her state of constitution previous to the coming on of labour; being in a very debilitated condition, both from the number of children, viz. 13, she had given birth to, as also her continued exposure to hardship; as the quantity of blood lost would not have materially affected any young person, but in her, the *sudden* loss gave her constitution a shock from which it had no power to rally.

We rather think the transfusion hastened her death, though we all dreaded a fatal termination before it was resorted to.

Robert Collins, M.D., *A Practical Treatise on Midwifery, Containing the Result of Sixteen Thousand Six Hundred and Fifty-Four Births, Occurring in the Dublin Lying-In Hospital, During a Period of Seven Years, Commencing November 1826* (London: Longman, Rees, Orme, Browne, Green & Longman, 1835), 127–9.

CHAPTER 6

Calling Dr. Darwin

Toward the end of his *Autobiography* (1887), assessing the process of his intellectual development, Charles Darwin writes: "My mind seems to have become a kind of machine for grinding general laws out of large collections of facts . . . I think I am superior to the common run of men in noticing things which easily escape attention, and in observing them carefully."[1] In his articulation of the link between general laws and "large collections of facts," Darwin draws attention to the relationship of evidence to conclusion, of part to whole, of individual to species. Making explicit the uniquely synecdochal logic of his scientific texts, Darwin casts himself as the Sherlock Holmes of Victorian natural philosophy, capable of understanding what others cannot even see, and of developing "general laws" for scientific and behavioral theories alike.

This logic prevails throughout his *Autobiography*; like *The Origin of Species*, Darwin's autobiographical text is a narrative of origins that recasts the larger questions of his intellectual life onto a smaller, personal framework. However, the translation of the phylogenetic, or group, narrative of origins, to the ontogenetic, or personal narrative, exposes a set of anxious displacements behind and within Darwin's self-construction. When he represents *himself* as the evolutionary subject, the generic and practical conventions of autobiography require the explication of a family structure, and specifically of a parent–child structure. Darwin's descriptions of his parents demonstrate anxieties regarding questions of gender and power, desire and knowledge. He represents himself as a subject engaged at once in a relationship of vexed desire for a mother who is dead, and of intense rivalry with a father who is all too present. The patterns of displacement and aggression produced through these relationships are the patterns that implicitly subtend Darwin's theories of origins, on the phylogenetic and the ontogenetic levels.

In his construction of an autobiographical persona in an evolutionary framework, Darwin directly anticipates the efforts that will be made in the next decade by Freud: both men utilize the discourse of science to comprehend the puzzle of human development, and both present their conclusions in narratives noteworthy for their literary qualities.[2] As a writer, Darwin, like Freud, consistently anticipates his critics through the meticulous analysis of physical evidence and the constant, self-conscious reformulation of his argument. On a more subtle level, however, Darwin, like Freud, *acts out* anxieties – particularly when they are related to questions of gender and power – through rhetorical structures that are symptomatic in their display of ambivalence and aggression.[3] In this chapter, I will analyze the ways in which Darwin acts out representational anxieties on the level of rhetorical presentation; thus the rhetorical becomes a lens through which to understand the ideologies of domesticity and desire displaced from home in particular to culture at large in Darwin's larger scientific project.

FIGURING THE MOTHER

In a discussion of his boyhood creative impulses, Darwin makes an explicit connection between creativity and creation:

I told another little boy (I believe it was Leighton, who afterwards became a well-known Lichenologist and botanist) that I could produce variously coloured Polyanthuses and Primroses by watering them with certain coloured fluids, which was of course a monstrous fable, and had never been tried by me. I may here also confess that as a little boy I was much given to inventing deliberate falsehoods, and this was always done for the sake of causing excitement. (23)

His "deliberate falsehood" causes excitement focused on his own generative powers; this "fable" represents an early desire for agency within the world of nature. Notably, however, such a production of agency is linked explicitly with the production of narrative; telling tales about nature generates excitement and attention for the child as for the man.

In a 1921 reading of this anecdote, Edward J. Kempf locates the source of "agency" in Darwin's body; the anecdote, he argues, "was told at the age when children are inclined to wonder seriously about the possible genetic qualities of their excreta."[4] For Kempf, an early practitioner of Freudian psychoanalysis in the project of literary theory, Darwin himself, rather than Darwin's text, is the object of analytic scrutiny. In Kempf's view, Darwin's various blindnesses to and manipulations of childhood memories lead to personal psychodramatic issues, rather than to his engagement with larger cultural dynamics reflected in his various modes of self-presentation. Thus for Kempf, Darwin's story "had the value of being a fertilization curiosity," in which Darwin, by urinating, was capable of producing "variously coloured Polyanthuses and Primroses." The boy has constructed himself as a paternal figure in relation to both the flowers he generates and the stories he generates. Darwin's story describes a myth of parthenogenetic fertility, in which generation occurs paternally, and in which the maternal is elided altogether: the source of flowers, or originary narratives, is Charles Darwin alone.

A footnote added to the *Autobiography* after its initial publication suggests that Darwin's "monstrous fable" is linked by complex means to the "generation" of Darwin himself. Darwin's son Francis adds the following explanatory account to his father's tale:

Rev. W. A. Leighton, who was a schoolfellow of my father's at Mr. Case's school, remembers [Charles Darwin] bringing a flower to school and saying that his mother had taught him how by looking at the inside of the blossom the name of the plant could be discovered. Mr. Leighton goes on, "This greatly roused my attention and curiosity, and I inquired of him repeatedly how this could be done?" – but his lesson was naturally enough not transmissible. (23, n1)

Leighton's story is noteworthy in its differences from Darwin's: rather than generating flowers himself, Darwin is shown, in Leighton's narrative, describing their proper names by "looking at the inside of the blossom." While Darwin's memory of the episode presents its events as a generative phantasy, Leighton's anecdote tells a tale of reading, of peeking inside a blossom and learning its secrets. The erotic symbolism of the two memories is quite notably different; Leighton's recollection seems to focus on the interaction of boy and blossom, a relationship mediated by the instructive presence of the mother. In Darwin's story, on the other hand, the mother-figure is elided altogether, in favor of a focus on one small but powerful boy. Darwin's version of this story is both more aggressive and more paternalistic, although its potency is twice undercut by qualification as "deliberate falsehood" and as "fable"; the apocryphal nature of the anecdote within the autobiography, in combination with Leighton's corrective version, signals its symptomatic complexity.

Kempf speculates on the significant differences between Darwin's and Leighton's stories:

Whether or not Darwin's mother actually propounded her enchanting riddle to her boy is not quite so important as the fact that he said she did, showing how

keenly his wishes relished the fancy that she had revealed to him the one secret
of life that fascinated her – the secret, which, if read, would reveal the origin
and creation of life and – himself. Children from seven to ten are usually
passionately fond of riddles. It is the trial and error method of finding the
answer to the omnipresent riddle as to their origin. Soon after this innocent
exchange of confidences with her boy, the beautiful mother died – went on a
long journey into the night . . . At ten, this boy was still collecting minerals with
much zeal, still searching for the answer to his mother's riddle and her wish that
he could know.[5]

Kempf sees a direct relationship between Darwin's scientific work and
the death of his mother in his youth, a relationship articulated, he
argues, in both Leighton's anecdote and in the version Darwin presents
in the *Autobiography*. "Looking at the inside of the blossom," exploring
the secrets of the scientific universe, signifies for Darwin as the means of
connection with his missing mother. Kempf argues that Darwin's fascination with "naming," with empiricism, and with origins is immediately
traceable to his desire to please, to imitate, and ultimately to recover his
mother, as well as his desire to understand the means by which his own
life was created. To act after her example is not only to indulge his
curiosity about flowers, but also to explore the acts and means of
physical generation, of sexuality. Empirical investigation, the observation of events and the generation of "general laws," functions for
Darwin as a complex means of articulating his powerful desire for a lost
mother, while compensating for that loss through the assertion of a male
generative phantasy.

Darwin mentions only briefly, and even then obliquely, his mother's
death, the most significant loss of his youth: "My mother died in July
1817, when I was a little over eight years old, and it is odd that I can
remember hardly anything about her except her death-bed, her black
velvet gown, and her curiously constructed work-table" (22). Darwin
repeats his mother's loss on the level of his narrative: she is lost to him in
memory, represented only by a few scattered objects, and thus remains
coextensive with those objects throughout the text. One of Darwin's
early biographers, in a book titled, appropriately enough, *Charles Darwin:
The Fragmentary Man*, responds to the simultaneous centrality and obli-
quity of this passage:

Even [his mother's] death made far less impression upon him than the local
burial of a dragoon which he witnessed about the same time, and certain details
of which . . . remained vivid after sixty years, though of the other, and one
would have supposed much more moving, event he could recall no more than

being sent for, going into his dying or dead mother's room and finding his father there (again the memory was of anything *but* his mother).[6]

In an "Autobiographical Fragment" that Darwin composed much earlier, in 1838, his memory of his mother's death is at once equally elliptical and far less dramatically embellished. He writes:

When my mother died I was 8 1/2 years old, and [Catherine] one year less, yet she remembers all particulars and events of each day whilst I scarcely recollect anything (and so with very many other cases) except being sent for, the memory of going into her room, my father meeting me – crying afterwards. I recollect my mother's gown and scarcely anything of her appearance, except one or two walks with her. I have no distinct remembrance of any conversation, and those only of a very trivial nature. I remember her saying "if she did ask me to do something," which I said she had, "it was solely for my good."[7]

Memory functions as an impediment for Darwin, blocking access both to his mother and to the scene of her death. His limited memory of her, however, is as the quintessential "good object"; she claims to act "solely for [his] good," and he recalls mourning her loss. Although he recollects her gown, this version of the maternal death-scene has not yet generated the series of objects through which she is later personated. In this much earlier version of his autobiographical record, the death of Darwin's mother is recorded in – and as – a rhetorical construction: her death is reported in the dash that divides his encounter with his father from his emotional response after the fact of the death. Represented variously by a series of objects or a series of dashes, Susannah Wedgwood Darwin is always already demarcated as absent.

Present in this text only by means of ellipsis and substitution, Darwin's mother figures the centrality of loss and repression in the *Autobiography* and in the developmental narrative that it describes. As a mother and as a woman, her status as an embodied presence is displaced by a series of objects that only ever remain, unanalyzed, a series of objects. Darwin constructs her person in terms of proximity through the vehicle of metonymy; the collection of things that surround her body literally effaces her physical presence. But at the same time, the convocation of bed, gown, and work-table remains provocatively suggestive, seductive even, for these objects delineate the spatial parameters of a body even as they attempt to describe a gesture of displacement. The combination of seduction and aversion locates the mother as a problematic but powerful figure within this passage and for the text as a whole.

As a rhetorical mode, metonymy is an extremely effective way to describe Darwin's evolutionary paradigm, which relies on a logic of non-teleology, but also of consistent renewal: in the evolutionary model, generations are contiguously related to but different from one another, configured as a chain of progression but, theoretically, not of teleology. Similarly, in Melanie Klein's description of infantile development, the chain of substitutions invoked against the threat of maternal loss bears a metonymic relationship to the maternal referent. Klein writes:

The process by which we displace love from the first people we cherish to other people is extended from earliest childhood onwards to things. In this way we develop interests and activities into which we put some of the love that originally belonged to people. In the baby's mind, one part of the body can stand for another part, and an object for parts of the body or for people. In this symbolical way, any round object may, in the child's unconscious mind, come to stand for his mother's breast. By a gradual process, anything that is felt to give out goodness and beauty, and that calls forth pleasure and satisfaction, in the physical or in the wider sense, can in the unconscious mind take the place of this ever-bountiful breast, and of the whole mother.[8]

In the terms of Klein's argument, all structures of substitution refer back to the mother, and especially to the maternal body. The subject's grid of positive associations is formulated initially with reference to the "ever-bountiful breast"; conversely, however, the subject's earliest aggressive impulses also occur within this referential structure, in the desire to destroy the breast, the body, the mother who has the power to withhold that bounty. The significance of metonymic substitution, then, refers to a structure of ambivalence directed toward the maternal object. The gesture of substitution or displacement functions as the attenuation of the conflicted emotional responses surrounding the division from – and, indeed, the connection to – the powerful mother. In Klein's terminology, the child's construction of its own subjectivity, authority, and agency depends on its ability to negotiate this particular conflict; thus the "epistemophilic impulse," the drive to and construction of knowledge, is predicated on an aggressive response to the danger of maternal loss.[9] That Darwin should use the vehicle of metonymy as a way of describing his mother's death represents, in this formulation, the perfect coincidence of vehicle and message: Darwin's displacement, as Klein suggests, is at once protective and suggestive, seductive and aggressive. As a means of expressing, rather than of occluding, his experience of his mother's death, Darwin introduces his own impeded memory and the vehicle of metonymy as critical signifiers within the *Autobiography*. In his representation of the mother-figure, Darwin's deployment of metonymy suggests a specificity of relationship between the mother and the rhetorical logic of the text.

In "The Agency of the Letter in the Unconscious," Lacan's reading of the metonymic structure extends the implications of the Kleinian paradigm. For Lacan, metonymy not only describes a reference back to maternal loss; it also describes the interaction of drive and substitution that constructs sexual desire. Lacan suggests that metonymy is the figure for infinite desire precisely because it presupposes a dynamic of perpetuation, of endlessness; he describes it as "being caught in the rails – eternally stretching forth towards the *desire for something else*."[10] Darwin's dead mother, receding from view in her only appearance in her son's autobiography, figures the infinite desirability of an object that can be neither appropriated nor demystified. For Darwin, the desirability of the maternal represents a desire for the originary, just as his impulse toward the originary is implicated in an impulse toward the maternal: in Darwinian evolutionary theory as in Freudian psychoanalytic theory, the "originary," the mother of all mothers, is located just over the horizon. Darwin's rhetorical figuration of the exchange of maternal loss for sexual desire is central to the terms by which he constructs his appropriation of the epistemophilic impulse, and therefore his appropriation of narrative and scientific authority, within the *Autobiography*.

Nancy Vickers suggests that the poetic strategy of description that presents a woman in terms of a series of scattered objects works to construct an inaccessible ideal, as well as to contain the actuality, the subjectivity, of that woman: "bodies fetishized by a poetic voice logically do not have a voice of their own; the world of making words, of making texts, is not theirs." In other words, to describe a woman through the vehicle of the blazon, in terms of fragmented, scattered body parts, is effectively to fragment and scatter the whole woman. The chivalric construction of an ideal thus divides the narrative representation of the woman, and of female desirability, from the agency of narrative production; the woman represented through the vehicle of the blazon is deprived of the opportunity to speak. Vickers, arguing that Petrarchism represents a powerful force in the textual construction of "woman," reads Petrarch's representation of the Actaeon–Diana myth as a struggle toward the rhetorical containment of a woman's power: "A modern Actaeon affirming himself as poet cannot permit Ovid's angry goddess to speak her displeasure and deny his voice; his speech requires her silence. Similarly, he cannot allow her to dismember his body;

instead he repeatedly, although reverently, scatters hers throughout his scattered rhymes."[11]

The implications of Vickers's argument for a reading of Darwin's *Autobiography* suggest the issues at stake for Darwin in the representation of his dead mother as a figure dispersed among several inanimate objects. In Kempf's terms, the "mother's riddle" is, for Darwin, the secret of human origins. In order for Darwin to pursue that riddle, it is necessary for him to circumscribe the sphere of maternal influence, particularly in the emotionally charged aftermath of her death. The gesture of dispersal and objectification signifies the circumscription of that power. Throughout the rest of the *Autobiography*, therefore, the "mother" is represented obliquely and doubly: through Darwin's persistent claims to poor memory; and through his elision, containment, and displacement of other women, particularly of the objects of his desire.

For throughout the *Autobiography*, the "Woman Question" is addressed only by means of rhetorical misdirection and the "scattering" of individual women as active agents in Darwin's life. An entire section of the *Autobiography* is dedicated to a detailed, stream-of-consciousness account of the men whose company Darwin has found most influential, including Lyell, Buckland, Murchison, Brown, Owen, Falconer, Hooker, Huxley, Herschel, Babbage, Spencer, Buckle, Smith, Macaulay, Stanhope, and Carlyle. In contrast to his detailed accounting of professional contacts, however, the same chapter opens with the following description of his wife:

You all know well your Mother, and what a good Mother she has ever been to all of you. She has been my greatest blessing, and I can declare that in my whole life I have never heard her utter one word which I had rather have been unsaid. She has never failed in the kindest sympathy towards me, and has borne with the utmost patience my frequent complaints from ill-health and discomfort. I do not believe she has ever missed an opportunity of doing a kind action to anyone near her. I marvel at my good fortune that she, so infinitely my superior in every single moral quality, consented to be my wife. She has been my wise adviser and cheerful comforter throughout life, which without her would have been during a very long period a miserable one from ill-health. She has earned the love and admiration of every soul near her. (96–7)

The function of this paragraph as a set-piece of domestic narrative is underscored by the fact that this is the only moment in the text in which Darwin uses the form of direct address. Earlier he had declared that this autobiography is intended to amuse him, "and might possibly interest my children or their children" (21), but it is only at this point that he shifts from public to private discourse. The effect of this rhetorical shift is to place his wife in the structural position of mother, and Darwin in the dual positions simultaneously of husband and son; in fact, Emma Wedgwood Darwin, his wife, was niece to his mother, Susannah Wedgwood Darwin. The contrast of this description with Darwin's detailed account of his professional relationships structures a distinction between private life and public life, in which women remain, undescribed, in the sphere of the private. The rhetorical invocation of privacy in this description implies that information about Emma Darwin is only available to those who know her already, and even they are presupposed to share Darwin's perceptions and conclusions. Despite its claims of Emma Darwin's centrality, however, the effect of this passage is to preserve her by means of rhetorical effacement in complete anonymity, the generic Victorian wife. Darwin's construction of this description demonstrates ambivalence through misdirection: that he has "never heard her utter one word which [he] had rather have been unsaid," that she has "never failed in the kindest sympathy," that he does "not believe she has ever missed an opportunity of doing a kind action" signifies ambivalence through the very accumulation of negative statements. Yet Emma Darwin's insignificant appearance here is apparently unreflective of her powerfully influential position over Darwin's personal and professional identities; her editorial influence shaped the posthumous production of his *Autobiography*, and her own letters, which fill two volumes, were published posthumously in 1915.[12] Around the time of his marriage in 1839, Darwin mysteriously lost the vigorous health that had enabled him to spend five years exploring with the *Beagle*, a fact that has been variously attributed to any number of physical and nervous diseases. The only fact that is certain is that Emma Darwin alone guarded and protected her husband; Kempf writes that Darwin obviously married a "mother image": "For over forty years she was his wife-mother-nurse."[13]

Emma Darwin, like Susannah, is meticulously represented as Other to the world of scientific and theoretical discourse presented in her husband's autobiography. But Melanie Klein suggests, like Kempf, that these two women bear a more direct relationship to Darwin's scientific pursuits than is first apparent. In *Love, Hate and Reparation*, Klein suggests that scientific exploration occurs as an attempt to regain access to, to reconstruct, the lost "good object" of infancy, the mother: "The drive to explore need not be expressed in an actual physical exploration of the world, but may extend to other fields, for instance, to any kind of scientific discovery. Early phantasies and desires to explore his mother's body enter into the satisfaction which the astronomer, for example, derives from his work."[14] Within the terms of Klein's argument, scientific exploration occurs in the service of two impulses, aggressive and reparative; these impulses describe the "depressive position," in which the infant desires the simultaneous presence and destruction of the mother-object.[15] Klein suggests that the activity of collecting, along with scientific exploration, contributes later to the adult's attempt to resolve tensions left over from turbulent infancy. She writes:

In the explorer's unconscious mind, a new territory stands for a new mother, one that will replace the loss of the real mother. He is seeking the "promised land" – the "land flowing with milk and honey." We have already seen that fear of the death of the most loved person leads to the child's turning away from her to some extent; but at the same time it also drives him to re-create her and to find her again in whatever he undertakes. Here both the escape from her and the original attachment to her find full expression.[16]

For Charles Darwin, who sailed around the world for five years on the *Beagle*, the activity of exploration is the act of reclaiming the lost mother, of exonerating himself from guilt in her disappearance, of supplementing his faulty memory of her loss. Simultaneously, however, he is now able to reclaim her on his own terms, as an adult, and through its strategic representation, to act as master of the scene.

Notably, then, Darwin's loss of mother – as well as his loss of memory regarding that mother – is inversely proportional to his investment in collecting, which he consistently describes as his "greatest passion"; at one point he writes, "It seems therefore that a taste for collecting beetles is some indication of future success in life!" (63). In contrast to his obscured memory of his mother, Darwin writes, "I am surprised what an indelible impression many of the beetles which I caught at Cambridge have left on my mind" (63); in support of his passion for beetles, he offers the following anecdote:

I will give a proof of my zeal: one day, on tearing off some old bark, I saw two rare beetles and seized one in each hand; then I saw a third and new kind, which I could not bear to lose, so that I popped the one which I held in my right hand into my mouth. Alas it ejected some intensely acrid fluid, which burnt my tongue so that I was forced to spit the beetle out, which was lost, as well as the third one. (62)

As a cautionary tale, this narrative suggests the potential dangers of a "zeal" for collecting. And as always within Darwin's *Autobiography*, the narrative's symbolic content participates symbolically in a larger set of theoretical issues: his overwhelming desire to possess all three beetles creates a situation first of pain, then of loss. That the pain is located in his mouth links this story symbolically with his attempts to narrate other painful stories in the text, most specifically, of course, with the story of desire, pain, and loss surrounding his mother's death. Both mother and beetle do injury – the first symbolic, the second literal – to Darwin's tongue, to his ability to tell the story of his life and his discoveries. These injuries produce rhetorical symptoms, made manifest in the representational anxieties surrounding three central issues: desire, pain, and loss.[17]

Thus there is a tension in Darwin's *Autobiography* between his inability to recollect and his drive to collect. Melanie Klein makes an explicit connection between an infant's primal love for the mother and its later love for objects or abstract concepts. The attempt to collect or codify these objects, to generate theories based on abstractions, signals a desire to reconstruct the primary, mother–child relationship; the relationship between mother and objects is not one of displacement but of symbolic equation. Darwin's passion for collecting recalls the only set of objects he collects, but which he actively chooses *not* to codify and analyze: the bed, gown, and curiously constructed worktable that belong to and signify as his mother. The epistemophilic impulse only breaks down at the scene of *actual* maternal loss, at the destruction of the truly good object. The mother functions as the missing link in both the evolutionary chain and the chain of signification.

As a narrative representation of a "family," the *Bildungsroman* of *The Origin of Species* is profoundly patriarchal and paternalistic, and is especially symptomatic of the narrative anxieties that persistently produce the "mother" as the text's most noteworthy absence. For with one or two exceptions, the question of gender difference in Darwin's major works, *The Origin of Species* (1859) and *The Descent of Man* (1871), is completely elided in favor of a universal paradigm that describes the genetic and reproductive capacities of "men" alone. Although Gillian Beer points out that Darwin "retains the idea of *natura naturans*, or the Great Mother, in [his] figuring of Nature," that mother remains simply a metaphor for the natural world, the untamed context in which the paternalistic line of evolution occurs.[18] In *The Origin of Species* Darwin describes the evolution of a species gendered male against the backdrop of "nature," rhetorically figured as female:

Man can act only on external and visible characters: Nature, if I may be allowed to personify the natural preservation or survival of the fittest, cares nothing for appearances, except in so far as they are useful to any being. She can act on every internal organ, on every shade of constitutional difference, on the whole machinery of life. Man selects only for his good: Nature only for that of the being which she tends. Every selected character is fully exercised by her, as is implied by the fact of their selection . . . How fleeting are the wishes and efforts of man! how short his time! and consequently how poor will be his results, compared with those accumulated by Nature during whole geological periods! Can we wonder, then, that Nature's productions should be far "truer" in character than man's productions; that they should be infinitely better adapted to the most complex conditions of life, and should plainly bear the stamp of far higher workmanship?[19]

"Nature" appears here in the guise of Darwin's mother, as well as his wife: if Nature selects only for the good "of the being which she tends," she is like Darwin's mother, who, he recalls, said she asked him to do something " 'solely for [his] good.' " In contrast to capitalistic, solipsistic "Man," Darwin's "Nature" is selfless, timeless, nurturing, and primarily invested in the well-being of her dependents, identical in form to his brief sketch of Emma Darwin in the *Autobiography*. By gendering these abstractions, Darwin maintains the division between ideality and reality, between private and public spheres, that characterizes his description of his wife. When he personifies "Nature" as woman and as mother, he appropriates the terminology of the chivalric ideal, gendering an abstraction in order to maintain the circumscription of female subjectivity.

FIGURING THE FATHER

Darwin's autobiographical representation of his mother's death betrays ambivalence about her, both in terms of her authority during life, and in terms of her premature "abandonment" of her son. His representation of his father's death is similarly vexed, but I want to argue that it involves a different set of representational and narrative issues. Darwin introduces the fact of his father's death in the context of a discussion of his own hypochondria:

Although I was employed during eight years on this work [a study of barnacles], yet I record in my diary that about two years out of this time was lost by illness. On this account I went in 1848 for some months to Malvern for hydropathic treatment, which did me much good, so that on my return home I was able to resume work. So much was I out of health that when my dear father died on

November 13th, 1847, I was unable to attend his funeral or to act as one of his executors. (117)

Despite his precision throughout this passage, despite the citation of his diary and his awareness that his voyage to Malvern occurred in 1848, Darwin shows a significant lapse of precision with respect to his "dear father's" death. The autobiography's editor, Nora Barlow, adds the following footnote to the passage: "The date of Dr. Robert's death is given as 1848 in *Life and Letters*. In the MS. the date is clearly written 1847 – a curious error" (117, n3). The death of Dr. Robert Darwin did, in fact, occur in 1848; Charles Darwin's parapraxis is a complex signifier of aggression and ambivalence.

When Darwin places his father's death in 1847 rather than 1848, he implies a causal relationship between that death and the prolonged disability which left him "unable to attend his funeral or to act as one of his executors." It is ironic, perhaps, that Dr. Robert Darwin was his son's physician. Rather than the loss of his doctor/father, however, it is the figure of his doctor/father that "caused" his illness. For Darwin's persistent ill-health is extremely useful to him, functioning as one of the central signifiers by which he challenges his father's authority, both as a medical man and as a socially important figure. Primarily, Darwin's illness enables him to reconstruct his lost maternal relationship with the wife who is dedicated to his care and recuperation, thus reclaiming the missing mother of his youth. And secondarily, it literalizes the disadvantage that the younger Darwin faces in his assertion of authority: Darwin succeeds in the world *despite* his illness, and despite the father who "strongly objected" (71) to the voyage of the *Beagle* and disapproved of his son's line of work. Charles Darwin reports his illnesses and his inadequacies as a direct challenge to his father, who is figured throughout the *Autobiography* as the center of both authority and vitality. By means of these challenges, Darwin is able to claim that position as his own.

Much contemporary backlash against Darwin's work came from natural theologists, who resisted a theory of evolution that was simultaneously organic and agnostic. Basil Willey writes that Darwin was thought "to have banished from the world the idea of God as Creator and Designer, and to have substituted the notion of 'blind chance,' thus undermining the basis of religious belief."[20] The question at the time was one about the sources and symptoms of power. But ironically, while natural theologists would have argued that there is no Father in the work of Darwin, the figure of the Father is not only present in his

Autobiography, but provides a powerful standard of identification for his son.[21] In Darwin's presentation and appropriation of the figure of the "Father" in this work, he attempts to appropriate the status of the "originary figure" for his own. But like the Holy Trinity of the original model, the Oedipal triangle presented in the *Autobiography* offers as its third term a Ghost: what is suppressed most literally in this text is the figure of the mother. Articulated over the circumscribed space of the woman, the mother, the Ghost, is the sense of powerful continuity from father to son, as well as the powerful rivalry of two competing intellects.

In order for Darwin to articulate the terms of his power, he must pay homage to an authoritative patriarchal structure while simultaneously appropriating it to his own ends. Significantly, then, the father-figure in Darwin's *Autobiography* is consistently God-like. In the sense that Darwinian evolution was culturally perceived as a direct challenge to the genetic powers of God, Darwin is multiply implicated in the act of father-slaying. For example, he offers the following anecdote of his childhood pranks:

I once gathered much valuable fruit from my Father's trees and hid them in the shrubbery, and then ran in breathless haste to spread the news that I had discovered a hoard of stolen fruit . . . About this time, or as I hope at a somewhat earlier age, I sometimes stole fruit for the sake of eating it; and one of my schemes was ingenious. The kitchen garden was kept locked in the evening, and was surrounded by a high wall, but by the aid of neighbouring trees I could easily get on the coping. I then fixed a long stick into the hole at the bottom of a rather large flower-pot, and by dragging this upwards pulled off peaches and plums, which fell into the pot and the prizes were thus secured. When a very little boy I remember stealing apples from the orchard, for the sake of giving them away to some boys and young men who lived in a cottage not far off, but before I gave them the fruit I showed off how quickly I could run and it is wonderful that I did not perceive that the surprise and admiration which they expressed at my powers of running, was given for the sake of the apples. (23–4)

In a single paragraph, Darwin documents three separate fruit-stealing schemes. Two of these, the first and the last, were accomplished for the fact of self-aggrandizement: he stages these scenes in order to make himself a young celebrity in the minds of his family, grateful for his discovery of a theft, and in the minds of the young men who admire his running. The second anecdote, which reports on the intricate scheme the boy developed for stealing from his father's *hortus conclusus*, positions the child as a young Satan-figure in his desire to infiltrate the garden. The "staging" and the narration of each of these scenes are implicated in a highly subversive goal: Darwin utilizes them to articulate a direct challenge to the Law of the Father. The theft of forbidden fruit, not once but three times, signifies an appropriation of the terms of "truth" and "knowledge."

As a challenge to conventional structures of authority, these three scenes incorporate and attempt to subvert both Biblical and Miltonic precedent.²² Notably, the second anecdote in particular contextualizes Darwin's autobiography in a generic and epistemological tradition that includes Rousseau. In the *Confessions*, another autobiographical text preoccupied with the problematic of maternal death, Rousseau describes a strikingly similar scene in which he steals an apple:

One memory of an apple-hunt that cost me dear still makes me shudder and laugh at the same time. These apples were at the bottom of a cupboard which was lit from the kitchen through a high lattice. One day when I was alone in the house I climbed on the kneading trough to peer into this garden of the Hesperides at those precious fruits I could not touch. Then I went to fetch the spit to see if it would reach; it was too short. So I lengthened it with one which was used for game – my master being very fond of hunting. I probed several times in vain, but at last I felt with delight that I was bringing up an apple. I raised it very gently, and was just on the point of grasping it. What was my grief to find that it was too big to pass the lattice! I resorted to the most ingenious devices to get it through. I had to find supports to keep the spit in position, a knife long enough to cut the apple in two, and a lath to hold it up. With time and perseverance I managed to divide it, and was in hopes of then bringing the pieces through one after the other. But the moment they were apart they both fell back into the cupboard. Kind reader, sympathize with me in my grief! . . . Next day, when the opportunity offered, I made a fresh attempt. I climbed on my perch, fastened the two spits together, straightened them, and was just going to probe . . . But unfortunately the dragon was not asleep; the larder door suddenly opened; my master came out, folded his arms, looked at me, and said "Bravo!" The pen falls from my hand.²³

Rousseau's apple-appropriation scene is at once more elaborate, more vexed, and more immediately dramatic than Darwin's is. The appearance of the "master" clearly halts the boy's attempts at apple-stealing, at father-slaying, and at narrative. Rousseau therefore makes explicit the implications of the act of theft: the boy's intricate machinations are thwarted simply by the master's appearance. While the tension between the object of desire and the forbidding father-figure remains unresolved in Rousseau's text, Darwin's successful appropriation of the paternal fruit demonstrates his success in the project of subversion. The redoubled nature of Darwin's gesture, as an allusion to Rousseau and a challenge to paternalistic authority, locates the *Autobiography* within a powerful intellectual tradition at the same time as it represents the direct subversion of theodicy.

Darwin's representation of his father demonstrates ambivalence through its rhetorical equivocations and often strained emotional justifications. The means by which he describes the father–son relationship are just as critical as the events he describes. The following is a typical example:

> When I left the school I was for my age neither high nor low in it; and I believe that I was considered by all my masters and by my Father as a very ordinary boy, rather below the common standard in intellect. To my deep mortification my father once said to me, "You care for nothing but shooting, dogs, and rat-catching, and you will be a disgrace to yourself and all your family." But my father, who was the kindest man I ever knew, and whose memory I love with all my heart, must have been angry and somewhat unjust when he used such words . . . I may here add a few pages about my Father, who was in many ways a remarkable man. (28)

This statement is a model of ambivalence. Darwin's inconsistent capitalization of the word "father" – Father, father, father, Father – persists throughout the *Autobiography* in no discernible pattern. If the keynote of the passage is his status at school, "neither high nor low," then that pattern of neither/nor is reflected throughout in the way he describes his father's response to his supposed "ordinariness." Robert Darwin and the boy's schoolmasters obviously misjudged the intelligence of their pupil; the prominence of Charles Darwin within Victorian intellectual circles is evidence enough of that fact. Within this context, though, Darwin's justification of his father's aggressive misjudgment rings hollow: if Robert Darwin had truly been "in many ways a remarkable man," he would not have made such a signal mistake about his own child. But Charles Darwin has competing desires regarding his father – the desire to exact revenge for this underestimation, as well as the desire to preserve his father's "remarkable" qualities intact for posterity. The ambivalence of the *Autobiography* therefore demonstrates Darwin's attempt both to preserve and to slay Robert Darwin; the authority of Charles Darwin is dependent on his ability to accomplish that task.

Thus Robert Darwin offers his son a model of authority to emasculate, even as he offers him a model to emulate. If Dr. Darwin was consistently God-like, he was also Freud-like, and in this regard offered his son a powerful precedent for scientific authority. Dr. Darwin, Charles explains, found great success in treating his female patients'

emotional ailments, as well as their physical ones, simply by listening
and by advising them on the volatility of male–female relationships.
"Owing to my father's skill in winning confidence he received many
strange confessions of misery and guilt. He often remarked how many
miserable wives he had known" (32). But as his son inadvertently
reveals, Dr. Darwin turns confidence into a confidence game. This is
one of a number of examples that Charles Darwin cites in the autobiography:

As a boy, I went to stay at the house of Major B –, whose wife was insane; and
the poor creature, as soon as she saw me, was in the most abject state of terror
that I ever saw, weeping bitterly and asking me over and over again, "Is your
father coming?" but was soon pacified. On my return home, I asked my father
why she was so frightened, and he answered he [was] very glad to hear it, as he
had frightened her on purpose, feeling sure that she could be kept in safety and
much happier without any restraint, if her husband could influence her,
whenever she became at all violent, by proposing to send for Dr. Darwin; and
these words succeeded perfectly during the rest of her long life. (40)

As an illustration of the means by which women were "contained" or
"kept in safety," this anecdote reveals the extreme of the logic Charles
Darwin appropriates in his "containment" of mother and wife through
rhetorical, rather than physical, means. The powerful figure of "Dr.
Darwin" is installed for Mrs. Major B – , as for his son, as the superego,
as the terrifying, punitive source of law and order. That the mere
invocation of Dr. Darwin's name is enough to silence this woman
signifies the extent to which the Law of the Father prevails within
Charles Darwin's universe.

Charles Darwin himself appropriates this model of authority to his
own ends, but not without ambivalence. Early in the *Autobiography*, he
writes, "I can say in my own favour that I was as a boy humane, but I
owed this entirely to the instruction and example of my sisters. I doubt
indeed whether humanity is a natural or innate quality" (26). He
represents his "humanity" in terms of his ability to restrain himself: "I
never took more than a single egg out of a bird's nest" (26–7); "I never
spitted a living worm" (27). But his representation of his personal
"power" vacillates wildly between extremes of humanitarianism and
outright cruelty:

Once as a very little boy, whilst at the day-school, or before that time, I acted
cruelly, for I beat a puppy I believe, simply from enjoying the sense of power,
but the beating could not have been severe, for the puppy did not howl, of

which I feel sure as the spot was near to the house. This act lay heavily on my conscience, as is shown by my remembering the exact spot where the crime was committed. It probably lay all the heavier from my love of dogs being then, and for a long time afterwards, a passion. Dogs seemed to know this, for I was an adept in robbing their love from their masters. (27)

Darwin is aware that beating the puppy reveals an investment in the manifestation of power over a smaller creature; as in the anecdote of his father and Mrs. Major B – , there is something sadistically, personally gratifying about his ability to demonstrate potency. His compensatory "passion" for dogs, however, conforms to what Melanie Klein describes as the depressive position: his guilt at damaging that puppy causes a disproportionate desire to adore all puppies, as an infant's desire to aggress against the mother is mediated by a need for that mother, and therefore the compensatory reassertion of the love-relationship. Darwin's "need" is demonstrated here in his ability to steal love, a rhetoric of theft that continues from his fruit-stealing adventures, a rhetoric that occurs consistently with reference to his father. "Robbing their love from their masters" is a means of stealing love, of appropriating the admiration of a dog for its master, or of a community for a Darwin. The rhetoric of theft represents Darwin's conversion-phantasy, in which all the admiration he describes as directed toward his father is made available to him. The pattern that Darwin describes here, in which his aggressive impulses are ultimately rewarded with slavelike adoration and the acknowledgment of his absolute mastery, is an appropriation of the epistemophilic impulse, in which knowledge is equated with sadism, with the expulsion of a mother, and with the appropriation of paternalistic mastery. The connection between this disturbing incident and Darwin's more subtle means of containing women becomes explicit in an appendix to the *Autobiography*, which reproduces notes scribbled on scraps of paper in 1837 or 1838, in which he debated the question of whether or not to marry. Under the heading "Marry," he lists the following reasons: "Children – (if it please God) – constant companion, (friend in old age) who will feel interested in one, object to be beloved and played with – better than a dog anyhow."[24]

Within the tension of the father–son relationship, the question of "memory" is a central signifier. "Memory" denotes not only Charles Darwin's ability or inability to recall the events of his youth. His reputation, the way in which he and his father will be remembered after death, is also implicated in his desire to construct his memories accurately, authoritatively, in his autobiography. Darwin writes:

I have heard my Father say he believed that persons with powerful minds generally had memories extending far back to a very early period of life. This is not my case for my earliest recollection goes back only to when I was a few months over four years old, when we went to near Abergele for sea-bathing, and I recollect the events and places there with some little distinctness. (21–2)

From the beginning, then, the fallibility of Darwin's memory, the limitations of his particular subject-position, present him with a distinct methodological challenge. Throughout the autobiography, as in his theoretical works, he praises the scientific mind as one that consistently attempts to universalize, taking the part, even the minute example, as evidence of a grander, invisible whole. But Darwin's desire to collect all the facts, to construct empirical chains of evidence leading to universal conclusions, is frustrated by the formal constraints of his project. For in the genre of autobiography, memory is a primary form of authoritative citation. Darwin's memory, unlike his father's, is faulty.[25] He writes of Robert Darwin:

My father possessed an extraordinary memory, especially for dates, so that he knew, when he was very old the day of the birth, marriage, and death of a multitude of persons in Shropshire; and he once told me that this power annoyed him; for if he once heard a date he could not forget it; and thus the deaths of many friends were often recalled to his mind. Owing to his strong memory he knew an extraordinary number of curious stories, which he liked to tell, as he was a great talker. He was generally in high spirits, and laughed and joked with every one – often with his servants – with the utmost freedom; yet he had the art of making every one obey him to the letter. Many persons were much afraid of him. (39)

Memory is what Darwin lacks and his father has. Memory is also the source of his father's good reputation, as well as his power as an authority-figure; that "many persons were much afraid of him" underscores Robert Darwin's representation as a god, powerful and potentially angry, in this text. In contrast, throughout the *Autobiography*, Darwin qualifies his own ability to remember events adequately, and contrasts his poor memory with his father's perfect one, his embattled position within contemporary scientific circles with his father's ease and authority as a community leader. As an index of comparison, the ability to remember constitutes the power differential between father and son; the rhetoric of memory becomes for Darwin the vocabulary of a struggle to prevail against the high standards of the father-figure.

Thus memory functions within this text and within the father–son relationship as the signifier of rivalry and competition – a competition that the son always fails. Clearly the most problematic instance of Charles's memory-failure occurs with reference to the death of his mother, yet memory is what gives Robert Darwin access to this dead woman, while it impedes Charles from that very connection. As represented through the figure of Robert Darwin, the ability to remember represents the ability to have, to possess, to master. Notably, then, Charles Darwin uses writing to supplement his inadequate memory: research allows him to accumulate data and to "master" a body of knowledge. And as Kempf suggests and Klein implies, such a gesture of intellectual mastery is linked with the desire to recuperate, to dominate, the "mother's riddle": the question of origins is always already a question of gender, power, and representation.

If collection and scientific exploration supplement the loss of the mother, then these activities supplement Darwin's loss of memory as well. Darwin comments that he needs a written text in order to prompt his memory:

I had, also, during many years, followed a golden rule, namely, that whenever a published fact, a new observation or thought came across me, which was opposed to my general results, to make a memorandum of it without fail and at once; for I had found by experience that such facts and thoughts are far more apt to escape from the memory than favourable ones. Owing to this habit, very few objections were raised against my views which I had not at least noticed and attempted to answer. (123)

Here Darwin articulates his resistance to challenge in the course of describing the measures he takes to disarm surprising "objections." The written text is central not only to Darwin's description of his work habits, however, but also to the psychological drama he describes in the *Autobiography*. When he writes about his scientific writings, he speaks of them as his offspring. For example, in the chapter entitled "My Several Publications," he describes the popular response to his first independent publication, *Journal of Researches*, published in 1845: "The success of this my first literary child always tickles my vanity more than that of any of my other books. Even to this day it sells steadily in England and the United States, and has been translated for the second time into German, and into French and other languages" (116). Darwin's delight at his "child's" success stands in marked contrast to his father's skepticism regarding his son's abilities. Darwin consistently constructs himself as the good father, and, for that matter, the good mother as well. The production of the texts describing his activities in research, exploration, and collection provides him with a supplementary parental structure, in which he is father and mother alike, and in which the "literary child" reflects positively on its progenitor. Thus he constructs a positive model for his own paternity, as well as a positive phantasy for his relationship with his own father.

Darwin's *actual* first child doesn't appear in the text for another fifteen pages, and even then young Francis Darwin acquires significance only by providing evidence for Charles Darwin's attempts to study the evolution of infantile expression: "My first child was born on December 27th, 1839, and I at once commenced to make notes on the first dawn of the various expressions which he exhibited, for I felt convinced, even at this early period, that the most complex and fine shades of expression must all have had a gradual and natural origin" (131–2). The "origin of species" is grounded explicitly in a Romantic notion of individual origins. When Wordsworth describes the sense of continual progression from father to son in the line "The Child is father of the Man," he posits a model of evolution within one individual as between two, collapsing the phylogenetic paradigm into the framework of ontogenesis. It is this redoubled sense of continuous, unbroken progression that Darwin struggles to "remember" in the *Autobiography*, despite the fact that his memories, when they exist, usually illustrate only fragmentation, ambivalence, and loss. At stake in Darwin's overdetermined descriptions of paternal continuity is a position of authority, within the autobiographical text as well as within the scientific and cultural discourses that the autobiography attempts to construct as continuous.

In his *Autobiography*, Darwin demonstrates a direct relationship between the origin of an individual and the origin of species, between ontogeny and phylogeny. The translation of the evolutionary model to the autobiographical mode makes clear the tensions regarding gender, gender roles, and questions of power that underpin, and often undercut, Darwin's representation of the "originary." Through the rhetorical presentation of his mother as effectively "missing," and through the accompanying representation of his father as a notably overdetermined figure of potency, he aligns himself – not unproblematically – with the powerful father. Thus Darwin's articulation of narrative authority occurs through the sacrifice of that mother to the all-powerful, all-knowing father. This parthenogenetic phantasy, the phantasy of continuity from "Father" to son, produces the "origin of species," and arguably, *The Origin of Species*.

CASE I. – The lady to whom [chloroform] was first exhibited during parturition had been previously delivered in the country by perforation of the head of the infant, after a labour of three days' duration. In this, her second confinement, pains supervened a fortnight before the full time. Three hours and a half after they commenced, and ere the first stage of the labour was completed, I placed her under the influence of the chloroform, by moistening, with half a teaspoonful of the liquid, a pocket-handkerchief, rolled up into a funnel shape, and with the broad or open end of the funnel placed over her mouth and nostrils. In consequence of the evaporation of the fluid, it was once more renewed in about ten or twelve minutes. The child was expelled in about twenty-five minutes after the inhalation had begun. The mother subsequently remained longer soporose than commonly happens after ether. The squalling of the child did not, as usual, rouse her; and some minutes elapsed after the placenta was expelled, and after the child was removed by the nurse into another room, before the patient awoke. She then turned round and observed to me that she had "enjoyed a very comfortable sleep, and indeed required it as she was so tired, but would now be more able for the work before her." I evaded entering into conversation with her, believing, as I have already stated, that the most complete possible quietude forms one of the principal secrets for the successful employment of either ether or chloroform. In a little time she again remarked that she was afraid her "sleep had stopped the pains." Shortly afterwards, her infant was brought in by the nurse from the adjoining room, and it was a matter of no small difficulty to convince the astonished mother that the labour was entirely over, and that the child represented to her was really her "own living baby."

Sir James Y. Simpson, Bart., "Cases Illustrative of the Use and Effects of Chloroform in Midwifery," in *Anaesthesia, Hospitalism, Hermaphroditism, and a Proposal to Stamp Out Small-Pox and Other Contagious Diseases*, ed. Sir W. G. Simpson, Bart., B.A. (Edinburgh: Adam & Charles Black, 1871), 207–8.

CHAPTER 7

Virginia Woolf's "Victorian novel"

[Mr. Ramsay, stumbling along a passage one dark morning, stretched his arms out, but Mrs. Ramsay having died rather suddenly the night before, his arms, though stretched out, remained empty.]

Virginia Woolf[1]

Psychoanalytic theories of subjectivity commence with the "death" of the mother, and Victorian narratives of domesticity and *Bildung* are similarly invested in the prior closure that enables a clean, unimplicated beginning. This cannot be said for *To the Lighthouse*, a novel that begins with a mother who is not only living but present and powerful. In its engagement with the material force of that power, incarnate in life as in death, this novel refigures the central conventions of life-writing in both Victorian and psychoanalytic contexts. Virginia Woolf, returning to tropes of maternal loss, interrogates their limitations and exposes their potential, and in this return, she begins to excavate the emotional, psychological, and representational power of the domestic within the worldly practices of language and art. In *To the Lighthouse*, artistic vision is melancholic, and Woolf exploits narrative conventions that allow her to personate that melancholia through the death of the mother. But she refuses to capitulate to the assumption that this is the end of the story – or the beginning of another story, the relevant story.

Moving the mother's death from its conventional place at the beginning into the middle of the novel unleashes Mrs. Ramsay from the constraining opposition of life and death and suggests that this woman, as a woman and as a mother, plays a pivotal role in the stories of those around her, even as she retains a private adventure story of her own. For this is a novel that deploys, to maximum pathos, the melancholic trope of Victorian fiction, maternal death, and through the vehicle of that death, displays the consequences of a highly productive introjection of the maternal influence. But Virginia Woolf, like George Eliot, rejects the most extreme implication of this trope, the implication that will return in the guise of D. W. Winnicott's theory of the "good-enough mother" who enables subjectivity through passivity and masochistic constraint. Mrs. Ramsay, unlike the psychoanalytic mother, has a private, interior life for more than half the novel, and through that interiority, she emerges as a subject, complex and resistant, on her own terms. While the reader's access to Mrs. Ramsay's private thoughts makes her sudden death all the more heartbreaking, Woolf travels in Eliot's path by refusing to allow the death of the mother to be the death of only a mother. And in doing so, she shatters the monolith constructed and maintained through the Victorian trope of maternal loss, suggesting in the process a new set of terms for understanding the overdetermined disjunction of domestic and artistic spheres of production.

For Mrs. Ramsay, beautiful and fecund, is no idealized domestic goddess. Her house is shabby, her children unruly, her matchmaking impulses shortsighted and sentimental. What is idealized, however, is a domestic mood that she creates, a mood sumptuous in its harmonies, secure in its attention to detail and to the feelings and needs of the many dependents of this house, adult and child alike. While the world of this text pays homage to Mrs. Ramsay's successful orchestration of that domestic sphere, Mrs. Ramsay herself is perpetually in excess of that homage, elusive of the many attempts to rein her into the confines of an image. Mr. Bankes muses:

For always, he thought, there was something incongruous to be worked into the harmony of her face. She clapped a deer-stalker's hat on her head; she ran across the lawn in goloshes to snatch a child from mischief. So that if it was her beauty merely that one thought of, one must remember the quivering thing, the living thing (they were carrying bricks up a little plank as he watched them), and work it into the picture; or if one thought of her simply as a woman, one must endow her with some freak of idiosyncrasy – she did not like admiration – or suppose some latent desire to doff her royalty of form as if her beauty bored her and all that men say of beauty, and she wanted only to be like other people, insignificant. (29–30)

Mrs. Ramsay's elusiveness and the fascination this entails for everyone from James to Lily Briscoe are a form of maternal loss even prior to the event of her death. By building in the elegiac mode before the actual elegiac occasion, Woolf constructs subjectivity as melancholic; like the novel's title, a prepositional phrase without a subject, subjectivity is constituted through the attenuation of the object of desire.[2]

Mrs. Ramsay, however, is as elusive to herself as she is to her loved ones, and in this, Woolf demystifies the maternal ideal by underscoring its relation to modernist representations of subjectivity more generally. Readers of this novel are distanced from this woman by the formality of the name "Mrs. Ramsay" – we are never invited to be on a first-name basis – but we are offered tantalizing glimpses of a private self all too rarely emerging in brief respites from household duties:

For now she need not think about anybody. She could be herself, by herself. And that was what now she often felt the need of – to think; well, not even to think. To be silent; to be alone. All the being and the doing, expansive, glittering, vocal, evaporated; and one shrunk, with a sense of solemnity, to being oneself, a wedge-shaped core of darkness, something invisible to others. Although she continued to knit, and sat upright, it was thus that she felt herself; and this self having shed its attachments was free for the strangest adventures. When life sank down for a moment, the range of experience seemed limitless. And to everybody there was always this sense of unlimited resources, she supposed; one after another, she, Lily, Augustus Carmichael, must feel, our apparitions, the things you know us by, are simply childish. Beneath it is all dark, it is all spreading, it is unfathomably deep; but now and again we rise to the surface and that is what you see us by. Her horizon seemed to her limitless. There were all the places she had not seen; the Indian plains; she felt herself pushing aside the thick leather curtain of a church in Rome. This core of darkness could go anywhere, for no one saw it. (62)

When Mrs. Ramsay is by herself, freed from the material apparition of her worldly body, she emerges into an entirely different kind of novel, an adventure novel, geographically unlimited and liberated from the closed doors and open windows that structure the quotidian domestic sphere. Through "a wedge-shaped core of darkness" reminiscent of the triangular purple blur in Lily's painting, Mrs. Ramsay achieves access to a self that has little to do with that which is lost to her family and friends following her death.

Through Mrs. Ramsay's interiority as well as her private adventure story, Woolf proposes a maternal narrative far in excess of those generic conventions commonly reified by the "mother"; constructing Mrs. Ramsay herself in *excess* of genre, Woolf challenges those conventions of genre so consistently articulated through the mother's containment. Freud argues in "Mourning and Melancholia" that the ferocity of the melancholic's hold on an idealized lost object exists in direct proportion to the uncontainability of the object, and thus to the subject's ambivalence,[3] and ambivalence toward the mother is palpable in *To the*

Lighthouse. One critic writes tendentiously (and rather misogynistically) of its negative aspects:

Superficially Mrs. Ramsay is a beautiful, positive creature, but gradually unveiled as the vision of Lily Briscoe unfolds, she is revealed as the negative force which usurps the lighthouse and thus prevents the integration of the family while she lives. Only after her death can James and Cam go to the lighthouse, and thus symbolically to their father. The action of the novel shows Mrs. Ramsay to be an absolute matriarch whose domination lives ten years beyond her Self.[4]

Such a demonization of Mrs. Ramsay responds implicitly to the power that accrues to the figure who is the center of the domestic world in death as in life. However, even as Woolf recurs to the form of Victorian fiction in order to challenge its most complacent assumptions about women and women's power, she appropriates its distinct, and distinctly pragmatic, formal advantages. I have argued throughout this book that the event of maternal death acts as a felicitous narrative structure in nineteenth-century Britain, and for women writers in particular, the absence in narrative of a maternal role-model can signify an opportunity for the construction of innovative templates for the young protagonist's identity. Thus from Burney's Evelina to Austen's Emma, from Gaskell's Margaret Hale to Eliot's Daniel Deronda, an emancipatory ethic of individualism, of self-creation, follows the fact of maternal absence.

Woolf, however, places Mrs. Ramsay's death in brackets in the middle of her novel, at once displacing and isolating the "center" of the text structurally and psychologically. In doing so, she frustrates conventions of plot, disrupting the imperial *Bildungsroman* of the Victorian and psychoanalytic child whose identity emerges full-blown in the wake of maternal loss. Mrs. Ramsay's death, bracketed from the text but central to it, figures not a narcissistic story of self-creation, but an aesthetic, a modernist, melancholic aesthetic. This aesthetic mode is embodied through desire for the beautiful missing mother, but it is dependent on her loss only as a vehicle for its articulation, not for its existence.

The final section of Woolf's novel overwrites the aesthetic of loss with the psychodramatic implications of maternal death, giving her characters and her readers a familiar vocabulary of Victorian domestic nostalgia for the expression of the abstract aesthetic issues that have gripped them from the first. When the world first begins to stir following Mrs. Ramsay's death and the other tragic events, worldly and domestic, of "Time Passes," it does so through the rebirth of a domestic sphere crystallizing around the memory of a mother, Mrs. Ramsay, far more explicitly and with far more pathos than in the Victorian convention. If "the entire action of the novel is unfolded symbolically in Lily Briscoe's painting,"[5] then Lily's late return to this painting, ten years later, signals her return to the image of Mrs. Ramsay, who is only now more literally elusive to the novel's life and art. For Lily has always been implicated in the iconography of maternity as she attempts to capture the triangular structure of mother and son sitting together in the window, in her painting as in her affective responses:

[Lily] could see it all so clearly, so commandingly, when she looked: it was when she took her brush in hand that the whole thing changed. It was in that moment's flight between the picture and her canvas that the demons set on her who often brought her to the verge of tears and made this passage from conception to work as dreadful as any down a dark passage for a child. (19)

Predicting the dark passage in which Mr. Ramsay first reaches out to find his wife already gone, this passage implicates the maternal body in artistic production. But for the child in the passage and the painter in the novel, the maternal body is that which must be left behind, the "passage from conception to work" entailing a more or less literal act of parturition in which articulation achieves itself independently of the maternal sphere.

This is the lesson that Woolf appropriates from Victorian novels that celebrate the structural implications of maternal loss, and for the sake of Lily Briscoe's "vision," aesthetic achievement is predicated on the transition from melancholia to mourning, on the ability to forsake the maternal object as an object. To the extent that Lily Briscoe's progress in *To the Lighthouse* operates as a plot, as the recuperation of a shattered domestic ideal, this is not a novel of melancholia like its Victorian ancestors, but rather a novel of mourning, suggesting a future beyond fixation on Mrs. Ramsay in the conclusion, "It was done; it was finished. Yes, she thought, laying down her brush in extreme fatigue, I have had my vision" (209). The structure of this novel would seem to suggest that the domestic achievements of the living mother and the aesthetic achievements of the living artist are mutually exclusive; after all, Woolf, writing elsewhere about the Victorian novel, famously declares that "Killing the Angel in the House was part of the occupation of a woman writer."[6]

In another sense, however, Woolf's novel utterly fails to "kill" Mrs. Ramsay or the Angel in the House. In its genuine celebration of the vastly imperfect but appealing depth of character represented in Mrs. Ramsay, and in its concluding nostalgia for the coherence that Mrs. Ramsay once gave this newly disparate, halting, stuttering, faulty domestic sphere, this novel mourns the loss of the mother, despairs of ever recapturing even the fictional sense of wholeness that her presence alone engenders. Lily Briscoe's "vision" achieves completion through, by, and from that loss, and *To the Lighthouse* ultimately repeats – with a heightened sense of emotional impact – the implications of the melancholic as its central aesthetic mode, recurring to the tragic inevitability of loss in the fragile domestic sphere, as in the fragility of artistic vision.

Melanie Klein writes of the "epistemophilic impulse," arguing that subjectivity originates as the child's aggressive response to a dawning awareness of vulnerability, through violence against the symbolic mother who is the token of such fragility:

Thus, not only does symbolism come to be the foundation of all phantasy and sublimation, but, more than that, upon it is built up the subject's relation to the outside world and to reality in general. I pointed out that the object of sadism at its zenith, and of the epistemophilic impulse arising and coexisting with sadism, is the mother's body with its phantasied contents. The sadistic phantasies directed against the inside of her body constitute the first and basic relation to the outside world and to reality. Upon the degree of success with which the subject passes through this phase will depend the extent to which he can subsequently acquire an external world corresponding to reality. We see then that the child's earliest reality is wholly phantastic; he is surrounded with objects of anxiety, and in this respect excrement, organs, objects, things animate and inanimate are to begin with equivalent to one another. As the ego develops, a true relation to reality is gradually established out of this unreal reality.[7]

"Reality," for Klein and for psychoanalysis throughout this period, is predicated on an aesthetic concept derived directly from those fictional and symbolic worlds that first constitute the psychodrama of the newly emergent subject. Fiction precedes reality as artistic vision shapes orientation with the material world; in the psychoanalytic *Bildungsroman*, subjectivity is a narrative of radical individualism that derives from symbolic acts of mother-slaying. But when Mrs. Ramsay, alone at night, sinks into herself, she emerges into an entirely different kind of novel. When Woolf foils the predicate of *Bildung*, she intervenes directly at the intersection of Victorian and psychoanalytic conceits of subject-formation.

Klein represents the mother as the fulcrum between fiction and "fact" and posits a tension between the mother and the epistemological framework from which she is excluded; independence – or aesthetic vision, or "a true relation to reality" – in psychoanalytic terms, is a vestige of the Victorian melancholic plot that features the bracketing or containment of the maternal subject. Even as psychoanalysis moves more aggressively toward an understanding of the mother's determining power in subject-formation, the story of subject-formation, both structurally and in terms of its narrative principles, remains melancholic to the end, predicated upon a beginning that is coincident with the mother's circumscription through objectification, idealization, demonization, or death.

If *To the Lighthouse* is Woolf's "Victorian novel," it is also her psychoanalytic novel, its participation in psychoanalytic tropes and conceits overdetermined from the moment of James Ramsay's opening Oedipal rage. While Woolf was writing *To the Lighthouse*, the Hogarth Press was publishing the earliest English translations of Freud's *Collected Works*, and *To the Lighthouse*, begun late in 1925 and published in 1927, immediately follows Joan Riviere's 1925 translation of "Mourning and Melancholia."[8] This novel represents more than just an intellectual engagement with the cultural context of Freud and object-relations theory, however.[9] Woolf claimed that writing *To the Lighthouse* was a form of psychoanalysis itself, the realization of an artistic vision achieved in direct proportion to her relations with her beloved dead mother. In her autobiographical "A Sketch of the Past," she describes the process of writing *To the Lighthouse*: "I wrote the book very quickly; and when it was written, I ceased to be obsessed by my mother. I no longer hear her voice; I do not see her . . . I suppose that I did for myself what psycho-analysts do for their patients. I expressed some very long felt and deeply felt emotion. And in expressing it I explained it and then laid it to rest."[10] Woolf articulates a personal transition achieved through her engagement with this novel, from a state of melancholic preoccupation with the mother who died on 5 May 1895, to a new liberation from the maternal ghost, a transition from a profoundly melancholic state to a willingness to forsake the object lost.

Prior to 1927, Woolf's mother was the formative "invisible presence" shaping her life:

Until I was in [my] forties – I could settle the date by seeing when I wrote *To the Lighthouse*, but am too casual here to bother to do it – the presence of my mother obsessed me. I could hear her voice, see her, imagine what she would do or say as I went about my day's doings. She was one of the invisible presences who after all play so important a part in every life. (80)

Revisiting her own mother's death, Woolf mourns not only the loss of the woman herself, but the loss of the domestic world of which she was the center, and the loss of innocence, too, that marked the transition to adulthood for the girl of thirteen: "How immense must be the force of life which turns a baby, who can just distinguish a great blot of blue and purple on a black background, into the child who thirteen years later can feel all that I felt on May 5th 1895 – now almost exactly to a day, forty-four years ago – when my mother died" (79).

The mother whose loss is memorialized through the reiterated date of her death, May 5th 1895, remains captive in Victorian England as her daughter writes almost half a century later from an England facing the imminent beginning of World War II. Thus the death of the mother – in this memoir and in *To the Lighthouse* – is a doubly "Victorian" phenomenon, an allusion to the conventions of Victorian fiction and to a childhood chora ruptured, the end of an era emblematized by the mother destined by death to remain forever Victorian. The writing process not only supplements that loss, but also cancels it in its ability to conjure the return of the beloved lost object.

And there is my last sight of her; she was dying; I came to kiss her and as I crept out of the room she said: "Hold yourself straight, my little Goat." . . . What a jumble of things I can remember, if I let my mind run, about my mother; but they are all of her in company; of her surrounded; of her generalised; dispersed, omnipresent, of her as the creator of that crowded merry world which spun so gaily in the centre of my childhood. It is true that I enclosed that world in another made by my own temperament; it is true that from the beginning I had many adventures outside that world; and often went far from it; and kept much back from it; but there it always was, the common life of the family, very merry, very stirring, crowded with people; and she was the centre, it was herself. This was proved on May 5th 1895. For after that day there was nothing left of it. I leant out of the nursery window the morning she died. It was about six, I suppose. I saw Dr. Seton walk away up the street with his head bent and his hands clasped behind his back. I saw the pigeons floating and settling. I got a feeling of calm, sadness, and finality. It was a beautiful blue spring morning, and very still. That brings back the feeling that everything had come to an end. (84)

Woolf presents an emotional stasis generated from the death of the mother, but the structure of her memoir is melancholic in its refusal to let Julia Stephen die, modeling instead aesthetic and emotional modes facilitated by the insistent centrality of her loss. Like the "Time Passes" section of *To the Lighthouse*, the memoir marks the chronological death of the mother, but then it returns to her in different guises, the next episode recalling Julia's youth and telling her story yet again. Psychologically, too, Woolf structures this event as a momentous beginning rather than a conclusion, a rupture so enormous that it requires an entirely new invention of self for a girl, a newly motherless daughter at the dawn of adolescence and the twentieth century:

The tragedy of her death was not that it made one, now and then and very intensely, unhappy. It was that it made her unreal; and us solemn, and self-conscious. We were made to act parts that we did not feel; to fumble for words that we did not know. It obscured, it dulled. It made one hypocritical and immeshed in the conventions of sorrow. Many foolish and sentimental ideas came into being. Yet there was a struggle, for soon we revived, and there was a conflict between what we ought to be and what we were. (95)

That revival underscores the coherence of Woolf's attempt to consolidate mourning and representation in *To the Lighthouse*, returning to the scene of the mother's death in order to make a statement about the centrality of that event to her vision of art, femininity, and the psychological underpinnings of the domestic sphere. These terms are uniquely "immeshed" for Woolf, and represent her departure from the conventions and ideological assumptions of both Victorian and psychoanalytic narratives. Throughout this book, I have argued for a profoundly interlocked relationship between these narrative forms, between mothers and melancholia, between maternal loss and the politics of representation, and in *To the Lighthouse*, through Virginia Woolf, these concerns come full circle. *To the Lighthouse* helps to consolidate modernist tropes of the melancholic through the implications of Mrs. Ramsay's death: under the influence of "Mourning and Melancholia" and the conventions of Victorian fiction, Woolf writes her "Victorian novel," and for her as for Freud, the mother is the figure whose loss is at once enabling and devastating. Within an intellectual context involved with both the Victorian and the psychoanalytic, Woolf addresses the powerful shaping force of the mother, for Mrs. Ramsay's death reiterates the centrality of her powerful presence, even in absence, within the economy of aesthetic production.

As Elizabeth Abel has so persuasively argued, Woolf writes *To the Lighthouse* at a moment in the history of psychoanalysis at which the question of the central, determining mother is particularly fraught. Melanie Klein presented her first series of lectures in London in 1925, at the home of Woolf's brother Adrian Stephen, prior to her permanent 1926 relocation to Britain; Klein's migration to London represented a political shift within the world of psychoanalysis, the full flowering of *British* psychoanalysis, as well as the beginning of a direct institutional challenge to Freudian phallocentric theories in favor of the mother-centered developmental theories of object-relations. Abel writes of Woolf's statement in *A Room of One's Own* that the mind " 'can think back through its fathers or through its mothers' ":

By exploring the consequences of this choice, Woolf joins in the narrative project on which psychoanalysis was embarking concurrently. In the central decade of her career, Woolf's narratives interrogate Freud's. "A woman writing," the sentence from *Room* concludes, "thinks back through her mothers." By questioning the paternal genealogies prescribed by nineteenth-century fictional conventions and reinscribed by Freud, Woolf's novels of the 1920s parallel the narratives Melanie Klein was formulating simultaneously and anticipate the more radical revisions that emerged in psychoanalysis over the next half century.[11]

Woolf's response to the institutional warfare between psychoanalytic fathers and mothers emerges in the Oedipal drama that is *To the Lighthouse* in its choice between living fathers and dead mothers, in a world shaped by the powerful hands of the mother who is now so tragically departed – but who remains influential nonetheless. Woolf's acknowledgment of the mother's forceful presence includes the metaphor of literary historical reconstruction foregrounded in *A Room of One's Own*, the process of "thinking back through our mothers," a project whose terms I have duplicated by placing Woolf in the context of a Victorian literary genealogy.

But the conjuring of the missing mother for Woolf is an even more complex project than such a literary historical emphasis might suggest. *To the Lighthouse* recalls the mother's forceful *presence* at the heart of domesticity, subjectivity, and art, a presence that Woolf utilizes to figure the stakes of aesthetic production; as Melanie Klein would argue, the mother's presence signifies in structures of language, gender, and power even – or perhaps most forcefully – when the mother herself is missing. In *To the Lighthouse*, Woolf offers the Ramsay family as an emblem of the ideological and psychodramatic components of melancholia within the modernist aesthetic. But even as Mrs. Ramsay's death provides an icon for that aesthetic, her life, constructed in excess of family, form, and art, confounds the implications of containment that give shape to narrative conventions of maternal death.

Notes

I THE LADY VANISHES

1 Oscar Wilde, *The Importance of Being Earnest*. The Importance of Being Earnest *and Other Plays* (New York: Signet, 1985), 177.
2 Sigmund Freud, *Inhibitions, Symptoms and Anxiety, The Standard Edition of the Complete Psychological Works of Sigmund Freud*, trans. and ed. James Strachey, twenty-six volumes (London: The Hogarth Press and the Institute of Psycho-Analysis, 1986), 20: 169. All quotations refer to this edition, and page numbers are cited parenthetically in the text.
3 Elizabeth Gaskell, *The Life of Charlotte Brontë*, ed. Alan Shelston (New York: Penguin, 1985), 57.
4 *Ibid.*, 58.
5 *Ibid.*, 87.
6 My reading of the *Bildungsroman* has depended on Franco Moretti's theory of this form, but Moretti's view of psychoanalytic *Bildung* is the opposite of mine. He writes:

> the *raison d'être* of psychoanalysis lies in *breaking up* the psyche into its opposing "forces" – whereas youth and the novel have the opposite task of fusing, or at least bringing together, the conflicting features of individual personality. Because, in other words, psychoanalysis always looks *beyond* the Ego – whereas the *Bildungsroman* attempts to *build* the Ego, and make it the indisputable centre of its own structure (*The Way of the World* [London: Verso, 1987], 10–11; italics in original).

This should underscore two different approaches to psychoanalysis: while Moretti's reading situates Freud in terms of his concern with pathology, I privilege a historical context of developmental and object-relations theories and situate Freud exactly within the generic tradition of developmental, ego-building narratives that also produces the *Bildungsroman*.
7 Sigmund Freud, *Beyond the Pleasure Principle, Standard Edition* 18: 16. On the narratological implications of this work, see Peter Brooks, *Reading for the Plot: Design and Intention in Narrative* (New York: Vintage, 1985).
8 Sigmund Freud, "Mourning and Melancholia," *Standard Edition* 14: 249–50.
9 Judith Butler, *Bodies That Matter: On the Discursive Limits of "Sex"* (New York: Routledge, 1993), 234–5. On melancholia and maternity, see also Julia

Kristeva, *Black Sun: Depression and Melancholia*, trans. Leon S. Roudiez (New York: Columbia University Press, 1989).

10 Judith Butler, *Gender Trouble: Feminism and the Subversion of Identity* (New York: Routledge, 1990), 57.

11 See Adrienne Auslander Munich, *Queen Victoria's Secrets* (New York: Columbia University Press, 1996); Margaret Homans, "'To the Queen's Private Apartments': Royal Family Portraiture and the Construction of Victoria's Sovereign Obedience," *Victorian Studies* 37:1 (Autumn 1993), 1–41; and Elizabeth Langland, "England's Domestic Queen and Her Queenly Domestic Order," in *Nobody's Angels: Middle-Class Women and Domestic Ideology in Victorian Culture* (Ithaca: Cornell University Press, 1995), 62–79.

12 Munich, *Queen Victoria's Secrets*, 187.

13 Adrienne Auslander Munich, "Queen Victoria, Empire, and Excess," *Tulsa Studies in Women's Literature* 6:2 (1987), 265.

14 *Ibid.*, 278.

15 Munich, *Queen Victoria's Secrets*, 193.

16 John Ruskin, "Of Queens' Gardens," in *Sesame and Lilies* (New York: Charles F. Merrill, 1891), 138.

17 Mrs. Ellis, *The Mothers of England: Their Influence and Responsibility* (New York: J. & H. G. Langley, 1864), 22.

18 Mary Poovey, *Uneven Developments: The Ideological Work of Gender in Mid-Victorian England* (Chicago: University of Chicago Press, 1988), 11.

19 Walter E. Houghton, *The Victorian Frame of Mind, 1830–1870* (New Haven: Yale University Press, 1957), 467.

20 Irvine Loudon, *Death in Childbirth: An International Study of Maternal Care and Maternal Mortality 1800–1950* (Oxford: Clarendon Press, 1992), 164–5. On the subject of medical practitioners' transmission of puerperal fever, see Oliver Wendell Holmes's controversial essay, "The Contagiousness of Puerperal Fever," *New England Quarterly Journal of Medicine* (April 1843), and on this subject more generally, Leonard Colebrook, "Puerperal Infection 1800–1950," in J. M. Munro Kerr, R. W. Johnstone, and Miles H. Phillips, eds., *Historical Review of British Obstetrics and Gynaecology, 1800–1950* (Edinburgh: E. & S. Livingstone, 1954), 202–25.

21 For a discussion of the implications of Simpson's implementation of obstetrical anesthetics, see Mary Poovey, "Scenes of an Indelicate Character: The Medical Treatment of Victorian Women," in *Uneven Developments*, 24–50.

22 Florence Nightingale, *Introductory Notes on Lying-In Institutions. Together with a Proposal for Organising an Institution for Training Midwives and Midwifery Nurses* (London: Longman, Green, 1871), 64–5, italics and brackets in original.

23 *Ibid.*, 68.

24 Robert Collins, M.D., *A Practical Treatise on Midwifery, Containing the Result of Sixteen Thousand Six Hundred and Fifty Four Births, Occurring in the Dublin Lying-In Hospital, During a Period of Seven Years, Commencing November 1826* (London: 1835), 383–4, italics in original.

25 *Ibid.*, 386–9.

26 D. C. O'Connor, "Contagion Viewed Practically," *Dublin Quarterly Journal of Medical Science* 38 (Dublin: 1864), 59.

27 Nightingale, *Introductory Notes,* 27–8.

28 *Ibid.,* 3.

29 *Ibid.,* 64.

30 J. Matthews Duncan, M.D., "The Mortality of Childbed," *Edinburgh Medical Journal* 15 (July 1869–June 1879), 402.

31 Robert Barnes, "Clinical History of the Eastern Division of the Royal Maternity Charity, During the Year Ending September 30, 1858," *Dublin Quarterly Journal of Medical Science* 28 (Dublin: 1859), 103. Barnes's quotation from the Birmingham Registrar is widely cited in contemporary obstetrical discourses, most influentially in Duncan's "The Mortality of Childbed," 402.

32 William Farr, *Vital Statistics: A Memorial Volume of Selections from the Reports and Writings of William Farr,* ed. Mervyn Susser and Abraham Adelstein (Metuchen, NJ: The Scarecrow Press, 1975), 275.

33 Charles Meigs, *Females and Their Diseases: A Series of Letters to His Class* (Philadelphia, 1848), quoted in Irvine Loudon, *Death in Childbirth: An International Study of Maternal Care and Maternal Mortality 1800–1950* (Oxford: The Clarendon Press, 1992), 49.

34 Collins, *A Practical Treatise,* 373–4.

35 Edward B. Sinclair and George Johnston, *Practical Midwifery: Comprising an Account of 13,748 Deliveries Which Occurred in the Dublin Lying-In Hospital, During a Period of Seven Years, Commencing November, 1847* (London: 1858), 50–1.

36 Taking the metaphor of objectification to a remarkably literal degree, R.W. Johnstone writes of the period between 1850 and 1900: "By far the most outstanding feature of anatomical research in obstetrics during the period under review was the study of frozen sections of the bodies of women dying during pregnancy, labour or the puerperium. It was what Freeland Barbour used to call 'the Ice Age' of obstetrical anatomy, and he himself was the leading exponent of it in this country" ("Labour," in Kerr *et al., Historical Review,* 50).

37 Farr, *Vital Statistics,* 276.

38 Moretti, *The Way of the World,* 214.

39 Farr, *Vital Statistics,* 279.

40 Loudon, *Death in Childbirth,* 4.

41 Farr, *Vital Statistics,* 278.

42 Roger Schofield, "Did the Mothers Really Die? Three Centuries of Maternal Mortality in 'The World We Have Lost,'" in *The World We Have Gained: Histories of Population and Social Structure,* ed. Lloyd Bonfield, Richard M. Smith, and Keith Wrightson (Oxford: Basil Blackwell, 1986), 260. Schofield reports a death rate of .46 for the period 1856–60, while in the early 1930s the rate was .45, and in 1981, .01 (231). Consensus among experts indicates a remarkable stability in British maternal mortality rates between 1837 and 1937, with a rate almost constantly in the vicinity of .45, except at

sites of epidemic infection. In 1936, the rate fell below 4 deaths per 1000 births and has fallen steadily since then, a fact attributable in part to such advances in medicine as the implementation of penicillin (see William Gilliatt, "Maternal Mortality – Still-Birth and Neonatal Mortality," in Kerr *et al.*, *Historical Review*, 258).

43 John Hawkins Miller, "'Temple and Sewer': Childbirth, Prudery and Victoria Regina," in *The Victorian Family: Structures and Stresses*, ed. Anthony S. Wohl (London: Croom Helm, 1978), 34–5.

44 Houghton, *The Victorian Frame of Mind*, 355.

45 Nina Auerbach, *Woman and the Demon: The Life of a Victorian Myth* (Cambridge, Mass.: Harvard University Press, 1982). A number of feminist studies of nineteenth-century fiction have addressed the question of maternal representation, largely focusing on female authorship, issues of childbirth, and the implications of the powerful mother–child continuum. See especially Margaret Homans, *Bearing the Word: Language and Feminine Experience in Nineteenth-Century Women's Writing* (Chicago: University of Chicago Press, 1989); Marianne Hirsch, *The Mother/Daughter Plot: Narrative, Psychoanalysis, Feminism* (Bloomington: Indiana University Press, 1989); and Elisabeth Bronfen, *Over Her Dead Body: Death, Femininity and the Aesthetic* (New York: Routledge, 1992).

46 Samuel Richardson, *Clarissa*, ed. Angus Ross (New York: Penguin, 1985), 1299. All quotations refer to this edition, and page numbers are cited parenthetically in the text.

47 Michel Foucault, "Panopticism," in *Discipline and Punish: The Birth of the Prison*, trans. Alan Sheridan (New York: Vintage, 1979), 201.

48 Moretti, *The Way of the World*, 5.

49 Claire Kahane, "The Gothic Mirror," in *The (M)Other Tongue*, ed. Shirley Nelson Garner, Claire Kahane, and Madelon Sprengnether (Ithaca: Cornell University Press, 1986), 336. See also "The Spectral Mother; or, The Fault of Living On," in April Alliston, *Virtue's Faults: Correspondences in Eighteenth-Century British and French Women's Fiction* (Stanford: Stanford University Press, 1996), 144.

50 On the novel of sensibility, see Janet Todd, *Sensibility: An Introduction* (New York: Methuen, 1986); G. J. Barker-Benfield, *The Culture of Sensibility: Sex and Society in Eighteenth-Century Britain* (Chicago: University of Chicago Press, 1992); and Jean Hagstrum, *Sex and Sensibility: Ideal and Erotic Love from Milton to Mozart* (Chicago: University of Chicago Press, 1980). On realism in the context of the *Bildungsroman*, see Moretti, *The Way of the World*, as well as Ian Watt, *The Rise of the Novel: Studies in Defoe, Richardson, and Fielding* (Berkeley: University of California Press, 1967); Michael McKeon, *The Origins of the English Novel, 1600–1740* (Baltimore: The Johns Hopkins University Press, 1987); and Peter Brooks, *The Novel of Worldliness: Crébillon, Marivaux, Laclos, Stendhal* (Princeton: Princeton University Press, 1969). On the Gothic novel, see Maggie Kilgour, *The Rise of the Gothic Novel* (London: Routledge, 1995), Robert Kiely, *The Romantic Novel in England* (Cambridge, Mass.: Harvard

University Press, 1972); and Judith Wilt, *Ghosts of the Gothic: Austen, Eliot, and Lawrence* (Princeton: Princeton University Press, 1980).

51 On the implications of Austen's satirical view of the cult of sensibility, see Marilyn Butler, *Jane Austen and the War of Ideas* (Oxford: Clarendon Press, 1975).

52 Jane Austen, *Northanger Abbey*, ed. Anne Henry Ehrenpreis (New York: Penguin, 1985), 37.

53 Charles Dickens, *Oliver Twist*, ed. Peter Fairclough (New York: Penguin, 1985), 46. All quotations refer to this edition, and page numbers are cited parenthetically in the text.

54 Jane Austen, *Emma*, ed. James Kinsley and David Lodge (New York: Oxford University Press, 1987), 4. All quotations refer to this edition, and are cited parenthetically in the text.

55 Hirsch, *The Mother/Daughter Plot*, 67. See also D. A. Miller, "The Danger of Narrative in Jane Austen," in *Narrative and Its Discontents* (Princeton: Princeton University Press, 1981).

56 For a reading of *Emma* in the context of Julia Kristeva's theory of melancholy in *Black Sun*, see Frances L. Restuccia, "A Black Morning: Kristevan Melancholia in Jane Austen's *Emma*," *American Imago* 51:4 (1994), 447–69.

57 Adrienne Rich, "Jane Eyre: Temptations of a Motherless Woman," in *On Lies, Secrets, and Silence* (New York: Norton, 1979), 91, 95, 106.

58 Margaret Oliphant, *Miss Marjoribanks* (New York: Penguin, 1989), 25. All quotations refer to this edition, and page numbers are cited parenthetically in the text.

59 Elizabeth Langland sees the novel's opening death as "an opportunity for social reorganization rather than as personal tragedy" (*Nobody's Angels*, 154).

60 Q. D. Leavis, Introduction to *Miss Marjoribanks* (London: Chatto & Windus, 1969).

2 PSYCHOANALYTIC CANNIBALISM

1 D. W. Winnicott, "This Feminism," in *Home is Where We Start From*, ed. Clare Winnicott, Ray Shepherd, Madeleine Davis (New York: Norton, 1986), 191.

2 Sigmund Freud, *Inhibitions, Symptoms, and Anxiety, Standard Edition* 20: 136–7.

3 Freud, "Mourning and Melancholia," *Standard Edition* 14: 249–50.

4 Freud, *The Interpretation of Dreams, Standard Edition* 5: 400–1, n3, italics in the original.

5 Otto Rank, *The Trauma of Birth* (New York: Harcourt, Brace & Co., 1929), 211.

6 Freud, *Inhibitions, Symptoms, and Anxiety*; see especially 170.

7 Freud, *The Ego and the Id, Standard Edition* 19: 58. See also "Analysis Terminable and Interminable," *Standard Edition* 23: 216.

8 Freud, *Inhibitions, Symptoms, and Anxiety*, 138–9.

9 Melanie Klein consistently spells "phantasy" with a "ph," rather than as "fantasy." In her introduction to *The Selected Melanie Klein* (New York: The Free Press, 1986), Juliet Mitchell explains that "the 'ph' spelling is used to indicate that the process is unconscious" (22). I have elected to use the spelling most commonly used by Klein and other object-relations theorists, in part to retain the implication that the processes they describe are pre-Oedipal and therefore pre-symbolic, as well as unconscious.

10 For more on both the phallic mother and the mother as erotic object, see "Female Sexuality," *Standard Edition* 21: 225–43, as well as Lecture XXIX of *New Introductory Lectures*, "Revision of the Theory of Dreams," *Standard Edition* 22: 24; also Lecture XXXIII, "Femininity," *Standard Edition* 22: 126–7 and 130. For more on the incest taboo, see chapter 1, "The Horror of Incest," in *Totem and Taboo*, *Standard Edition* 13: 1–17, as well as "'A Child is Being Beaten': A Contribution to the Case of Sexual Perversions," *Standard Edition* 17: 187–90. Case-studies in which Freud discusses the incest taboo include the case of the Wolf-Man, "From the History of an Infantile Neurosis," *Standard Edition* 17: 100–2; and the case of Little Hans, "Analysis of a Phobia in a Five-Year-Old Boy," *Standard Edition* 10: 130–5.

11 Sigmund Freud, "Female Sexuality," *Standard Edition* 21: 228.

12 *Ibid.*, 230.

13 Sigmund Freud, *Beyond the Pleasure Principle*, *Standard Edition* 18: 15. Further quotations refer to this edition, and page numbers are cited parenthetically in the text.

14 See especially Jacques Derrida, "Freud's Legacy," 292–337, in *The Post Card*, trans. Alan Bass (Chicago: University of Chicago Press, 1987), and Elisabeth Bronfen, "The Lady Vanishes: Sophie Freud and *Beyond the Pleasure Principle*," *South Atlantic Quarterly* 88:4 (Fall 1989).

15 Jacques Lacan, "Of the Subject Who is Supposed to Know," in *The Four Fundamental Concepts of Psycho-Analysis*, ed. Jacques-Alain Miller, trans. Alan Sheridan (New York: Norton, 1981), 239.

16 Lacan, "Tuché and Automaton," *The Four Fundamental Concepts*, 63.

17 Julia Kristeva, *Revolution in Poetic Language*, trans. Margaret Waller (New York: Columbia University Press, 1984), 50; see also 241, n21 and 258, n10.

18 *Ibid.*, 68–9.

19 *Ibid.*, 68.

20 Jane Gallop, "Reading the Mother Tongue: Psychoanalytic Feminist Criticism," *Critical Inquiry* 13 (Winter 1987), 322.

21 J. Laplanche and J.-B. Pontalis, *The Language of Psycho-Analysis*, trans. Donald Nicholson Smith (New York: Norton, 1978), 278.

22 In "The Origins of Transference" (1952), Klein claims that the infant's negotiation of a relationship with and against the mother prefigures all future transferential relationships (reprinted in Mitchell, *The Selected Melanie Klein*, 201–10).

23 For important discussions of the relationship between Anna Freud and Melanie Klein, see Phyllis Grosskurth, *Melanie Klein: Her World and Her Work*

(New York: Knopf, 1986) and Elisabeth Young-Breuhl, *Anna Freud: A Biography* (New York: Summit Books, 1988). For additional background on the developing practice of child analysis, see Karl Abraham, "The First Pregenital Stage of the Libido" (1916), "An Infantile Theory on the Origin of the Female Sex" (1923), "An Infantile Sexual Theory Not Hitherto Noted" (1925), and "The Influence of Oral Erotism on Character-Formation" (1924), all reprinted in Karl Abraham, *The Selected Papers of Karl Abraham, M.D.*, trans. Douglas Bryan and Alix Strachey (London: The Hogarth Press and the Institute of Psycho-Analysis, 1973). See also "Love for the Mother and Mother Love" (1939), in which Alice Balint argues that "love for the mother is originally a love without a sense of reality, while love and hate for the father – including the Oedipus situation – is under the sway of reality," reprinted in Michael Balint, *Primary Love and Psycho-Analytic Technique* (London: The Hogarth Press and the Institute of Psycho-Analysis, 1952), 116–17.

24 Ernest Jones, "The Phallic Phase," *Papers on Psycho-Analysis* (London: Maresfield Reprints, 1948), 438. Quoted in Grosskurth, *Melanie Klein*, 202.

25 Sayers argues that these female analysts, three of whom were analyzed by Karl Abraham, used their life-experiences as women, mothers, and daughters to assert the centrality of women, mothers, and daughters in their work (Janet Sayers, *Mothering Psychoanalysis* [New York: Penguin, 1991]). See also Madelon Sprengnether, *The Spectral Mother: Freud, Feminism, and Psychoanalysis* (Ithaca: Cornell University Press, 1990).

26 Joan Riviere, "Hate, Greed and Aggression," in Melanie Klein and Joan Riviere, *Love, Hate and Reparation* (New York: Norton, 1964), 17.

27 Winnicott, "This Feminism," *Home*, 191.

28 Winnicott, "The Mother's Contribution to Society," in *Home*, 124–5.

29 Riviere, "Hate," 8–9.

30 Klein, "The Importance of Symbol Formation in the Development of the Ego," in Mitchell, *The Selected Melanie Klein*, 96.

31 *Ibid.*, 97–8.

32 Klein, "The Psychological Principles of Infant Analysis" (1926), reprinted in *ibid.*, 66.

33 Freud, *The Interpretation of Dreams, Standard Edition* 4: 100.

34 Klein, "The Psycho-Analytic Play Technique," in Mitchell, *The Selected Melanie Klein*, 51–2.

35 Melanie Klein and Joan Riviere, *Love, Hate and Reparation* (New York: Norton, 1964), v. All quotations refer to this edition and are cited parenthetically in the text with the designation *LHR*.

36 Mitchell explains Klein's replacement of the Freudian concept of the libidinal "phase" – oral, anal, genital – with the less teleological term "position": "Melanie Klein introduces a concept that presents the moment of ego organization – she substitutes a structural for a developmental notion. This facilitates the making of a connection between adult psychoses and infant development – a 'position' is an always available state, not something one passes through" (*The Selected Melanie Klein*, 116).

37 D. W. Winnicott, "The Use of an Object and Relating Through Identifications," in *Playing and Reality* (New York: Routledge, 1990), 86, italics in original.

38 *Ibid.*, 88.

39 *Ibid.*, 94.

40 *Ibid.*, 89, italics in original.

41 For an extended analysis of the mirror-function of the mother, see Heinz Kohut, *The Analysis of the Self* (New York: International Universities Press, 1971), especially 124.

42 Winnicott, "The Mirror-Role of the Mother and Family in Child Development," in *Playing and Reality*, 112, italics in original.

43 *Ibid.*, 112–13.

44 *Ibid.*, 117.

45 Winnicott, "Transitional Objects and Transitional Phenomena," in *Playing and Reality*, 2.

46 *Ibid.*, 6, italics in original.

47 *Ibid.*, 11.

48 *Ibid.*

49 Winnicott, "*Sum*, I Am," in *Home*, 63.

50 Winnicott, "The Mother's Contribution to Society," 123.

51 Winnicott, "The Use of an Object," 92.

52 John Ramsbotham, M.D., *Practical Observations in Midwifery, with Cases in Illustration* (2nd Edition, revised, in one volume) (London: 1842), 46.

53 Winnicott, "This Feminism," 188.

54 *Ibid.*, 192–3.

55 Winnicott, "The Pill and the Moon," in *Home*, 196–7.

56 *Ibid.*, 197.

57 *Ibid.*, 200–1.

58 *Ibid.*, 207.

59 *Ibid.*, 207–8.

60 *Ibid.*, 207.

61 John Ruskin, "Of Queens' Gardens," in *Sesame and Lilies* (New York: Charles F. Merrill, 1891), 138.

3 BROKEN MIRROR, BROKEN WORDS: *BLEAK HOUSE*

1 Barbara Johnson, "My Monster/My Self," in *The Critical Difference* (Baltimore: The Johns Hopkins University Press, 1987), 147.

2 Paul de Man, "Autobiography as De-Facement," in *The Rhetoric of Romanticism* (New York: Columbia University Press, 1984), 76. All references are to this edition, and page numbers are cited parenthetically in the text.

3 Charles Dickens, *Bleak House*, ed. Norman Page (New York: Penguin, 1971), 84–5. All references are to this edition, and page numbers are cited parenthetically in the text.

4 Marcia Renee Goodman, "'I'll Follow the Other': Tracing the (M)other in

Bleak House," *Dickens Studies Annual* 19 (1990), 154. See also Judith Wilt, "Confusion and Consciousness in Dickens's Esther," and Virginia Blain, "Double Vision and the Double Standard in *Bleak House*," both in *Charles Dickens's Bleak House*, ed. Harold Bloom (New York: Chelsea House, 1987).

5 D. A. Miller, *The Novel and the Police* (Berkeley: University of California Press, 1988), 65.

6 *Ibid.*, 86.

7 D. W. Winnicott, "Transitional Objects and Transitional Phenomena," in *Playing and Reality* (New York: Routledge, 1971), 1–25. See also Melanie Klein, "Love, Guilt and Reparation," in Melanie Klein and Joan Riviere, *Love, Hate and Reparation* (New York: Norton, 1964).

8 Ironically, Lady Dedlock's first name is "Honoria." In her incarnation as a woman of suspect virtue, however, she is quite distinct from Coventry Patmore's Honoria, locus classicus of the ideal of domestic virtue exalted throughout *The Angel in the House*.

9 Jacques Lacan, "Seminar on 'The Purloined Letter,'" trans. Jeffrey Mehlman, in *The Purloined Poe: Lacan, Derrida and Psychoanalytic Reading*, ed. John P. Muller and William J. Richardson (Baltimore: The Johns Hopkins University Press, 1988), 40.

10 In her reading of *David Copperfield*, Mary Poovey notes a similar habit with Agnes and uses it to link Agnes's domestic labors with David's labor as a professional writer:

> Despite numerous references to Agnes as her father's housekeeper, whatever domestic tasks she performs or oversees are signified only by her basket of keys. That these keys stand for actual labor is suggested only indirectly . . . In both his representations of David's writing and Agnes's housekeeping, in other words, Dickens displaces the material details and the emotional strain of labor onto other episodes – thereby conveying the twin impressions that some kinds of work are less "degrading" and less alienating than others and that some laborers are so selfless and skilled that to them work is simultaneously an expression of self and a gift to others. (*Uneven Developments: The Ideological Work of Gender in Mid-Victorian England* [Chicago: University of Chicago Press, 1988], 101)

Poovey's analysis is suggestive for a reading of *Bleak House*, as well, for Esther acts as both a domestic laborer and a writer, and thus represents a combination of the characteristics most central to Agnes and David.

11 Jane Gallop, *Reading Lacan* (Ithaca: Cornell University Press, 1985), 148.

12 For a suggestive reading of the significance of handkerchiefs in *Oliver Twist*, see John O. Jordan, "The Purloined Handkerchief," *Dickens Studies Annual* 18 (1989), 1–17.

13 *Studies in Conduct: Short Essays from the "Saturday Review"* (London: Chapman & Hall, 1867), 139.

4 WILKIE COLLINS AND THE SECRET OF THE MOTHER'S PLOT

1 Michel Foucault, *The History of Sexuality*, vol. 1, *An Introduction*, trans. Robert Hurley (New York: Vintage, 1980), 35.

2 Wilkie Collins, *The Woman in White* (1859–60), ed. Julian Symons (New York: Penguin, 1985), 105. Further quotations refer to this edition, and page numbers are cited parenthetically in the text.

3 Tzvetan Todorov, "The Typology of Detective Fiction," in *The Poetics of Prose*, trans. Richard Howard (Ithaca: Cornell University Press, 1977), 42–52.

4 The *sujet supposé savoir*, for Lacan, is the figure whose supposed stability and omniscience give the analysand sufficient security of context to elicit transference and thus desire; in the essay "Of the Subject Who is Supposed to Know," this illusory figure is emblematized alternately by the analyst, God, Freud, and the phallic mother. The important point, however, is that the *sujet supposé savoir* is necessarily fictive, an introjected melancholic construct temporarily projected outward, suggesting, for Lacan, the inherently narcissistic character of desire. See Jacques Lacan, "Of the Subject Who is Supposed to Know," in *The Four Fundamental Concepts of Psycho-Analysis*, ed. Jacques-Alain Miller, trans. Alan Sheridan (New York: Norton, 1981), 230–43.

5 *Webster's New Collegiate Dictionary* (Springfield, Mass.: Merriam-Webster Inc., 1983), 1249.

6 U. C. Knoepflmacher, "The Counterworld of Victorian Fiction and *The Woman in White*," in *The Worlds of Victorian Fiction*, ed. Jerome H. Buckley (Cambridge, Mass.: Harvard University Press, 1975), 362.

7 Jacques Derrida, *Of Grammatology*, ed. and trans. Gayatri Chakravorty Spivak (Baltimore: The Johns Hopkins University Press, 1976), 61. In the translator's preface to this edition, Spivak describes Derrida's "trace" as follows: "Derrida's trace is the mark of the absence of a presence, an always already absent present, of the lack at the origin that is the condition of thought and experience" (xvii).

8 *Ibid.*, 65. Italics in "original."

9 Jacques Lacan, "The Signification of the Phallus," in *Ecrits: A Selection*, trans. Alan Sheridan (New York: Norton, 1977), 286.

10 Alice A. Jardine, *Gynesis: Configurations of Women and Modernity* (Ithaca: Cornell University Press, 1985), 187–8.

11 Derrida, *Of Grammatology*, 145.

12 Jean-Jacques Rousseau, *The Confessions*, trans. J. M. Cohen (New York: Penguin, 1953), 19.

13 Derrida, *Of Grammatology*, xvii. Freud's most explicit invocation of the language of the trace occurs in the brief 1925 essay, "A Note upon the 'Mystic Writing-Pad,'" *Standard Edition* 19: 227–32.

14 Lacan, "The Mirror Stage," in *Ecrits*, 1–2. Julia Kristeva's critique of the distinction between imaginary and symbolic, or pre-Oedipal and Oedipal, argues that the pre-Oedipal or semiotic space of maternal presence is a

determining presence within symbolic functioning. See especially "The Semiotic and the Symbolic," part 1 of *Revolution in Poetic Language*, trans. Margaret Waller (New York: Columbia University Press, 1984).

15 Lacan, "Of the Subject," in *The Four Fundamental Concepts*, 239.

16 D. A. Miller, *The Novel and the Police* (Berkeley: University of California Press, 1988).

17 Wilkie Collins, "Preface [1860]," *The Woman in White*, ed. Harvey Peter Sucksmith (New York: Oxford University Press, 1989), xxx.

18 Barbara Johnson, "The Frame of Reference: Poe, Lacan, Derrida," in *The Purloined Poe: Lacan, Derrida, and Psychoanalytic Reading*, ed. John P. Muller and William J. Richardson (Baltimore: The Johns Hopkins University Press, 1988), 243.

19 Unsigned review, *The Times*, 30 October 1860, 6, reprinted in *Wilkie Collins: The Critical Heritage*, ed. Norman Page (Boston: Routledge & Kegan Paul, 1974), 97.

20 Unsigned review, *Dublin University Magazine* 57 (February 1861), 200–3, reprinted in Page, *Wilkie Collins*, 105.

21 D. A. Miller argues that the uncanny effect of *The Woman in White* is grounded in the body: the effects of reading a sensation novel are sensory, and it is the "acting out" of effect in *The Woman in White* that focuses both the novel's "readings" and its anxieties, as those readings are staged within the narrative itself. "The novel makes nervousness a metonymy for reading, its cause or effect. . . The association of nervousness with reading is complicated – not to say troubled – by its coincident, not less insistent or regular association with femininity" (*The Novel and the Police*, 151).

22 Page, *Wilkie Collins*, 98.

23 See, for example, the unsigned review in the *Saturday Review* 10 (25 August 1860), 249–50, reprinted in Page, *Wilkie Collins*, 85.

24 Sigmund Freud, *Fragment of an Analysis of a Case of Hysteria*, Standard Edition 7: 48.

25 Jane Gallop, "Keys to Dora," in *In Dora's Case: Freud – Hysteria – Feminism*, ed. Charles Bernheimer and Claire Kahane (New York: Columbia University Press, 1985), 209.

26 *Ibid.*, 213.

27 *Ibid.*, 213–14.

28 Barbara Fass Leavy is one of the few critics who are conscious of the tendency, active in both the novel and in much of its criticism, to elide the fact of Anne Catherick's significance. She writes, "Even U. C. Knoepflmacher's brilliant study of the book reads as if there are only two heroines in it, Laura Fairlie and Marian Halcombe. Anne Catherick is virtually dismissed as a 'deranged outcast,' whose chief importance, apparently, is as a foil for her half-sister Laura" (Barbara Fass Leavy, "Wilkie Collins's Cinderella: The History of Psychology and *The Woman in White*," *Dickens Studies Annual* 10 [1982], 91).

29 Collins, *The Woman in White*, ed. Sucksmith, 373. I retain the Oxford

University Press version of this "narrative" because its editor has elected to reproduce it graphically as a tombstone. In contrast, the Penguin edition privileges its narrative qualities, collapsing the lines into a conventional paragraph (426).

30 Leavy, "Wilkie Collins's Cinderella," 127.

31 René Girard, *Violence and the Sacred*, trans. Patrick Gregory (Baltimore: The Johns Hopkins University Press, 1977), 145, italics in original. For discussions of the terms of mimetic desire, see especially René Girard, "'Triangular' Desire," in *Deceit, Desire, and the Novel*, trans. Yvonne Freccero (Baltimore: The Johns Hopkins University Press, 1965), 1–53, and also "From Mimetic Desire to the Monstrous Double," in *Violence and the Sacred*, 143–68.

32 Eve Kosofsky Sedgwick, *Between Men: English Literature and Male Homosocial Desire* (New York: Columbia University Press, 1985).

33 Toril Moi, "The Missing Mother: The Oedipal Rivalries of René Girard," *Diacritics* 12 (1982), 27–8.

34 Unsigned review, *Critic* 21 (25 August 1860), 233–4, reprinted in Page, *Wilkie Collins*, 82.

35 Laurie Langbauer, "Women in White, Men in Feminism," *Yale Journal of Criticism* 2:2 (1989), 223.

5 DENIAL, DISPLACEMENT, *DERONDA*

1 George Eliot, *Daniel Deronda*, ed. Barbara Hardy (New York: Penguin, 1986), 202–3. All quotations refer to this edition, and page numbers are cited parenthetically in the text.

2 Judith Wilt, *Ghosts of the Gothic: Austen, Eliot, and Lawrence* (Princeton: Princeton University Press, 1980), 173.

3 Claire Kahane, "The Gothic Mirror," in *The (M)Other Tongue*, ed. Shirley Nelson Garner, Claire Kahane, and Madelon Sprengnether (Ithaca: Cornell University Press, 1986), 336.

4 See especially Melanie Klein, "A Contribution to the Psychogenesis of Manic-Depressive States" (1935), in *The Selected Melanie Klein*, ed. Juliet Mitchell (New York: The Free Press, 1986).

5 Sigmund Freud, *The Interpretation of Dreams, Standard Edition* 4: 260–1.

6 *Ibid.*, 261–2.

7 Sander Gilman, *The Jew's Body* (New York: Routledge, 1991), 126–7.

8 Steven Marcus, "Literature and Social Theory: Starting In with George Elliot," in *Representations: Essays on Literature and Society* (New York: Random House, 1975), 212n. Despite the notoriety of this observation, it is noteworthy that to find this quote, the reader of Marcus's text must also "look down": circumcision appears only in a footnote at the end of the essay, a footnote which only arises itself in response to a rhetorical question: "Are we back in that Victorian swamp in which the state of medical science was used as an excuse for pronouncements about existential terrors?" (212). Marcus's multiply qualified footnote reads in its entirety:

How much so has only recently been disclosed by a graduate student of mine, Lennard Davis. Mr. Davis has discovered a detail – or a missing detail – in *Daniel Deronda* – that throws the whole central plot of the novel out of kilter. Deronda's identity is a mystery to him and has always been. It is only when he is a grown man, having been to Eton and Cambridge, that he discovers that he is a Jew. What this has to mean – given the conventions of medical practice at the time – is that he never looked down. In order for the plot of Daniel Deronda to work, Deronda's circumcised penis must be invisible, or nonexistent – which is one more demonstration in detail of why the plot does not in fact work. Yet this peculiarity of circumstance – which, I think it should be remarked, has never been noticed before – is, I have been arguing, characteristic in several senses of both George Eliot and the culture she was representing.

Despite the fact that most critics who invoke this passage, myself included, attribute the circumcision to Marcus, in Marcus's own text it is a moment at least as overdetermined and displaced as the event it describes in the novel: located in small print at the bottom of the page, written off (as citation) as really the discovery (property) of another man (graduate student), who dared to see what has never been seen before.

9 Marianne Hirsch, "Fraternal Plots: Beyond Repetition," in *The Mother/Daughter Plot: Narrative, Psychoanalysis, Feminism* (Bloomington: University of Indiana Press, 1989), 70–1.

10 Joanne Long Demaria, "The Wondrous Marriages of *Daniel Deronda*: Gender, Work, and Love," *Studies in the Novel* 22:4 (Winter 1990), 409.

11 *Ibid.*, 411.

12 Cynthia Chase, "The Decomposition of Elephants: Double-Reading *Daniel Deronda*," *PMLA* 93:2 (March 1978), 218.

13 *Ibid.*, 222.

14 *Ibid.*, 224.

15 F. R. Leavis, *The Great Tradition* (London: Chatto & Windus, 1960), 122.

16 Chase argues that the relationship she focuses on, between the narratives of Hans Meyrick and Daniel Deronda, "is in one sense a subtler version of the opposition between Gwendolen and Deronda" ("The Decomposition of Elephants," 215).

17 Rosemarie Bodenheimer, "Ambition and Its Audiences: George Eliot's Performing Figures," *Victorian Studies* 34:1 (1990), 27.

18 Laura Mulvey, "Visual Pleasure and Narrative Cinema," *Screen* 17 (Autumn 1975), 7. Kaja Silverman argues that the filmic scene is predicated on loss, and very specifically, on the loss, editing out, or marginalization of the original maternal voice (*The Acoustic Mirror: The Female Voice in Psychoanalysis and Cinema* [Bloomington: Indiana University Press, 1988]).

19 Catherine Belsey, "Re-reading the Great Tradition," in *Re-Reading English*, ed. Peter Widdowson (New York: Methuen, 1982), 134.

20 In Freud's discourse, the phallic mother *is* a spider: in "Femininity," he writes: "You may well doubt whether you have gained any real advantage from this when you reflect that in some classes of animals the females are the stronger and more aggressive and the male is active only in the single act of

sexual union. This is so, for instance, with the spiders" (115). As a gloss on this thought, he later makes the connection explicit: "According to Abraham (1922) a spider in dreams is a symbol of the mother, but of the *phallic* mother, of whom we are afraid; so that the fear of spiders expresses dread of mother-incest and horror of the female genitals" (*New Introductory Lectures, Standard Edition* 25: 24).

21 Virginia Woolf, *A Room of One's Own* (New York: Harcourt Brace Jovanovich, 1957), 50.

22 Neil Hertz, *The End of the Line: Essays on Psychoanalysis and the Sublime* (New York: Columbia University Press, 1985), 230.

6 CALLING DR. DARWIN

1 Charles Darwin, *The Autobiography of Charles Darwin, 1809–1882*, ed. Nora Barlow (New York: Norton, 1958), 139, 140–1. All quotations refer to this edition, and page numbers are cited parenthetically in the text.

2 For an analysis of the literary qualities of Freud's prose, particularly in his case-study of Dora, see Steven Marcus, "Freud and Dora: Story, History, Case History," in *In Dora's Case: Freud – Hysteria – Feminism*, ed. Charles Bernheimer and Claire Kahane (New York: Columbia University Press, 1985), 56–91.

3 For Freud's elaboration of the concept of "acting out," see "Remembering, Repeating, and Working-Through," *Standard Edition* 12: 145–56.

4 Edward J. Kempf, *Psychopathology* (St. Louis: C. V. Mosby Company, 1921), 214.

5 *Ibid.*, 214. Kempf argues that Susannah Wedgwood Darwin's fascination with her father-in-law Erasmus Darwin's work, especially his *Zoonomia*, was the source of *her* engagement with the riddle of origins (212–13).

6 Geoffrey West, *Charles Darwin: The Fragmentary Man* (London: George Routledge & Sons, 1937), 45.

7 Charles Darwin, "An Autobiographical Fragment Written in 1838," in Charles Darwin and Thomas Henry Huxley, *Autobiographies*, ed. Gavin de Beer (New York: Oxford University Press, 1983).

8 Melanie Klein, "Love, Guilt and Reparation," in Melanie Klein and Joan Riviere, *Love, Hate and Reparation* (New York: Norton, 1964), 102–3.

9 For a discussion of the "epistemophilic impulse," see Melanie Klein, "The Importance of Symbol-Formation in the Development of the Ego," in *The Selected Melanie Klein*, ed. Juliet Mitchell (New York: The Free Press, 1986), 96–8.

10 Jacques Lacan, "The Agency of the Letter in the Unconscious," in *Ecrits: A Selection*, trans. Alan Sheridan (New York: Norton, 1977), 167.

11 Nancy Vickers, "Diana Described: Scattered Woman and Scattered Rhyme," in *Writing and Sexual Difference*, ed. Elizabeth Abel (Chicago: University of Chicago Press, 1982), 107, 109.

12 See Mrs. Henrietta Emma Darwin Litchfield, *Emma Darwin: A Century of Family Letters*, ed. Henrietta Litchfield (London: J. Murray, 1915).

13 Kempf, *Psychopathology*, 244. Kempf attributes Darwin's illness to an anxiety neurosis, while Douglas Hubble, in an article titled "The Evolution of Charles Darwin," suggests that "Charles suffered not from an organic disease but from an autonomic disorder," from an illness deriving from emotion and conscious thought (*Horizon* 80 [1946], 83). In a note following the text of Darwin's *Autobiography*, editor Nora Barlow writes:

> The nausea, giddyness, insomnia and debility from which he suffered, follow the now familiar pattern of the ills of other eminent Victorians, with the Victorian Hydropathic establishment, the sofa and the shawl as characteristic hall-marks. Charles Darwin's forty years of invalid existence, moreover, were an unexpected sequel to his youthful vigour, for his strength and endurance were well above the average, as Captain Fitz-Roy has recorded in his accounts of various incidents during the *Beagle* Voyage... Yet health anxieties did trouble Charles Darwin even in the early days before the voyage, so that his marriage to a deeply sympathetic wife can hardly have done more than increase a deep-seated tendency. Her over-solicitude helped to cast that faint aura of glory on the Symptom, an attitude that was carried on into adult life by several of their children. (240–1)

For a discussion of Darwin's illness, as well as an annotated bibliography suggesting arious diagnoses, see Barlow's note, "On Charles Darwin's Ill-Health," *Autobiography*, 240–3.

14 Klein, "Love, Guilt, and Reparation," 105.

15 *Ibid.*, 104.

16 *Ibid.*, 102–3.

17 In *The Interpretation of Dreams*, Freud analyzes at some length the "May-Beetle Dream," in which one of his patients, "an elderly lady," has symbolized anxieties about her daughter, her husband, and sexuality in a dream about two beetles escaping from a box. Freud and his analysand connect this dream with the contradiction of appearance and character expressed in George Eliot's *Adam Bede*. See *The Interpretation of Dreams, Standard Edition* 4: 289–92.

18 Gillian Beer, *Darwin's Plots: Evolutionary Narrative in Darwin, George Eliot and Nineteenth-Century Fiction* (Boston: Routledge & Kegan Paul, 1983), 9.

19 Charles Darwin, *The Origin of Species* (New York: New American Library, 1958), 90. The gender construct that Darwin invokes is a variation on the ancient division between (female) receptacle and (male) logos; in the *Timaeus*, still another originary narrative, Plato describes the receptacle: "Therefore we must not call the mother and receptacle of visible and sensible things either earth or air or fire or water, nor yet any of their compounds or components; but we shall not be wrong if we describe it as invisible and formless, all-embracing, possessed in a most puzzling way of intelligibility, yet very hard to grasp" (Plato, *Timaeus*, trans. Desmond Lee [New York: Penguin, 1977]).

20 Basil Willey, "Darwin and Clerical Orthodoxy," quoted in Monica Correa Fryckstedt, "Defining the Domestic Genre: English Women Novelists of the 1850s," *Tulsa Studies in Women's Literature* 6:1 (Spring 1987), 22.

21 For an uncannily similar description of father–son ambivalence, as well as

for a contemporary discussion of evolutionary theory, see the autobiography of Edmund Gosse, *Father and Son* (1907) (New York: Norton, 1963).

22 Milton plays a multiply significant role in Darwin's *Autobiography*. Darwin announces at one point that *Paradise Lost* was the only book he brought with him on the voyage of the *Beagle*, the trip which provided him with the raw material to construct *The Origin of Species*. Gillian Beer comments on this connection:

> Darwin was to rejoice in the overturning of the anthropocentric view of the universe which Milton emphasizes, yet his language made manifest to Darwin, in its concurrence with his own sense of profusion, destiny, and articulation of the particular, how much could survive, how much could be held in common and in continuity from the past. Milton gave Darwin profound imaginative pleasure – which to Darwin was the means of understanding. (*Darwin's Plots*, 36)

23 Jean-Jacques Rousseau, *The Confessions*, trans. J. M. Cohen (New York: Penguin, 1984), 42. For an analysis of the implications of Rousseau's own originary crisis, the death of his mother at his birth, see Jacques Derrida, *Of Grammatology*, trans. and ed. Gayatri Chakravorty Spivak (Baltimore: The Johns Hopkins University Press, 1976), 144–52.

24 Charles Darwin, "The pencil notes of 1837–38: 'This is the Question,'" Note Three to Darwin's *Autobiography*, ed. Barlow, 232–3.

25 Darwin refers to his poor memory throughout the *Autobiography*, and indeed, a slip of the memory was responsible for the central crisis of his later career. Samuel Butler accused him in print of harboring a grudge against him, a misunderstanding perpetuated by the fact that Darwin forgot to mention that a certain article had previously been published elsewhere, and therefore could not possibly be an attack on Butler. For an overview of the Samuel Butler controversy, see the second appendix to Darwin's *Autobiography*, ed. Barlow, 167–219, which reproduces the articles and correspondence in question.

7 VIRGINIA WOOLF'S "VICTORIAN NOVEL"

1 Virginia Woolf, *To the Lighthouse* (New York: Harcourt Brace & Company, 1927), 128. All quotations refer to this edition, and page numbers are cited parenthetically in the text.

2 On *To the Lighthouse* as an elegiac novel, see Peter Knox-Shaw, "*To the Lighthouse*: The Novel as Elegy," in *Virginia Woolf: Critical Assessments*, vol. III, *Critical Responses to the Novels from* The Voyage Out *to* To the Lighthouse, ed. Eleanor McNees (East Sussex: Helm Information Ltd., 1994), 699–721. On melancholia and the death of the father, see Gillian Beer, "Hume, Stephen, and Elegy in *To the Lighthouse*," in Harold Bloom, ed., *Virginia Woolf's* To the Lighthouse: *Modern Critical Interpretations*, (New York: Chelsea House, 1988), 75–94; as well as Perry Meisel, *The Absent Father: Virginia Woolf and Walter Pater* (New Haven: Yale University Press, 1980), and Mark Spilka, *Virginia*

Woolf's Quarrel With Grieving (Lincoln: University of Nebraska Press, 1980).
3 Sigmund Freud, "Mourning and Melancholia," *Standard Edition* 14: 251.
4 Glenn Pederson, "Vision in *To the Lighthouse*," in McNees, *Virginia Woolf*, 556.
5 *Ibid.*, 574.
6 Virginia Woolf, "Professions for Women," in *The Death of the Moth and Other Essays* (New York: Harcourt, Brace, & Company, 1942), 238.
7 Melanie Klein, "The Importance of Symbol Formation in the Development of the Ego" (1930), in *The Selected Melanie Klein*, ed. Juliet Mitchell (New York: The Free Press, 1986), 97–8.
8 For a discussion of the Hogarth Press in its relationship to Freud, psychoanalysis, and the International Psycho-Analytic Library, see "Freud and the Freudians," in J. H. Willis, Jr., *Leonard and Virginia Woolf as Publishers: The Hogarth Press, 1917–41* (Charlottesville: University Press of Virginia, 1992), 297–328. See also Perry Meisel and Walter Kendrick, *Bloomsbury/Freud: The Letters of James and Alix Strachey, 1924–1925* (New York: Basic Books, 1985).
9 The question of whether Woolf herself actively read psychoanalysis during this period remains open; Elizabeth Abel writes:

> [Woolf] claims to have avoided reading Freud until 1939, a deferral that must have required some effort, since from 1924, when Leonard Woolf agreed to James Strachey's request to take over publication of the International Psycho-Analytical Library, the Woolfs' own Hogarth Press published the English translation of every text Freud wrote, as well as nearly seventy additional volumes of the International Psycho-Analytical Library . . . Woolf's letters and diaries make it clear that she was involved in the publication process, but with one exception . . . she appears to have avoided opening the books, which she consistently represents as objects to be handled rather than as texts. (*Virginia Woolf and the Fictions of Psychoanalysis* [Chicago: University of Chicago Press, 1989], 14)

10 Virginia Woolf, "A Sketch of the Past," in *Moments of Being*, second edition, ed. Jeanne Schulkind (New York: Harvest/HBJ, 1985), 81. All quotations refer to this edition, and page numbers are cited parenthetically in the text.
11 Abel, *Virginia Woolf*, 3. See also my chapter 2, "Psychoanalytic Cannibalism." J. H. Willis writes of this historical moment: "The twenties and thirties thus saw the rise of the second generation of psychoanalysts who began to expand and extend the practice into areas only suggested by Freud and his early followers. A number of brilliant and gifted women made their appearance in international psychoanalytic circles at this time" (*Leonard and Virginia Woolf*, 321). During this period of growth and innovation, Willis points out, the Woolfs' Hogarth Press was at the vanguard of developments, particularly as they involved important female psychoanalysts, publishing Melanie Klein's *Psycho-Analysis of Children* and Helene Deutsch's *Psychoanalysis of the Neurosis* in 1932, as well as Anna Freud's *The Ego and the Mechanism of Defence* in 1937.

Index

CAMBRIDGE STUDIES IN NINETEENTH-CENTURY
LITERATURE AND CULTURE

General editors
Gillian Beer, *University of Cambridge*
Catherine Gallagher, *University of California, Berkeley*

Titles published